"Shannon Cramer writes with faithful h vites others to come alongside her and ... planting seeds of hope in even the most trying of times. As a pastor, I look forward to sharing this book with parishioners in our community who are struggling with chronic pain and illness."

—MARK MOFIELD,
senior pastor, Melrose Baptist Church

"Shannon Cramer's book is a mixture of her raw story of battling chronic diseases and a spiritual guide to fighting battles like hers. With her robust theological perspective, she brings scripture to bear in these situations. I would unreservedly recommend this book to anyone facing a long-term battle."

—MATT MERRILL,
senior pastor, Crestwood Church

"If you suffer from chronic illness and pain and have asked the why questions—with no answers—you will find help and hope in this book. Shannon Cramer vulnerably shares her ten-plus-year journey with uncommon honesty. She offers a blueprint to rebuild your life on an unshakeable foundation supported by God's truths. You will experience peace and joy that defy your circumstances."

—BILL GILMOUR,
author of *Aftermath of Jennifer Kesse's Abduction*

"As Christians, we affirm Immanuel, 'God with us,' but we often forget Immanuel, 'God as us.' Life's rhythms and reasons aren't always wrapped in knowing why the planet tilts toward suffering and chaos but in the beautiful, mysterious, yet defining truth that Jesus walked this sideways earth as one of us. Shannon Cramer's words gently (and humorously) remind us that rather than knowing why hardships endure, knowing Immanuel as 'God as us' presents the greatest cure for body, mind, and soul."

—PEYTON GARLAND,
author of *Tired, Hungry, and Kinda Faithful*

"Shannon Cramer is a writer with a heart of service. She graciously and vulnerably shares her experience with chronic illness in this must-read book for anyone living with an autoimmune disorder or simply walking through a dark patch of their human experience, looking for hope."

—HANNAH BUNN WEST,
author of *Remarkable Women of the Outer Banks*

"Shannon Cramer's book is truly insightful, inspirational, and life-changing. I was walking a very dark path when I was diagnosed with my chronic disease. Her book helped me find my way back into God's loving arms and into the light."

—JIM,
GPA warrior (granulomatosis with polyangiitis)

"Shannon Cramer's *How to Keep Believing When You're Suffering* is a perfect Christian tool for anyone who's grappling with a chronic condition and seeking tranquility. A heartfelt and inspirational read!"

—SHERRI,
survivor of chronic back pain

"This book is a must-read for anyone struggling with a new diagnosis and a valuable source of encouragement for those who have been walking with chronic illness for a long time. Relevant and motivating."

—EMILY,
mom with psoriatic arthritis

"In early adulthood, with proven academic success and youthful zeal, Shannon Cramer began a slow slide into the abyss of suffering and despair. In this articulate and inspirational account, she walks us out of the darkness brought on by three medical conditions into grace and light using Scripture and her own powerful testimony. Readers will be drawn in by her courage and this summation: 'My life has been richer because of disability.'"

—LINDA VIGEN PHILLIPS,
author of *Crazy*

"As the chronic warrior that she is, Shannon has poured her heart and soul into writing a book which serves to demystify and debunk the challenges of living with physical disability as a child of God. Whilst never shying away from the incredible frustrations she faces carrying out some of the simplest daily tasks, she confronts and disarms the debilitating nature of her conditions with the truths found in the word of God and in the character of his Son Jesus Christ."

—**DAWN FRANCIS,**
founder, *MakeMeAvailable*

How to Keep Believing
When You're Suffering

How to Keep Believing When You're Suffering

A Guide to Braving Chronic Illness

SHANNON CRAMER

RESOURCE *Publications* · Eugene, Oregon

HOW TO KEEP BELIEVING WHEN YOU'RE SUFFERING
A Guide to Braving Chronic Illness

Resource Publications
An Imprint of Wipf and Stock Publishers
199 W. 8th Ave., Suite 3
Eugene, OR 97401

www.wipfandstock.com

PAPERBACK ISBN: 978-1-6667-8493-0
HARDCOVER ISBN: 978-1-6667-8494-7
EBOOK ISBN: 978-1-6667-8495-4

01/05/24

Glory be to my Strength and my Song.
All my love to you, Jesus, for making everything possible.

For my treasured Parker,
Thank you for always seeing me.

Contents

Acknowledgments | xi

Introduction: The Way Forward | xiii

PART 1   YOU ARE NOT ALONE

Introduction   Meet Immanuel | 3

Chapter 1   Jesus Understands the Loneliness of Being Different | 6

Chapter 2   Jesus Lived with Limitations and Loss | 11

Chapter 3   Jesus Knew Fear and Deep Sorrow | 17

Chapter 4   Jesus Experienced Betrayal and Abandonment | 21

Chapter 5   Jesus Felt Forsaken by God | 25

Chapter 6   Jesus Understands Your Physical and Emotional Pain | 29

PART 2   HARMFUL MINDSETS TO TOSS

Introduction   Take Out the Trash | 37

Chapter 7   Deliverance from Guilt | 39

Chapter 8   Discern False Condemnation from Godly Sorrow | 45

Chapter 9   Respond to Accusations of "Not Enough Faith" | 50

Chapter 10   Overcome Lies with God's Truth | 55

Chapter 11   Curb Your Anxiety | 59

Chapter 12   Lose the Obsession with "Normal" | 64

PART 3   ATTITUDES TO CULTIVATE

Introduction   Garden Something Good | 69

Chapter 13   Move from Fretful → Fruitful God Time | 71

Chapter 14   Believe That God Is for You | 76

Chapter 15   Esteem Yourself through God's Eyes | 80

Chapter 16   Practice an Attitude of Gratitude | 83

Chapter 17   Be Empowered by God's Past Faithfulness | 87

Chapter 18   Know You Win in the End | 90

Chapter 19   Cultivate a Balanced View of Healing | 94

Begin Planting | 99

PART 4   HOPE IN THE RULE BREAKER

Introduction   Did You Know God Has a Rebellious Streak? | 103

Chapter 20   The Least Are the Greatest | 106

Chapter 21   Weakness Is Strength | 110

Chapter 22   Redeemed for Good | 117

Chapter 23   History Is Not Set in Stone | 121

PART 5   PRINCIPLES OF POSITIVE PRAYER

Introduction   Healthy Homes | 127

Chapter 24   Tell God the Truth | 129

Chapter 25   Shift Your Focus to God's Promises | 133

Chapter 26   Pray God's Promises with Power | 138

Chapter 27   Practice a Self-last Prayer Structure | 141

Chapter 28   Quickly Connect Throughout Your Day | 145

Chapter 29   Discerning God's Voice in Times of Stress | 147

PART 6   PRAYERS FOR SPECIFIC NEEDS

Introduction   If the Shoe Fits . . . | 157

Chapter 30   Prayers for the Dark Night of the Soul | 158

Chapter 31   Ask for an Attitude Adjustment | 163

Chapter 32   Pray for What You *Really* Want from Healing | 166

Chapter 33   Peace That Passes Understanding | 169

Chapter 34   Mustard Seed Faith | 172

Chapter 35   Revelation of God's Love | 175

Chapter 36   The Benjamin Button Prayer | 177

Chapter 37   Pray for Fulfilled Desires | 180

Chapter 38   Ask for a New Dream | 183

Chapter 39   When You're Ready—Pray Big | 186

Chapter 40   Pray to Remember Disability | 189

PART 7   SEEKING GOD WHEN YOU ARE SUFFERING

Introduction   Celebrating Chapstick Kissing Explorers | 195

Chapter 41   Simply Show Up | 197

Chapter 42   Focus on Being with God vs. Doing for Him | 201

Chapter 43   Place Importance on Internal Transformation | 204

Chapter 44   Tools to Increase Your Awareness of God's Presence | 208

Chapter 45   Tips for Serving with Disability | 212

Chapter 46   Church and Community | 218

PART 8   TRANSFORMED THROUGH TRIALS

Introduction   Harness the Harvest | 226

Chapter 47   Difficulties Can Draw You Closer to God | 229

Chapter 48   Strengthened by Struggle | 234

Chapter 49   Crazy Gratitude | 238

Chapter 50   Contentedness | 241

Chapter 51   The Gift of Priorities | 244

Chapter 52   You Are Uniquely Equipped to Comfort Others | 248

Chapter 53   More Blessings Available to You Now | 253

Chapter 54   What Joy Awaits | 257

Confessions from the Valley | 261

Conclusion   Comfort for the Road | 263

Appendix 1: Overcome Lies with God's Truth | 267

Appendix 2: Principles of Positive Prayer | 281

Appendix 3: Prayers for the Dark Night of the Soul | 290

Appendix 4: My Favorite . . . | 293

Bibliography | 299

Acknowledgments

PARTNERING WITH GOD AND so many of my brothers and sisters in Christ to bring this book to life was an absolute joy. It truly took a village:

To Immanuel, Hosanna! You have reclaimed my brokenness more powerfully than I could imagine and your blessings are wondrous to behold.

To my husband Parker, you are my best friend, my number one editor, and the one I am delighted to adventure through life with. You enabled this to happen, my love, and I pray God credits it to your account.

Mom and Dad, you equipped me with everything I needed to get through life's unexpected challenges by raising me to know Jesus. But mom gets extra credit for being my research assistant, late-night editor, and The Grammar Queen.

Laurie, my mother-in-law and friend, I know your constant prayers have opened doors for me. I am grateful for your unwavering support.

For my M&M's—Mark Mofield and Matt Merrill—two trusted men of ministry, thank you for all the golden nuggets of advice and for ensuring the scriptural soundness of this work.

To Dr. Xavier Preud'Homme, Dr. Domenic Sica, and Dr. Matthew Brengman—this book was possible because you fought for my quality of life. Thank you for innovating on behalf of medical zebras. Kathy, thank you for listening to God's prompting and connecting me to help when I most needed it.

Emily, Melissa, Corinne, Pat, and Rachel F.— each of you invested so much in this book. Mandy, Rachel H., and Chantal, you paved the way with your support and prayers. Most importantly, all of you have invested so much into me. Each one of you makes me a better person and I am honored by your marvelous friendships.

To my Crestwood Cheerleaders, my immense gratitude for your steadfast encouragement. This is a group victory!

To Sheryl, Peyton, and Hannah, wear your wonder women capes proudly for answering a million social media and new author questions.

Sherri, Benton, and Cam, this book is better for your insight. Wise aunts and uncles you are!

Bill, Linda, and Dawn, thank you for lending your time and your voice to my work. May God bless your own endeavors.

To Stephanie and her incredible tribe—we are awestruck at your generosity which is breathing life into dreams we once thought were impossible. Whatever God has planned for our journey, you make us sing with thankfulness.

I celebrate the hardworking team at Wipf and Stock Publishers. Thank you for seeing value in this book and making a way for it to bring hope to the chronic illness community.

To all the children of my heart—James, Peter, Emma, Caroline, Casey, Elise, Paul, Hailey, Addison, Natalia, Sophia, Ethan, Liam, Hailey, and Harper—life is not always easy, but God is always good. Whatever your futures have in store, live boldly and with great courage because God's love is with you. He will catch you every time.

Lastly, to my readers and to everyone who entrusted me to share their experiences—may we all see God redeem our stories.

Introduction

The Way Forward

Praise be to the God and Father of our Lord Jesus Christ, the Father of compassion and the God of all comfort, who comforts us in all our troubles, so that we can comfort those in any trouble with the comfort we ourselves have received from God. —2 Cor 1:3–4

"Excuse me? This can't be happening. Not to me. Not at twenty-three . . . I just graduated college with honors and married the most wonderful man. Our entire future is ahead of us. We have prayed and mapped out beautiful dreams. Parker and I are going to transform lives through teaching, have four amazing kids, and explore this unclear calling we feel towards ministry. That is the plan. I know I've been having bizarre symptoms, but this has to be a colossal misunderstanding."

The compassionate sorrow in my doctor's eyes confirms the terrible truth, "I am so sorry. There is still so much we don't understand about this disorder. The symptoms will be more manageable with treatment, but you will have them for the rest of your life. I can help you file for disability when you're ready."

Think again, doc. Frankly, this disorder has no idea who it is messing with. I'm the kid who started saving her birthday money for a car at age eight. I had a summer job from the time I was twelve and won $75,000 in college scholarships. I am responsible, hardworking, and driven. I was illustrating my first life plan in crayon when other kids were doodling stick figures.

Most importantly, I am God's beloved child and he has work for me to do. It is only a matter of time until Jesus restores my strength.

***

Hi. My name is Shannon and I'm a narcoleptic. I prayed for healing every day for years after my diagnosis—fully believing God could restore me. However, instead of getting better, new symptoms appeared. I was diagnosed with two additional disorders: gastroparesis and post orthostatic tachycardia syndrome. *Where was God? How could he allow my circumstances to snowball so badly out of control?*

I have been asking tough questions and navigating chronic illness with Jesus for over a decade now. Life has not been what I expected. But Jesus has been so much more than I dared to imagine.

Whether you are newly disabled or have been coping with a chronic condition for years, we all need encouragement from believers who understand what we are going through. So, before we dig into the purpose of this book, here is a quick glimpse of what it is like to be me:

MY STORY IN A NUTSHELL:

I look like a normal young woman on the outside. But on the inside? I have the energy levels of an eighty-year-old. My hardwiring is a mess.

Narcolepsy is not the laughable need for naps that pop culture makes it out to be. It is a glitch in the immune system that causes your body to attack your sleep cells. Once my cells reached a critical low, my body lost its ability to control the quality of my rest. I can sleep for ten hours, take a two-hour afternoon nap, and still feel exhausted.

The fatigue narcoleptics experience is equivalent to what a healthy person would feel after forty-eight hours of sleep deprivation. To put my reality into perspective, think about spy movies. Any spy flick worth its salt has a scene where the hero is interrogated after being kept awake by the enemy agent. Sleep deprivation is *Torture 101* because our bodies were designed for rest. It is nearly impossible to physically function or maintain mental focus when your sleep is severely compromised. Imagine trying to hold down a job or have quality of life in that condition.

Gastroparesis is partial paralysis of the stomach. In other words, the upper half of my digestive tract moves at the speed of a sloth. I've had a chronic cough for the last eight years due to food refluxing back up. Gone are the days of chocolate, tacos, and hamburgers. Everything I eat is low fat, low fiber, and gluten-free in order to be easily digestible. I never thought I would actually miss salads!

The rapid onset of this paralysis was frightening. I lost sixty pounds in eighteen months. Three surgeries later, I am able to maintain my weight by eating six mini-meals a day. I have breakfast, elevenses, lunch, afternoon tea, first dinner, and second dinner like a hobbit.

My last condition, post orthostatic tachycardia syndrome (POTS), is a communication disorder between the brain and the autonomic nervous system (ANS). The ANS is responsible for everything that happens in your body that you don't consciously think about. It controls your heart rhythms, breathing, blood pressure, digestion, urination, pupil dilation, and circulation. Weird things happen when your brain sends out screwy signals. The experiences of POTS patients vary widely because so many different body systems can be affected.

My most prominent symptom is low blood volume. Having low blood volume means that my heart works three times as hard and that my other organs don't always get the blood supply they need for peak function. I'm constantly on the verge of being dehydrated and am especially sensitive to heat. This is treated by running fluids intravenously. I have a port (similar to one a cancer patient would have) through which I infuse eight liters of fluid weekly. Running a bag of fluid takes a minimum of two hours and limits my mobility because I have to wheel a pole around with me.

If children ask, I tell them that the doctor gave me a special hose because—like a mermaid—my body needs a whole lot of water to be healthy. One little boy looked at me with wide eyes and exclaimed, "You are going to be the healthiest person in the whole world!" From his lips to God's ears.

By the time I was diagnosed with my third disorder, I realized God wasn't going to heal me according to my time table. Nor could I keep waiting for deliverance if I wanted to stay sane and make the most of my life. It was time to ask: "How am I going to live like this?"

What I needed was a survival guide for overwhelmed Christians with chronic conditions. Reconciling my body's condition with my faith was essential to my peace of mind. Was there a roadmap for hardships? Something with practical steps I could follow to help me keep believing? *How to Love God When You're Losing It* from the *For Dummies* series would have been perfect.

Today, I am thankful I never found that edition. Because that is when Jesus found me. Completely overcome by disability, he gathered me into his arms.

Christ has been carrying me ever since. With exquisite tenderness he's been leading me through this desert season one baby step at a time. And now, by his most wonderous grace, we are working together to write the book I once searched for. Classic Jesus—he is a simply stunning Savior.

WHAT YOU CAN EXPECT FROM THIS BOOK:

This book is for all my brothers and sisters who wonder:

> *How can I keep believing in God's goodness when he hasn't healed me or answered my prayers? How do I move beyond grief, disappointment, and anger to have faith in God's promises for me? Is it possible to genuinely be positive about my future when I'm facing a lifetime of chronic illness? Can I trust Jesus to repurpose my shattered life? What steps can I take to begin moving forward?*

Fellow warrior, in your hands is a battle plan. It is not a collection of mandatory rules you must follow *but an arsenal of life-giving tools for you to use as needed.* May they help you hold onto God, even as he holds onto you. Within these pages you will:

- Meet your teammate—Jesus. He intimately understands your situation and your feelings of grief.

- Acquire strategies for overcoming guilt, anxiety, and feelings of inadequacy.

- Refresh your mind with key biblical truths that promote awareness of God's love for you. You will always have worth—and a future to look forward to—because your identity is in Christ.

- Discover how God's ways are not our ways. *Spoiler:* He loves breaking the rules to your advantage.

- Build a healthy foundation for your prayer life and reclaim prayers that have run away with worry. You can connect honestly with God *and* develop habits that give your prayers a positive focus.

- Learn tips for discerning God's voice in stressful seasons.

- Discover helpful prayers for when you need peace, faith, or a divine attitude adjustment.

- Gather practical ideas for spiritually growing when you're just trying to keep going.

- Find an honest examination of how God has used disability to change me. Has he shifted my perspective in the decade following my initial diagnosis? May a transparent look at my frustrations and celebrations inspire you to hope.

For more than ten years, Jesus has been making a way for me to have hope, peace, and joy with chronic illness—things I once thought were impossible. Even when our bodies remain broken, God is capable of healing our hurts and our hearts. He can illuminate our darkest nightmares with triumph (John 1:5). May the comfort I have received from him encourage and empower you.

Now it's your turn. Jesus is your way forward.

Jesus answered, "I am the way and the truth and the life."
—John 14:6

Part 1

You Are Not Alone

Two are better than one, because they have a good return for their labor: If either of them falls down, one can help the other up. But pity anyone who falls and has no one to help them up. Also, if two lie down together, they will keep warm. But how can one keep warm alone? Though one may be overpowered, two can defend themselves. A cord of three strands is not quickly broken. —Eccl 4:9–12

Introduction

Meet Immanuel

"The virgin will conceive and give birth to a son, and they will call him Immanuel" (which means "God with us"). —Matt 1:23

"Why . . . ?" is the universal cry of our souls when the unthinkable happens. It is a raw and valid question. But, as someone who has tried to console herself with the theology of suffering, may I share a useful tidbit? *Why . . .* is an incomplete starting point.

Don't get me wrong—it is helpful and reassuring to develop a biblical understanding of suffering. I believe that suffering is not from God but is a byproduct of our fallen world. I know that God has a plan to bring all suffering to an end. Meanwhile, I have faith that God is powerfully reclaiming the brokenness of this world by working through it to accomplish his purposes. And I absolutely believe that we can become more like Jesus through suffering.

But let's get real: knowing *why* God allows suffering is cold comfort when you are hurting. If this is your only source of encouragement, God will seem remote and callous. For me, understanding *why* simply wasn't enough to heal my relationship with him.

My faith and my "new normal" needed a way to coexist. So what was I missing? Where could I find an ingredient strong enough to overcome my feelings of abandonment and repair my friendship with God?

At the grocery store. I will admit—it's a lot to ask of Food Lion's cereal aisle. But God seems to enjoy springing spiritual revelation on me in unlikely places.

My mom and I weigh our breakfast options as a woman with a bright floral scarf wound around her head passes us. She must be a cancer patient. "God, help her," I silently pray before turning back to duke it out between

Quaker Oatmeal Squares and Honey Bunches of Oats. *What the heck . . . life's short.* I toss Cinnamon Toast Crunch in the cart and turn to see my mom wrapping the stranger in a heartfelt embrace.

What in the world? Amazed at my mom's courage, I tiptoe forward to hear her share:

> I am a breast cancer survivor. I know today is really tough, but you are not alone. Just keep taking it one day at a time, and you will make it through this. I promise things are going to get better.

Grabbing my mom's hand, the woman tearfully replies,

> Thank you for stopping me; I really needed to hear that today. It's good to know that someone understands.

Their words sear through my defenses exposing the deepest hunger of my soul: I need more than a Jesus who is distantly sympathizing with me from the perfection of heaven. I could spend the rest of my days trying to wrap my head around the mysteries of God's ways, but it will never be enough. Perhaps, the missing ingredient I need to move forward is something so much simpler . . . *I need to know that Jesus understands my pain.*

Is that what you want? The comfort of someone who knows exactly what you are going through? To know you are not alone?

If this is the Jesus you need today, *he lives.* He has chosen the name Immanuel, which means "God with us." His very name is a promise to you, and to me, that we are not alone. Our Savior came in the flesh to get up close and personal with the messiness of human existence. To experience our struggles for himself. Jesus always understands our hurts—because he's lived them.

How can this be since Jesus was able bodied? While Christ's earthly body was "normal," his incarnation (choice to become human) came with many challenges. In this section, you'll discover that Jesus experienced the frustrations we face on a daily basis: loneliness, limitations, loss, fear, and pain.

Fellow warrior, what cannot be borne alone can be shouldered with the help of a friend. Especially when his name is Immanuel. When nothing else could rekindle my hope, realizing that Jesus is present in my suffering became my pathway to freedom. It may seem like a surprisingly simple baby step, but it gave me a partner. I didn't have to rebuild my life or my faith alone.

Neither do you. Take hold of Jesus' hand and brave your first step.

For we do not have a high priest who is unable to empathize with our weaknesses, but we have one who has been tempted in every way, just as we are—yet he did not sin. Let us then approach God's throne of grace with confidence, so that we may receive mercy and find grace to help us in our time of need. —Heb 4:15–16

Chapter 1

Jesus Understands the Loneliness of Being Different

Like one from whom people hide their faces he was despised, and we held him in low esteem. —Isa 53:3b

"YOU ARE ONE IN a million." I love those words when my husband whispers them in my ear. I would be ecstatic to hear that phrase from the lottery commission. But coming from my doctors? The statistic makes me cringe. The combination of my three disorders makes me an exceedingly rare individual. I would rather not be medically "interesting," thank you very much.

We live in a culture where everyone wants to stand out. However, being different because of a disability is not quirky, cool, or fun—it is lonely. I had no idea loneliness could come in so many layers before experiencing chronic illness.

For starters, inability to work is physically isolating from others. I cried countless mornings after Parker left for work in the first year of our marriage. I was unbearably lonely during those long hours by myself but too exhausted to put forward the effort it takes to make friends in a new city. I hated being the twenty-something-year-old whose only honest response to the question, "What do you do?" was "I'm chilling at home until I get some health problems under control (*followed by awkward laughter in an attempt to lighten the mood*)." What a conversation killer!

In addition, I was emotionally hungry for understanding. My loved ones could not relate to what I was going through. Casual acquaintances often had ignorant (and occasionally hurtful) reactions to my differences. I ached to find just one person who could completely identify with my challenges.

God has brought me a long way from those desperate first years. However, loneliness remains one of the hardest side effects of chronic illness for me to accept. I miss attending afternoon events, joining my gal pals on spur-of-the-moment adventures, and being able to lay beside Parker comfortably on the couch. Despite twelve years of practice, my heart still hurts when I'm unable to participate because of my restrictions. Some days, I feel as if I am watching the world sail by from my lone island.

Are you feeling similarly marooned and isolated? Then make a little room under your palm tree. *Jesus understands the loneliness of being different because he had the distinction of being the most unique person in history.* One hundred and seventeen billion people have walked the face of our planet.[1] Only one has been fully human and fully divine. Jesus is in a league entirely of his own.

FAR FROM HOME:

Immanuel knows that physical limitations separate us from our loved ones in painful ways. In order to come to earth, Jesus had to leave the only home he had ever known—heaven. To gain insight into the loneliness of Jesus the man, we need to start with Jesus the heavenly king. What does his life in paradise look like?

Try to imagine the spiritual fullness of the atmosphere Christ came from. The Bible teaches that Jesus has been reigning in heaven with God since the beginning of time. Creation itself springs from him, and he fashions everything from forests to family trees with his Father. He sits at the right hand of God, receiving constant worship in a kingdom where there is no evil, suffering, or pain. Together, their love is the light that illuminates all darkness and the source of all life.[2]

Wow. I cannot fathom such soul-satisfying companionship. My tiny human brain can only grasp the merest hint of who God is. First Corinthians 13:12 ERV reveals that,

> Now we see God as if we are looking at a reflection in a mirror [*cloudy picture (CEV), blurred image (GW), or dim likeness (NIRV)*]. But then, in the future, we will see him right before our eyes.

---

1. Kaneda and Haub, "How Many People Have Ever Lived on Earth?," para. 3.
2. John 1:1, John 1:3, Heb 1:3, Rev 22:3, John 1:4–5

As God's child, you are on an upward journey in your relationship with the Father. Your current knowledge of God is like a keyhole offering a brief glimpse of what is to come. It is as if you have fallen in love with someone from a grainy photograph.

However, when you cross the threshold into heaven, you will experience God on an entirely new level. You will wake up from the faded picture to find yourself enveloped in your true love's embrace. In an eclipse of profound revelation, black and white will become vibrant technicolor. Your longed-for hopes will explode into reality!

If this image gives you warm fuzzies, thank Jesus. We can eagerly anticipate a deeper connection with God in heaven because Jesus undertook the reverse journey:

> Instead, he gave up everything, even his place with God.
> He accepted the role of a servant, appearing in human form.
> —Phil 2:7 ERV

What an outrageous exchange. Jesus temporarily gives up the ideal connection with God. He trades flawless companionship in order to come to a world where his differences make him a puzzle to everyone. How lonely would that be?

Take a minute to think about it. All of Jesus' relationships on earth were a bit odd. He was a son who was his parents' Savior, a sibling who was sinless, a mortal teacher whom mother nature obeyed, and a carpenter who was building a heavenly kingdom. Because of his divinity, he never had a friend or family member who "could put an arm around him . . . and say, 'I know exactly what you're going through.'"[3] He was an outsider.

Sounds like one hell of a road trip. And that's before things got *really* ugly.

LIFE ON THE OUTSKIRTS:

Human nature has an unfortunate tendency towards middle school behavior—when confronted by someone new or different, it closes ranks against the outsider. We dislike it when the unfamiliar threatens our world view or reminds us of our own insecurities. So, we shut our eyes to what challenges us and hold those who make us uncomfortable at arm's length. It is easier than confronting our fears or changing how we think.

This distancing reaction is always hurtful. Similar to racism, disabled individuals are often left out and undervalued when communities are not

---

3. Bloom, "Jesus Understands Loneliness," para. 6.

intentionally inclusive. Many of us have been on the receiving end of belit- tling behaviors (i.e., false assumptions, patronizing attitudes, character as- sassination, and name calling.) All of these behaviors point a finger at the different individual and label them "other—not one of us." An *outcast.*

As a middle-class white American, I never thought I would be able to personally identify with this term. Then, (in the interval between my narco- lepsy and POTS diagnosis) I spent five years stumping multiple specialists. Frustrated with their inability to figure me out, some of these doctors re- sorted to name calling. I was accused of being depressed or overly-anxious. I was called a hypochondriac and an attention seeker.

It felt like a sucker punch. In a way I wish it had been—that would have been less harmful than being rejected by the doctors I needed to help me. Every time a specialist declared that my symptoms were in my head, I second guessed myself. I lost crucial months (in which preventable damage was done) because I was too discouraged to seek help. The word "outcast" began to ricochet around my mind like a poisonous pinball.

Have the repercussions of disability left you feeling unwanted and unloved? Do you need proof that public opinion is not a reliable measurement of per- sonal worth? Then use this chapter's key verse to silence shame and renew your inner strength. Isaiah 53:3 is your fight song:

> Like one from whom people hide their faces he was despised,
> and we held him in low esteem. —Isa 53:3b

The Bible is clear . . . *Jesus was an outcast.* It seems impossible that these words should describe him. Jesus was the only perfect person to ever grace this earth and he unquestionably deserved the admiration of us lesser mortals. Who had the audacity to find fault with God's Son? The men who should have been his most loyal supporters—the religious leaders.

Now, that's a sucker punch. The chief priests were in the profession of serving God. They should have been the first people to recognize Jesus' true identity and join his ministry. Instead, the priests were blinded by narrow expectations and petty jealousies. In the process of looking for a militant messiah who would free Israel from Roman rule, they dismissed the man who could save their souls. They hated Jesus' popularity with the poor and were embarrassed when he challenged them to be more merciful. How dare this Nazarian nobody question their spiritual authority and upset the status quo?

The angry priests lashed out in a smear campaign to discredit Jesus. They called him:

- A Sinner (John 9:24)

- A Blasphemer (John 10:33)

- A Traitor to Rome (John 19:12)

- Satan Himself (Matt 12:24)

Woah. Epic job fail. The high school coach who cut Michael Jordan from the varsity team and the publishers who rejected J.K. Rowling's *Harry Potter* made trifling career mistakes by comparison. The chief priests could not have been more off base when sizing up the blameless Son of God. They either had major stones or were acting out of sheer stupidity.

I am leaning towards the latter. Because when the name calling didn't work, the priests escalated to the ugliest act of prejudice—violently devaluing human life. They tortured Jesus, drove him *outside* of the city walls, nailed him to a cross, and left him to die like a criminal on the *outskirts* of Jerusalem (Heb 13:12).

The cross is the final testament to how misunderstood Jesus was during his lifetime. He was an outsider from start to finish.

The next time someone questions your value as a disabled individual, stop and consider how Jesus was treated. He was misunderstood by everyone. People doubted whether or not he had anything worthwhile to give. He was called names that couldn't have been further from the truth. You, my friend, are in *very* good company.

Secondly, remember that Jesus did not allow being categorized as an outcast to define him. *Being misunderstood by others has no power over you when you understand who you are.* Jesus knew that even when people pegged him dead wrong, they were pointing to something true: He was indeed the *outcast* Son of God. Jesus willingly allowed himself to be *cast out* of heaven so that *no one will be alone on their island* (Phil 2:6–8).

Do not think less of yourself because your life is unconventional. You are much more than a chronic condition. Who are you? You are a child of the living God. You are Jesus' treasure. You are valued. You are chosen. You are loved.[4]

Listen, my dear brothers and sisters: Has not God chosen those who are poor in the eyes of the world to be rich in faith and to inherit the kingdom he promised those who love him? —Jas 2:5

4. 1 John 3:1, Deut 7:6, Eph 2:10 NLT, 1 Pet 2:9, 1 John 4:8–10

Chapter 2

Jesus Lived with Limitations and Loss

The Word became flesh and made his dwelling among us.
—John 1:14

EVERY DISABILITY COMES WITH its own set of limitations. My most frustrating symptom is fatigue. The tiredness I battle as a narcoleptic makes me feel like one of the walking dead. POTS amplifies this fatigue further because my brain signals my heart to beat very quickly. My record pulse is 170 beats per minute. Was I having an intense cardio workout? Nope: I was chilling on the couch!

It's little wonder I fight against debilitating exhaustion when I'm running stationary marathons. I struggle to balance my part-time work with the afternoon naps and rest days I need to avoid crashing. The brain fog I push through to accomplish even simple tasks feels like wading through molasses. As a previously active person who still has big dreams for my life, I find this zombie existence infuriating.

Beneath these daily frustrations lies a profound sense of loss. I grieve all the parts of myself I have needed to give up in order to conserve energy for the non-negotiable aspects of life. Motherhood, investing in more friendships, travelling, painting, singing, gardening, and owning pets are among the casualties of my fatigue. Each thwarted desire and sacrificed joy, feels like a lost piece of myself. Sometimes I fear I'm at risk for losing the essence of who I am.

Perhaps your most debilitating symptom is sensory deprivation, immobility, chronic pain, or immune deficiency. While limitations vary widely by diagnoses, we are all coping with loss as a result of our physical conditions. You and I both know how maddening it is when you can't perform tasks that

used to come easily or enjoy life on your own terms. The good news is . . .
Jesus gets our frustration.

Our Savior's incarnation came at a very steep price. Jesus had to sup-
press some of his godly characteristics in order to have the "human" experience. This was not a one-time choice but a continuous commitment. As a
fully divine being, Jesus made thousands of choices every day to opt "in" to
the limitations of a human body. What godly traits did that require him to
opt out of?

The Three Big A's.[1] To become Immanuel, Jesus intentionally suspended his
ability to be:

- *All-Powerful*
- *All-Knowing*
- *All-Present*

This staggering self-denial makes Christ the expert on personal limitations and loss. Jesus gave himself up for us long before the passion of the
cross. His sacrifice truly began with a baby's first breath.

OUR *ALL-POWERFUL* SAVIOR LIMITED HIMSELF WITH PHYSICAL NEEDS:

Jesus is the very definition of self-sufficient strength. In his divine state he
is "the radiance of God's glory and the exact representation of his being,
sustaining all things by his powerful word (Heb 1:3)." God the Son can hold
the universe together without eating organic, cleansing his toxins, or needing eight hours of beauty sleep to be his best self. He is effortlessly awesome.

I would save the world as the all-powerful King of Kings if those were
my credentials. Yet Jesus chose a far tougher assignment—the inconve-
nience of a human body. Beginning his mission as a newborn meant he
had to rely on fallible human parents for his care. Mary and Joseph carried
him wherever he needed to go. They helped him sit up until his abdominal
muscles developed. Christ had to endure the humiliation of another person wiping him. Imagine how fragile Jesus felt going from infinite power to
helpless infant.

---

1. Thank you to my wonderful friend Emily Walker for suggesting *"The Three Big
A's!"*

Remarkably, Immanuel continued to opt "in" to physical needs as he grew into adulthood and began his ministry. On earth, he got snack attacks. I think of the Snickers' commercials, "You're not you when you're hungry," every time I read about that poor little fig tree Jesus withered to its roots for failing to provide him with fruit snacks (Mark 11:12–20). Sounds like sweet and gentle Jesus experienced low blood sugar episodes. Who knew holy Christ could get hangry?

Human Jesus also had to make do with limited energy. John's gospel relates how he arrived in a Samaritan village and, "*tired* from the long walk, sat *wearily* beside the well about noontime (John 4:6 NLT)." How that simple word "tired" blesses my narcoleptic heart! Jesus could have been a human Energizer Bunny with the power source he had flowing through his veins. Yet, he elected to sit "wearily" beside a well. What type of Savior is this?

A Savior I can fall in love with. This tired and worn-out Jesus speaks to me. The fact that he chose to experience the fatigue I find so frustrating tells me more about the depth of his love than his raw power ever could. It is inspiring that he had to accept help from other people, make decisions about how to spend his energy, and take time out to regroup. *Jesus understands the frustration of physical weaknesses because he had a human body just like you and me.*

GOD'S *ALL-KNOWING* SON EMBRACED A LEARNING CURVE:

Heavenly Jesus is all-seeing and completely formed. He knows everything from the deep secrets of God to where you stashed your favorite Halloween candy. But instead of emerging from Mary's womb as a fully baked wonderkid, Christ "increased in wisdom and stature, and in favour with God and man (Luke 2:52 KJV)."

What is the astonishing implication of this statement? Jesus—who is constant and perfect— was not born knowing everything. He had to learn and grow for the very first time.

Growing is hard work. Like all children, young Jesus had to discover the world through his five senses and develop his speech. Joseph showed him how to hammer a nail. A rabbi taught him to read the Torah. What would it be like to learn to count, when you are the one who numbers the stars?

The word "wisdom" in Luke 2:52 has a deeper meaning which is even more shocking. It is translated from the Greek word *sophia* which refers to "both human *and divine wisdom*," including "knowledge, intelligence, and understanding."[2] Dang. Jesus couldn't even get a free pass on his Bible trivia. Growing in divine wisdom means that he wasn't born babbling the Beatitudes or healing a sick cow from his cradle in the hay. Immanuel had to develop his relationship with God and grow into his identity as Messiah. How much patience would it take to sit through "Sabbath" school lessons at the knee of a teacher you created?

Jesus did not go to all that trouble for the orange juice and animal crackers. His decision to begin life with the limited knowledge of a pint-sized person had you at the center of its heart. As people with chronic conditions, all of us have had to relearn skills or find new ways of doing things. We have adapted to challenging new circumstances. A ready-made savior would not be able to relate to that kind of learning curve. But a Bethlehem baby? He gets growing pains.

JESUS FORFEITED HIS ABILITY TO BE *ALL-PRESENT*:

Divine Jesus can simultaneously interact with every person on our planet without breaking a sweat. It's a perk of being God. Now, imagine he loaned you the ability to be in multiple places at once for the span of a single day. How would you use his omnipresence?

I would attend a funeral. I dearly loved and was privileged to know Parker's kind-hearted Grandad. Unfortunately, his death came at an impossible time for me.

I normally teach preschool two mornings a week. But every September I work four days in a row in order to get my classroom set up for the new school year. This wouldn't be a big deal for a healthy person—for me it is an Ironman Triathlon.

News of Grandad's death came on day four when my body was on the brink of collapse. Going out of town for a few days to attend the funeral would put me out of commission for a week. I would jeopardize my job and be more of a burden than a comfort to the mourners. Parker and I agreed it would be better for everyone if I stayed home, but to this day I regret that necessity. If I could tap into Jesus' divine ability to be all-present, I would go back in time to honor Grandad *and* be a state away resting up for the first day of school.

I try not to dwell on what I was capable of before disability as a general rule. But when tiredness separates me from my loved ones, I crave the energetic "get-it-done" Shannon I used to be. In such moments, my sanity

2. Renn, *Expository Dictionary of Bible Words*, 1051.

is anchored by a Jesus who understands that limitations demand tough choices—a Jesus who missed funerals.

Jesus was in Bethany when he received the news that his friend Lazarus was ill (John 11:1–4). He couldn't send his clone ahead or teleport himself to Lazarus' bedside without breaking his commitment to experience life as a human. In heaven, he had been (and would return to being) the ultimate multitasker. *But here on earth Jesus was just like us: he could only deal with one person or situation at a time.*

I suspect it was very painful for Jesus to deny his ability to be "all" to everyone. When he finally reaches Lazarus' home, his friend has been dead and buried for four days. He is too late to prevent Lazarus' death.

My heart is so touched by what happens next. On seeing the heartbreak of Lazarus' sisters Mary and Martha, Jesus is deeply moved. The divine Son of God does something beautifully and entirely human—he cries (John 11:35).

It does not matter that Jesus is there to raise Lazarus from the dead. Or that he is about to disperse the stench of the grave with his breath of life. It does not even matter that Immanuel knows in the next few minutes the sisters' sorrow will be eclipsed by joy. Jesus cries because he is moved by the grief of his friends and by the pain Lazarus suffered. Their hurt is real to him. Christ weeps for the sorrow they have already experienced.

These are the tears of the Lord who loves you. Christ traded his ability to be *all-present* because he is *all-compassionate*. Jesus' heart is always with you in loss.

However much our abilities have diminished, we can't begin to touch the productivity scale-back Christ experienced when he left heaven to become a man. For thirty-three years, Jesus suppressed his *Three Big A's* in favor of countless frustrations. Wasn't there a simpler way?

Beloved, Jesus is not concerned with simple. He is committed to standing in solidarity with you through your limitations. Hebrews 2:17 explains that, "For this reason he had to be made like them, fully human in every way, in order that he might become a merciful and faithful high priest in service to God, and that he might make atonement for the sins of the people." Jesus knew you needed someone on your team. So he came in human weakness in order to win you to himself.

Talk about a crazy play. But Christ's life is a reminder that the challenges of God's children are never quite what they seem. Out of Jesus' losses, God birthed a family. There is great hope for your ashes yet.

He has sent me . . . to bestow on them a crown of beauty instead of ashes . . . —Excerpted from Isa 61:1–3

Chapter 3

Jesus Knew Fear and Deep Sorrow

Then he said to them, "My soul is crushed with grief to the point of death." —Matt 26:38 NLT

THE FIERCEST BATTLE OF my life has not been against chronic illness, it has been against fear. I still don't like to think about how afraid I was during the first year after my diagnosis. The physical symptoms were alarming. The realization that I was not going to have the future I'd imagined for myself? That was utterly terrifying.

Fear of losing my dreams was unlike any bully I had previously encountered. It was a palpable monster looming over all aspects of my life—dogging my every step. I felt like I was sharing a studio apartment with the Incredible Hulk.

At night, I'd wake up screaming from nightmares of my college professors telling me it would be impossible for me to teach. My mind reeled with the accusation, "Failure" until I struggled to breathe.

By day, I broke into cold sweats thinking about the challenges ahead. I was haunted by the idea that I had become a burden to others. The hollowness of being unable to be the wife I wanted to be frequently made me feel like I was going to vomit. I would not wish this relentless fear on my worst enemy. I was walking a tightrope in an attempt to cling to my sanity.

Harder still, my fear was coupled by a cruel taunt, "If you were a better Christian, if you loved God more, you wouldn't be afraid." Guilt over feeling afraid stood in the way every time I tried to bring my fears to God. It seemed like one more way I was failing.

Do you feel like you're on the edge of an abyss? Like fear is threatening to swallow you whole? Are you keeping your fears from God because you think they are unchristian? Then let's be bold together and ask, "Jesus, did you ever feel afraid?"

Travel with me to the garden of Gethsemane. Shhh . . . tiptoe past the snoring disciples, and allow your eyes to adjust to the inky blackness of the night. Just beyond that gnarled olive tree someone is in distress. Who is the man hunched over in the dirt crying out for God's mercy?

The anguished man is Jesus (Matt 26:37). How unexpected to see him trembling in the distraught posture I know so well. Immanuel knows that he is about to be crucified, experience separation from God, and be punished for the sins of all people. We have found him during his dark night of the soul.

What is Christ praying as he prepares to face the cross? Is he crying out for courage? Seeking God's strength? As we inch closer, his prayer reaches our ears, "My Father! If it is possible, let this cup of suffering be taken away from me (Matt 26:39 NLT)."

Come again? Those are not the words I thought we'd hear. Did Jesus really ask God for a way out? Why would he plead with God when he came to earth to be crucified in the first place?

Jesus prayed for deliverance because he was afraid. Isn't fear what prompts any of us to ask God for another way? No one prays for an escape when life is good. Instead, we cry out for mercy in our hardships, pain, and heartaches. We plead with God when we are afraid of a future without the person we love, facing a risky surgery, or need rescuing from unbearable symptoms. It is when we dread whatever "cross" lies before us that we echo Christ's cry, "Father, take this away from me!"

Jesus words suggest he is seriously stressed. But his body confirms it. Jesus was having physical symptoms as a result of his inner torment. The gospel of Luke says that he, "was in such agony of spirit that his sweat fell to the ground like great drops of blood (Luke 22:44 NLT)." That may seem a little far-fetched, but Luke was a physician. Was the doc trying to spice up his gospel? Or was Jesus actually sweating blood?

Modern medical practitioners recognize an extremely rare occurrence called hematohidrosis. Persons experiencing severe physical or emotional stress can have a spike in blood pressure that bursts the capillaries which feed into their sweat glands. As a result, the individual sweats blood. Studies of this phenomenon say, "*Acute fear* and intense mental contemplation are the most frequent causes."[1] Documented cases include a soldier preparing to go to battle, persons facing execution, and a case that occurred during the London Blitz. Based on Luke's observations at the garden of Gethsemane, I would add Jesus to this list.

Isn't it freeing to know that Jesus didn't face the cross as if it was going to be a cinch? That he can relate to your feelings of fear? He experienced dread to the extreme point of sweating blood and yet still was sinless. How did Christ keep fear from winning?

Push PLAY on Jesus' prayer, "My Father! If it is possible, let this cup of suffering be taken away from me. Yet I want your will to be done, not mine (Matt 26:39 NLT)."

Jesus was sinless because he did not allow fear to control his actions. Instead, he called on a faith that outweighed his fear. He shifted his focus to God's will and unfailing goodness. He remembered that his death would bring life to his brothers and sisters and trusted God to redeem his sacrifice. Ultimately, it is Jesus' faith in his Father that gives him the strength to turn from his fears and towards the cross.

Immanuel shows us that the key to overcoming fear is standing on God's perfect love (1 John 4:18). This love is the only foundation firm enough to hold us when everything else seems to be slipping away (Isa 54:10).

The next time anxiety paralyzes you, follow Christ's example. Remind disability that it is not your identity because first and foremost you are a child of God (1 John 3:1). Proclaim over the wreckage of your broken dreams that you are a new creation in Christ and that he is calling you to things far greater than you can imagine (Eph 1:18–19a). Linger in the limitless love of the Father you belong to and can never be separated from (Rom 8:38–39).

Lastly, remember that feelings of fear are not sin. Fear only becomes sin when you allow it to perpetually rule your life. If guilt about your fearful feelings is keeping you from God, then point to Jesus on his knees in the garden. He proved that fear is a natural reaction to daunting circumstances. He even allowed himself time to grieve and regroup.

Faith is moving forward when you are afraid. Anyone can run into battle when they are unaware of the horrors of war. But the truly courageous know what lies ahead and go anyway. Like Jesus we go—because we know there is something more important worth fighting for.

---

1. Jerajani et al., "Hematohidrosis," 290–92.

If all you have strength for today is a baby step, then Jesus rejoices that you are toddling. Every small step towards following God, caring about others, and living with purpose is a triumph. So lay your fears at Jesus' feet. He knows just how much strength moving forward takes.

But the Lord is faithful, and he will strengthen you and protect you from the evil one. —2 Thess 3:3

Chapter 4

Jesus Experienced Betrayal and Abandonment

Jesus answered, "Die for me? I tell you the truth, Peter—before the rooster crows tomorrow morning, you will deny three times that you even know me. —John 13:38

MANY OF US HAVE been wounded by fair weather friends who leave when the strain of disability/chronic illness becomes inconvenient. As a college senior, I lost my three closest friends. Frightened and stressed, I am sure I was no picnic as a friend or roommate. I know I dropped the ball in my relationships. But it was still painful to be deserted by women I admired when my friendship was no longer fun. Three years of shared killer cookies, classes, and road trips—forgotten.

Few experiences are as emotionally scarring as being abandoned by those you love when you need them the most. Nearly a decade later the sting has softened, but my heart still aches for what could have been when I see photos of their reunions on Facebook.

It encourages me that the most flawless friend in human history also experienced betrayal and abandonment. Who would unfriend Jesus? But Immanuel routinely lost disciples when the call to follow him was confusing or challenging (John 6:66). Judas became the world's most famous backstabber when he sold Jesus' whereabouts to the religious leaders who put him to death. Yet, there was an even closer friend who deserted Jesus in his hour of need: Peter.

JESUS' BETRAYAL:

Peter was one of Jesus' best friends. He had experiences with Jesus that were unique and precious. Peter walked with Christ on the waves and was the first disciple to proclaim that Jesus was the long-awaited Messiah. He, James, and John formed Jesus' inner circle. The trio had the privilege of seeing Jesus transfigured in all of his heavenly brilliance and watched awe-struck as he resurrected a little girl from the dead. They were also his chosen companions when he was deeply troubled in the garden of Gethsemane.

Peter had an all-access pass to Jesus' life. He witnessed Christ's triumphant/tough moments and passionately declared himself to be "all in" as a disciple. When Jesus warns Peter that he will deny him, Peter exclaims, "Even if I have to die with you, I will never disown you (Matt 26:35)."

But what happens when Jesus is arrested and Peter has the opportunity to live up to his promises? His bravado fails him. Peter denies Jesus not once, not twice, but three times. That burns. Jesus was aware of Peter's actions on the outskirts of the trial even while he was facing his accusers. When Peter denies him for the third time, Luke 22:61 says, "The Lord turned and looked straight at Peter."

What an incredibly private moment amidst the tumult of Jesus' trial and torture. Yes, Christ felt the lash of the whip, but he also felt the sting of Peter's betrayal. Jesus understands wounds inflicted by desertion.

LEARNING FROM JESUS' RESPONSE (JOHN 21:15–19):

How did the risen Christ address Peter's denial? Jesus gives Peter the opportunity to atone for his mistake by professing his love. Notice that after Peter's declaration Jesus didn't snap back, "Then why did you deny me?" Instead, his loving response is "Follow me (v. 19)" and "Take care of my sheep (v. 16)."

In one conversation, Jesus reinstates Peter as a disciple, gives him a purpose, and makes him a leader. He does not condemn Peter or rehash the past for a little passive aggressive payback. By saying little, Jesus says it all: Peter is freely forgiven and now it is time to move on. Two truths from this interaction grabbed my attention and helped my own hurts to heal.

First, Peter did not deny Jesus because he found God's Son inadequate. For many years, I blamed myself for losing my college friends. Who would want to be friends with someone who is disabled, weak, and scared? What did I have to offer? These insecurities handicapped my efforts towards developing new friendships. If I couldn't give as much as I had been able to in the past, would I be rejected again?

But Jesus' self-esteem didn't suffer from Peter's disappearing act. He didn't waste a single moment wondering if he had been a bad friend. Genie may rock the cave of wonders, but Jesus would trounce him in a sing-off of a "Friend Like Me."[1] Christ understood that Peter's actions were a reflection of Peter's own brokenness. Peter denied Jesus because he was afraid of being persecuted.

Likewise, my friends didn't abandon me because I had nothing to offer. The wane of these relationships mostly came down to bad timing. My world was unraveling as their lives were just beginning. They were busy making decisions about where they would live, work, or go to graduate school. Their bright futures were calling. I was an anomaly, and I am sure they found my hardships frightening. Perhaps the outcome would have been different if we'd met later when we all had more life experience.

Understanding that it wasn't my fault allowed me to feel good about myself again. Jesus has been teaching me to extend grace to myself and to value the friend I am able to be as a disabled person. He's been showing me that even though I have slowed down, my unique combination of kindness, genuine concern, thoughtfulness, and loyalty are still there. And as I've begun to "re-love" myself, God has blessed me with friends who value me . . . . narcolepsy and POTS included.

Secondly, Jesus did not condemn Peter as a bad person because he made one (or three) poor choices. Therefore, I must also extend grace towards friends who have let me down. I'll admit that in the anger of being rejected, it was tempting to vilify my college friends.

But our lives are all a combination of personal failures and successes. Beyond being fair weather friends at age twenty-two, they have become women who are a blessing to their families and communities. All things considered; they are excellent people.

Jesus has looked past millions of my mistakes to see my promise. I am trying to adopt his vision. While I still mourn the loss of my friends, Jesus has helped me to forgive them in my heart. I pray that God blesses them with health, happiness in their families, joy in their work, and that they never read this book because I do not want them to be burdened by guilt. I genuinely wish them well. Whenever twinges of loss threaten me

---

1. Hit song from Disney's *Aladdin* (1992).

with sadness, I remember that I have one friend who I can never burn out. Dearest Immanuel, I have never had a friend like thee.

Even if my father and mother abandon me, the Lord will hold me close. —Ps 17:10 NLT

Chapter 5

Jesus Felt Forsaken by God

And at three in the afternoon Jesus cried out in a loud voice, "Eloi, Eloi, lema sabachthani?" (which means "My God, my God, why have you forsaken me?"). —Mark 15:34

GOD, WHY HAVE YOU *forsaken me?* Is that the cry hidden in your heart today? Have you had too many disappointments to believe that God is for you? Do you feel like a target as tough blows come one after the other? Are you wondering if God has forgotten you or if he even cares about you at all?

Most of us immediately go into fix-it mode when those we love are sick or hurting. If my nephew or goddaughter scrapes their knee, I am by their side with a choice of Care Bear or Scooby Doo Band-Aids before they can work up a decent cry. If Parker's had a bad day, I am running to Food Lion for an apple crumble pie. And when someone dares to suggest in December that my long-haired indoor/outdoor cat is looking "fat," my claws come out in defense of Vinny's "winter fluff." (His cold weather fur is an impressive optical illusion, but I swear he only weighs the recommended ten pounds.)

We want instant relief for our loved ones. So, when God doesn't use his power to help us in the ways we hope for or expect, it feels like abandonment. When our health declines, our business fails, or our child dies we wonder, *"God, where are you?"* Confused and hurt, we withdraw into ourselves feeling forsaken and beneath his notice. Or we beat God to the punch and angrily reject him before we can feel rejected. *Either way, our feelings make our pain worse by distancing us from our one source of comfort.*

All Christians go through times of brokenness when God seems far away. These tough seasons can be crossroad moments in your spiritual journey. Will your faith be governed by feelings or grounded in Scriptural fact?

Jeremiah 17:9a teaches, "The heart is deceitful above all things and beyond cure." While grief is valid and important, feelings cannot be the only foundation of our truth because emotions are changeable creatures. The inevitable outcome of a faith based solely on feelings is bitterness when life doesn't turn out as planned.

God's word is an unchanging measure of truth (Matt 24:35). Practicing faith in Scripture is not about blind believing or replacing reality with fairy tales: it is about being open to the possibility that the Bible represents a truth higher than your feelings. It is choosing to engage with God through your doubt, anger, and grief rather than running away from him. It is taking action to investigate what the Bible says about suffering, praying through your problems, and repeating God's promises until they stick in your heart.

This type of faith is not easy and takes time. It took two years of constant reminders for my wounded heart to begin seeing the Lord's work in my life. Over and over I told myself in moments of disappointment and anger that Jesus' very name, Immanuel, was a proclamation that God had not abandoned me. At times it felt emotionally grueling to engage when I wanted to barricade my heart in numbness. *But remaining open to God while I wrestled with him had one definite advantage over giving in to doubt—it kept my hope alive.*

If you long for hope that you are not alone, begin to foster it. Cling to these two biblical truths:

TRUTH #1 — A SIMILARITY:

Jesus understands the acute pain of feeling abandoned by God. "My God, my God, why have you forsaken me?" were Christ's last anguished words as a human. He cried them through lips battered beyond recognition as he hung suffocating on the cross. Why was it necessary for Jesus to die tortuously alone?

God is absolutely holy and completely good. Therefore, he can have no part of sin. That is a problem for God's people. Isaiah 59:2 says, "But your iniquities have separated you from your God; your sins have hidden his face from you." Human sin is an obstacle to our relationship with him, and before Jesus, there was no easy workaround.

The Old Testament Israelites tried (and repeatedly failed) to follow a lengthy set of rules to make themselves right with God. Not even the priests could live up to God's standard of holiness. A veil—representative of the consequences of sin—separated the priests from the synagogue chamber where God's presence dwelled. Unauthorized priests who went beyond the curtain and trespassed upon God's holiness died (Lev 16:2).

Sin separates people from God and results in death (Rom 6:23). *Period*. No human being is worthy of standing before the flawless Father on the strength of his/her own merit. Tough luck Mary Poppins. You may be practically perfect in every way, but there aren't enough spoonfuls of sugar in the universe to make your sins appear sweet to God. For "We all, like sheep, have gone astray, each of us has turned to our own way (Isa 53:6a)."

Mercifully, we have a shepherd who loves his lambs and "the Lord has laid on him the iniquity of us all (Isa 53:6b)." Jesus not only bore our sins but also the terrible consequence of them—painful separation from God. His cries from the cross were more than an expression of hurt feelings. Jesus was voicing fact. He was quite literally forsaken to face undeserved punishment entirely alone.

TRUTH #2—THE KEY DIFFERENCE BETWEEN JESUS' EXPERIENCE AND OURS:

It seems so unfair. How could God turn away from Jesus, even for a moment? Isaiah 53:10 provides insight into God's motivation, "Yet it was the Lord's will to crush him and cause him to suffer, and though the Lord makes his life an offering for sin, he will see his offspring and prolong his days, and the will of the Lord will prosper in his hand."

Jesus was allowed to suffer so that you could become God's offspring. Your brother willingly agreed to shed his innocent blood because he wanted "to bring you safely home to God (1 Pet 3:18 NLT)." He took up the cross we deserved and credited us with his perfect life so that we can enter God's holiness. And with his final breath on earth, the veil in the synagogue was torn in two!

Now that is a curtain call. There is no longer a barrier between you and God's presence because Jesus has destroyed the power of sin and death for every believer. Robed in Christ's righteousness, God is with you, for you, and his Holy Spirit lives in you. You are family.

Your adoption has major perks. Even when you feel forgotten by God, you have his promise in Hebrews 13:5 that, "Never will I leave you; never will I forsake you." For "neither death nor life, neither angels nor demons, neither the present nor the future, nor any powers, neither height nor depth, nor anything else in all creation, will be able to separate us from the love of God that is in Christ Jesus our Lord (Rom 8:38–39)." He further vows to stand by you through seasons of doubt, fear, and anger. For, "if we are faithless, he will remain faithful (2 Tim 2:13)." God will never turn his face away from you or leave you to fend for yourself.

The key difference between your feelings of being forsaken and Immanuel's? *Jesus actually was forsaken by God in his moments on the cross, so that you never will be.* But even though Christ experienced this worst-case scenario, let us remember the implications of the resurrection:

> Ultimately, the One who died forsaken is raised in the glory of God. Christ's story does not end in disgrace but in the complete revelation of the power of the Father. The eternal relationship of the Father and Son is restored and we are welcomed into everlasting life. —Rev. Mark Mofield

Wow. I owe God an apology. I don't understand all the mysteries of his sovereignty or why some prayers go unanswered. But just like I try to fix the hurts of those I love, he is working to fix things for me. God and Jesus fought to protect me from hell, death, and the consequences of my sin. A home awaits me in heaven where one day all wrongs will be righted. Until then, God has given me the immediate relief of his promises and his presence. And that beats a Scooby Doo Band-Aid any day.

When doubts filled my mind, your comfort gave me renewed hope and cheer. —Ps 94:19

Chapter 6

Jesus Understands Your Physical and Emotional Pain

He was despised and rejected by mankind, a man of suffering, and familiar with pain. Like one from whom people hide their faces he was despised, and we held him in low esteem. Surely he took up our pain and bore our suffering, yet we considered him punished by God, stricken by him, and afflicted. But he was pierced for our transgressions, he was crushed for our iniquities; the punishment that brought us peace was on him, and by his wounds we are healed. —Isa 53:3–5

EVERY DISABLED INDIVIDUAL HAS their own unique blend of physical discomfort and emotional pain. We are mixes of shooting sciatica, live-wire neuropathy, vicious heartburn, or phantom pain tossed together with lost abilities, strained relationships, financial fears, or shattered dreams. But none of us want to drink from the cup of chronic pain and suffering solo.

We only have to look to the cross to know that Jesus experienced physical and emotional pain during his life. Crucifixion was a barbaric form of execution. The torture Jesus suffered at the hands of Roman soldiers left his body "disfigured beyond that of any human being and his form marred beyond human likeness (Isa 52:14)."

Christ's outward appearance reflected the ravages of his innocent soul when he became sin for us (2 Cor 5:21 ESV). Jesus endured the pain of being wrongfully accused, betrayed by his friends, ripped from God's presence, and having his human life cut short. "He was humiliated and received no justice. Who can speak of his descendants? For his life was taken from the earth (Acts 8:33 NLT)." Utterly alone, Immanuel simultaneously shouldered the sins of every human life (Luke 22:44 NLT, 1 John 2:2).

Jesus wins *Most Suffered in a Moment* hands down. But as someone fighting against the corrosive weariness of ongoing suffering, I have additional questions. God always gives me the greatest revelations of his love when I trust him with my toughest queries. So today, I'm not holding back . . . I want to know:

> *Jesus,*
>
> *Isaiah 53:4 says that you "bore my suffering." Thank you for bearing a depth of suffering in your hours on the cross that I cannot fathom. Yet my rebellious mind argues that at least your anguish ended quickly. Ongoing suffering is so crushing, it would comfort me to know whether you can relate specifically to my pain. It frustrates me that there are no gospel accounts of you being sick.*
>
> *Why then does Isaiah 53:4 (NRSV) read, "Surely he has borne our infirmities and carried our diseases"? How does the pain you faced in your hours on the cross equate to the accumulated hurt of an entire lifetime of disability? Do you know how exhausting it is to live with narcolepsy and POTS day in and day out? How heartbreaking it is to be forced to give up the future you've worked towards?*

God grew his answer in my heart over the course of several years. But it has revolutionized the cross for me. I pray he guides my words so that you may have a deeper revelation of his love.

ONE WITH CHRIST:

Jesus' sacrifice on the cross paid for your salvation and opened the doors to heaven. But the cross is about so much more than your future—it is about your present. The cross intimately and permanently connects you to Christ this very day. It enables Immanuel to continue to be *"God with you,"* while you await your heavenly home.

Christians consider the Holy Spirit to be the part of the Trinity that dwells inside us. (And indeed he does). But look carefully at the prayer request Jesus made for future believers when his death was drawing near. Amazingly, Jesus asks the Father to grant, "that the love you have for me may be in them and that *I myself may be in them* (John 17:26)."

Move over Holy Spirit and make some room . . . Immanuel has arrived. The Bible is clear that we have been made one with Christ:

> But if you give yourself to the Lord, you and Christ are joined
> together as one person. —1 Cor 6:17 TLB

> And Christ lives within you, so even though your body will die
> because of sin, the Spirit gives you life because you have been
> made right with God. —Rom 8:10 NLT

Can you grasp the magnitude of what this means? The cross made it possible for Jesus to live inside of us. Jesus was not just "God with us" for a few decades two thousand years ago, he is "God with us" *still*. You are bound together with him. The implications of your union are astounding.

Advantage #1—Jesus Understands Your Suffering:

First, Jesus does not apply a general understanding of pain to your situation. *He understands your suffering specifically because his spirit is joined to yours.* He experiences life with you.

For me, this means that when reflux makes me cough until my lungs are exhausted, Jesus' lungs burn. His heart beats quicker when mine races. Through me he knows the cruel irony of being malnourished despite being able to afford quality food.

Perhaps through you he has borne lupus, slowly shut down with ALS, or watched his world fade permanently to black. Christ has wept into his pillow nightly from the guilt of burdening his family, waited on the results of a life-changing x-ray, and endured the humiliation of being bathed by a stranger. He has even coped with diseases scientists haven't identified. Living inside each believer, he is present in all our suffering and has experienced every type of pain.

Jesus' love is always all-in. He personally shares the hurts of his people. Jesus reinforced this truth when he preached that his followers will be confused at the final judgement. They will inquire,

> Lord, when did we see you hungry and feed you, or thirsty and
> give you something to drink? When did we see you a stranger
> and invite you in, or needing clothes and clothe you? When did
> we see you sick or in prison and go to visit you? —Matt 25:37–39

And Jesus will respond, "*Truly I tell you, whatever you did for one of the least of these brothers and sisters of mine, you did for me* (v. 40)."

Furthermore, when the Risen Christ confronted Saul about jailing/executing Christians, did he say, "Saul, Saul, why do you stone Stephen?" Or

"Why do you arrest Lydia?" No! He asked, "Saul! Saul! *Why do you persecute me* (Acts 22:6)?"

United with us, Jesus experiences our hunger, thirst, loneliness, helplessness, illnesses, and broken dreams firsthand. We look forward to the day when he will make all things new. But Jesus realized that we would need more than a distant promise to navigate the troubles of this life. We would need *him*. So, Christ took up the cross and became one with his people.

In all their suffering he also suffered, and he personally rescued them. In his love and mercy he redeemed them. He lifted them up and carried them through all the years. —Isa 63:9 NLT

Advantage #2—You Have Christ's Strength:

Our second advantage becomes clearer with a quick lesson in Livestock 101. A yoke is a special harness for two animals (such as oxen) which allows them to shoulder burdens as a team. It serves two functions. First, the yoke spreads the weight of the load in order to make each ox's job easier. Secondly, it combines the oxen's' strength. This allows the team to accomplish tasks that would be difficult for a single ox.

Occasionally, a young or weak ox is paired with a stronger one to learn the ropes. The bigger ox's strength protects the weaker animal from carrying too much weight. Meanwhile, the young ox is taught how to move forward by an experienced partner.

Jesus is stronger than all the world's oxen combined. He yoked himself to you so that he can share your burdens by taking them upon himself. But that yoke works two ways. The equally glorious flipside is that you are also yoked to his strength. Christ lives in you—giving you his courage, perseverance, and resiliency. You have direct access to his wisdom and are covered daily by his mercy. Jesus encourages,

> Come to me, all you who are weary and burdened, and I will give you rest. Take my yoke upon you and learn from me, for I am gentle and humble in heart, and you will find rest for your souls. For my yoke is easy and my burden is light.—Matt 11:28–30

Young ox (wink wink), you are on a winning team. Jesus is the ultimate victor over pain and is a capable coach. Immanuel lives within you and is also known as Wonderful Counselor (Isa 9:6). Your only job is to look to him for guidance. As you fix your eyes on Jesus, he will carry you triumphantly through all seasons.

All praise to God, the Father of our Lord Jesus Christ, who has blessed us with every spiritual blessing in the heavenly realms because we are united with Christ. —Eph 1:3 NLT

YOU ARE NEVER ALONE:

I have yet to find my grocery store stranger—that one other person who can completely relate to my struggles. I am ok with that now. Immanuel found me when I needed to be understood, and he knows *exactly* what it is like to be me.

Jesus is your greatest source of comfort because he uniquely understands your sorrows. He has wrapped you up in his embrace and is whispering to your heart the very last words he spoke before ascending to heaven, "I am with you always, even to the end of time (Matt 28:20 WE)."

That is exceedingly good news—because Christ is *the* mighty ally of choice. "He is able to save completely those who come to God through him, because he always lives to intercede for them (Heb 7:25)." Jesus is simultaneously walking in your shoes and advocating for you in heaven. He is entirely qualified to represent your needs because he understands the complexity, messiness, and frustrations of earthly existence.

This very minute he stands before the Father passionately pleading your cause. So, take heart! Even if disability makes you *one in a million*, your life is in the capable hands of Jesus: *the one and only Immanuel.*

The Word became flesh and made his dwelling among us. We have seen his glory, the glory of the one and only Son, who came from the Father, full of grace and truth. —John 1:14

Part 2

Harmful Mindsets to Toss

We demolish arguments and every pretension that sets itself up against the knowledge of God, and we take captive every thought to make it obedient to Christ. —2 Cor 10:5

Introduction:

Take Out the Trash

. . . let us drop every extra weight, every sin that clings to us and slackens our pace, and let us run with endurance the long race set before us. —Heb 12:1 VOICE

Hebrews 12:1 urges us to leave our baggage behind in order to run our Christian race well. But as an individual with all the athleticism of a sea cucumber, I like to relate this verse to a topic more in my wheelhouse: noses.

Parker calls me the *"Super Sniffer."* Strangely, it is a quirk shared by many narcoleptics. I can tell what my husband has eaten for a snack with a kiss—an apple and goldfish crackers. My preschool students can never sneak out of the bathroom without washing their hands. I can evaluate food freshness with the accuracy of a "best by" date and locate a misplaced gym sock with a few strategic inhalations.

If I could share one piece of wisdom in my capacity as a human bloodhound it is this: If you do not want your house to stink, you have to regularly take out the trash. I am the first person to take out a half empty bag of trash after a few warning whiffs from yesterday's chicken fat or cantaloupe rinds. Otherwise, the stench will begin to permeate the house. You can fanatically Febreze, but lurking beneath the sweet perfume there is still a putrid sourness. The only way to absolutely be free of the odor is to remove the garbage.

Fellow journeyer, our souls also require regular housekeeping. Five years ago, I wanted nothing more than to put my house in order—to leave behind my grief and move forward. But I realized something rotten was still poisoning the air. I needed God to help me get rid of the stink of guilt, anxiety, and discontentment, as well as the lingering aroma of lies I'd been believing. Only then would I be able to breathe deeply of his goodness and run my race unencumbered.

Moving forward requires leaving behind the unhealthy thought patterns that have been holding you back. It is time to let go.

Chapter 7

Deliverance from Guilt

Therefore, [there is] now no condemnation (no adjudging guilty of wrong) for those who are in Christ Jesus . . . —Rom 8:1 AMPC

Note to Reader:

In my early years of disability, I constantly worried that I was somehow being punished for my sins. The next three chapters address the variations of guilt I experienced and the scriptural tools that finally set me free. However, if guilt about being sick is not a problem for you—praise God! Skip to Chapter 10 "Overcome Lies with God's Truth."

For those of you who need a jailbreak, Jesus can deliver you from guilt this day. I ask that you read the next few chapters carefully before drawing conclusions. The concepts surrounding sin/sickness are complex, and a statement taken out of context (or a partial truth) can be as harmful as a lie. I pray these pages are a safe place for you to discover how Christ awaits everyone in need of healing with outstretched arms and unfailing love.

Do you feel guilty about being sick? Have you been asked hurtful questions about whether sin could be a barrier to your healing? Are unexplained feelings of shame causing you more stress than your disabilities themselves?

The idea that sickness is a punishment for sin has been deeply rooted in the human psyche for centuries. What boggles my mind, is that this prejudice is still heartbreakingly visible within the modern church.

I didn't realize how ingrained this belief is until after I became disabled. Not only did others insult me—*my own mind* was plagued by the idea that I somehow deserved my conditions. Did God hold my moments of anger and doubt against me? Perhaps if I had handled narcolepsy more gracefully, he would have answered my prayers before I developed POTS and gastroparesis.

Years of deteriorating health compounded my guilt until shame followed me everywhere. It was the elephant in the room on the day Parker and I met with our church deacon, Pat, to pray for healing. No way was I going to tell her about the mammoth weight I was carrying. I had been burned too many times before.

Thankfully, that wise woman of faith saw straight through my pretenses. Pat pierced me with her gaze and spoke a truth I had secretly been waiting years to hear, "Shannon, God wants you to know this is not your fault."

Her words rang through my soul like a liberty anthem.

To carelessly shackle a person who is already fighting disease with guilt is a terrible misuse and abuse of God's word. As disabled believers it is vital we know God's stance on sickness so that we can protect our hearts from painful emotional damage. So, what does the Bible *actually* say about disease? Does Jesus think sickness is caused by sin? To find out, let's visit two stories in the gospel of John.

STORY #1—A MAN BORN BLIND (JOHN 9:1–41):

Our first story begins when Jesus sees a blind beggar. Curious, his disciples ask him, "Rabbi, who sinned, this man or his parents, that he was born blind (v. 2)?"

You don't need a law degree to spot the leading nature of their question. The disciples live in a survival of the fittest culture where life is tough—even for the abled bodied. It seems logical to them that anyone with the added burden of disability probably did something to tick off the Big Man upstairs.

Jesus' response is revolutionary, "neither this man nor his parents sinned, but *this happened so that the work of God might be displayed in his life* (v. 3)."

What a victorious proclamation! Jesus declares that the man's blindness has nothing to do with punishment. Instead, God is redeeming his beloved child's brokenness. Furthermore, God is revealing his glory through the life of a man he sees as special and significant.

The most powerful part of this miracle is not the restoration of a man's sight—it is the healing of a wounded soul. Jesus gives someone who has been misjudged his entire life the gift of dignity. His words of affirmation confirm that God loves this man and has chosen him for an important mission. From the moment Jesus opens the blind man's eyes, his story offers a vision of hope to all disabled believers. Instead of wondering, "Is God punishing me?" we can ask, "Is God calling me to a higher purpose?"[1]

STORY #2—A PARALYZED MAN (JOHN 5:1–15):

Rewind a few chapters in the gospel of John to join Jesus beside the pool of Bethesda. Don't let the name fool you: Bethesda was less serene suburban spa and more field hospital. Here, "crowds of sick people—blind, lame, or paralyzed" gathered (John 5:3).

Jesus zeros in on one paraplegic amidst this sea of hurting people. He instructs the man to get up and go home. Can you imagine the man's skepticism being overtaken by joy as he tentatively rose to his feet? His wonder at putting weight on limbs that have been useless for thirty-eight years? While the man marvels at his restored mobility, Christ vanishes into the crowd.

When they meet again, Jesus gives the man this advice, "Now you are well; so stop sinning, or something even worse may happen to you (John 5:14)."

Wait just a minute, Jesus. You seem to be implying there is a cause/effect relationship between the man's behavior and his paralysis. So, sickness can be caused by sin?

Sometimes. Logically we know that our actions have natural consequences. Chain smoking causes lung damage. Under-exercising while over-eating leads to obesity. Promiscuity increases your risk of contracting sexually transmitted diseases. Perhaps the paralyzed man had fallen in with a bad crowd and was injured while trying to hurt someone else. The Bible doesn't share those details.

But here is the catch . . . health nuts also get lung cancer. Innocent victims of horrific abuse contract HIV. People who did nothing to cause their disorder later exacerbate their symptoms by failing to follow their doctors' instructions. Disease is a complicated problem that comes with countless back stories. The issue of guilt/innocence is often unclear.

---

1. For a better understanding of the interplay between God and suffering, read the *Note to Reader* at the beginning of "Part 8: Transformed Through Trials" or the section *Like Our Father* in "Confessions from the Valley."

SAME KIND OF DIFFERENT:

Where does that leave those of us who are worried our sickness is a result of sin? In need of a better question. Shelve the difference of the blind man's innocence and paralyzed man's guilt for a moment. Instead, let's explore the *remarkable similaritie*s between their two stories:

1. Both men had been ill for a very long time:

One man has been blind from birth and the other immobile for thirty-eight years. Decades of disability have worn away their strength until they've faded into the background of life to focus on survival.

2. Jesus is the one to initiate contact:

The New Testament is full of stories where invalids approach Jesus. But did you notice that neither the blind or paralyzed man cries out for healing? Instead, Jesus recognizes their quiet desperation and he reaches out to them. We have a Savior who comes for us—even when we are oblivious to his presence or too weak to ask for help.

3. Jesus cares about their physical wellness:

Each man receives healing and the opportunity to live a full life.

4. Jesus cares about their spiritual well-being:

Both men immediately face opposition from the religious leaders in the afterglow of their miracles. The Pharisees are outraged that Jesus healed them on the Sabbath. They throw the man born blind out of the temple screaming, "You were steeped in sin at birth; how dare you lecture us (v. 34)?" Can you imagine how shredded he must have felt by their accusations?

What happens next brings tears to my eyes every time I read it. John 9:35 says, "Jesus heard that they had thrown him out, and when he found him . . ." Translation? Christ learns that the church is trying to take the joy of the formerly blind man's healing away by forcing him back into a sinner's identity. *And Jesus won't stand for it. The Savior of the World stops what he is doing and goes to find a hurting man (who never asked for his help) for the second time!*

I have only been able to find one other gospel account where Jesus actively goes in search of a specific individual. Guess who it is? *The previously paralyzed man.* Like the blind man, Jesus seeks him out to correct damage done by the Pharisees.

True—he does advise the man to turn from sin during this second meeting. But I suspect Christ's tones conveyed a tender concern for the future that struck a chord with the man's heart. Because for the first time since the paralyzed man regained his mobility, he recognizes his miracle worker. His healer is Jesus.

Consider the evidence of these similarities and ask yourself a new question: Did Jesus treat the innocent man differently from the one who contributed to his condition? No! It was incredibly important to him that both men understand their value to God. Regardless of the *origins* of their sicknesses, the *outcomes* are the same: *Jesus is merciful.* Blind eyes see. Lame legs leap. Two hearts find healing through their identity in Christ.

LOVE'S BOTTOM LINE:

You too are a new creation in Christ. This is the identity that defines you, not your sins. For now, you live in a fallen world where there are natural consequences for your actions and the actions of others. However, as a believer, you can be confident that God is not punishing you with sickness because:

> *On this side of the cross, God never punishes his children with disability, disease, or sickness.*

There is zero wiggle room in this statement. How can I be so sure?

The Bible says that "Everything [the Lord] does is just and fair (Deut 32:4a)." God is the embodiment of justice. Keep this thought at the forefront of your mind. Now, consider that earthly courts practice protection against Double Jeopardy. This prevents an individual from being tried/punished twice for the same offense. Most humans agree that it would be unfair to repunish a person who has already paid the price for their crimes.

God is infinitely more just and merciful than any human being. So, in an outrageous act of love Jesus willingly paid the price for your sins. Isaiah 53:5 ERV proclaims, "he was being punished for what we did. He was crushed because of our guilt. He took the punishment we deserved, and this brought us peace. We were healed because of his pain." Jesus satisfied the divine judgement you deserved once and for all.

Do you realize what this means? *Jesus' sacrifice makes it utterly impossible for any negative situation in your life to be a punishment from God.* God will never lash out at you or make you pay for your failings with a divorce, disability, or death of a loved one. He simply cannot punish you because Jesus was punished in your stead. Choosing to punish you after Christ sacrificed himself would be an act of injustice that would unravel the very fabric of God's being. It would require the Lord to rob the cross of its power, forfeit his goodness, and cease to be holy. It is absolutely unthinkable.

Let us approach the issue of sin/sickness as resurrection people. Regardless of whether false feelings of shame have blinded you to God's purposes or justifiable guilt has paralyzed you from moving forward—the bottom line is the same. Take your lingering feelings of guilt and point them to the cross. That is where your punishment hangs. *By the blood of Jesus, you are forgiven and free.*

It is for freedom that Christ has set us free. —Gal 5:1a

Chapter 8

Discern False Condemnation
from Godly Sorrow

*Stand firm, then, and do not let yourselves be burdened again by a
yoke of slavery. —Gal 5:1b*

Do you ever feel like you have a debate team living inside your head? I
do. As soon as I embrace Christ's deliverance from guilt the devil's advocate
side of my brain begins to argue, "Isn't some guilt good and necessary?" Fair
point. Only sociopaths have a guilt free existence, so appropriate levels of
remorse are important for moral growth.

The Bible teaches a concept called godly sorrow (2 Cor 7:8–11). Godly
sorrow is healthy grief over sin which inspires a person to make positive
behavioral changes. For example, most of us have experienced genuine regret after speaking harshly to a loved one. Godly sorrow prompts you to
apologize, make efforts to repair the relationship, and silently count to ten
the next time you feel tempted to respond in anger. That is all good.

What's tricky is that both godly sorrow and false condemnation (un-
true/unmerited feelings of shame) are accompanied by similar feelings of
guilt. If you are a people pleasing perfectionist like me, these look-alike feelings can be problematic. It is entirely too easy to fall back into destructive
patterns of false condemnation when you are naturally hard on yourself.
Now that I am free from believing God is punishing me with sickness, I
want to safeguard myself against future wrong thinking.

So, how can we identify which feelings of guilt are appropriate (godly
sorrow) and which are unhealthy (false condemnation)? Here is a simple
screening tool you can use to expose false condemnation and shut it down.
I pray these two tips help you live in victory:

TIP #1—FALSE CONDEMNATION IS VAGUE AND SPIRITUALLY PARALYZING:

Do you feel as if you did something to cause your sickness but can't figure out what that "something" is? Are you overwhelmed with generalized feelings of guilt or failure? False condemnation plagues its victims with a constant sense of shame that does not have a clear origin. An internal transcript of my falsely condemning thoughts would read:

> *My health is going from bad to worse. Doctors can't figure out what is wrong with me and God is not answering my prayers. It must be my fault. I've always been a screwup and can never do anything right. Why would God bother with a failure like me? I don't know where I went wrong, but I must have done something to deserve this.*

Sound familiar? If so, ask yourself whether or not vague accusations make sense from God's perspective. Would a good and gracious God expect you to repent from a "mystery" sin he refuses to reveal to you?

No way. God's desire is to help you turn from sin so that you can enjoy a stronger relationship with him. Making you feel ashamed of a sin you cannot identify would do nothing to serve his purpose. When you can't put a finger on the behavior that led to your illness—you are experiencing the unmerited guilt of false condemnation.

The danger of these false feelings is that they will imprison you in a vague sense of unworthiness until you are too ashamed to ask for God's help. Alienated from your one source of comfort, you become spiritually paralyzed. It is a struggle to live effectively for Christ when you are distracted by discouragement.

Godly sorrow is the opposite in every way. It happens when the Holy Spirit convicts you of a specific sinful action or self-destructive behavior pattern. (For example, Jenny realizes her liver damage is due to years of alcohol abuse.) The apostle Paul described godly sorrow in his letter to the Corinthians:

> For the kind of sorrow God wants us to experience leads us away from sin and results in salvation. There's no regret for that kind of sorrow . . . Just see what this godly sorrow produced in you! Such earnestness, such concern to clear yourselves . . . You showed that you have done everything necessary to make things right. —Excerpts from 2 Cor 7:10–11

Paul is clear that "there's no regret" for godly sorrow. Notice how he praises the Corinthians for their earnest efforts to clear their names and their determination to put things right. *Godly sorrow is markedly different from the paralyzing effect of false condemnation because it is action oriented. It is a catalyst for change.*

Godly sorrow will always encourage you to partner with your helper, the Holy Spirit, to become more Christ-like (John 14:26). It does not taunt you for your past failures, but reminds you of who you are as God's child. It is a force that is future focused and dedicated to empowering you. This is how godly sorrow would speak to Jenny about her alcoholism:

> *Jenny,*
>
> *You are hurting yourself and the people you love. It is time to stop drinking because I have amazing plans for your life. I know you're thinking about all the times you failed to sober up in the past, but today is a new day. I have forgiven you, and you need to forgive yourself so that we can move forward.*
>
> *Hold on to me. We can do this together. I know it's a difficult battle, but you are beloved, strong, and smart. I promise I will not let you go. So, let's take the first step. Call your AA sponsor.*

Can you hear how different the voice of godly sorrow is from the accusations of false condemnation? False condemnation weighs you down with shame, while godly sorrow lifts your eyes to the future. One voice sneers "worthless," while the other proclaims, "Let's make these changes because you are of great worth to me." False condemnation breaks connection with God. But godly sorrow builds relationship as you join forces with the Holy Spirit to pursue a more Christ-like you.

TIP #2—WOULD A DOCTOR CONNECT YOUR BEHAVIOR WITH YOUR PHYSICAL CONDITION?

This second rule of thumb is vitally important. It is difficult to think objectively when you are desperate to figure out, "Why has this happened to me?" False condemnation loves to take advantage of your need for answers by convincing you that your disability is the result of a specific—yet unrelated—behavior. To regain a balanced perspective, ask yourself whether a medical professional would find a relationship between your behavior/condition. *If the answer is "no," you are experiencing false condemnation!* Practice with these examples:

Example 1: Sophie's hands are swollen and painful from osteoar-
thritis. Performing simple household tasks has become increasingly uncomfortable. Every time her hands hurt, she remembers
how she regularly shoplifted as a teenager. Sophie has not stolen
anything since she became a Christian forty years ago. However,
she still worries that God is punishing her for her earlier thefts.

Example 2: Dakota also suffers from severe arthritis in his hands.
But he has always had a problem with unchecked rage. His fists
have acted as a channel for his anger over decades: punching
holes in walls, denting cars, and destroying furniture. He's repeatedly sustained serious fractures to both hands.

Both Sophie and Dakota see a connection between their behavior and
their current condition. But what would a doctor say? While Dakota's hands
are a logical end result of years of abuse, Sophie's arthritis could not have
been caused by shoplifting. She is experiencing false condemnation and
projecting her inability to forgive herself onto God.

The good news of Christ for every Sophie is that God forgives us when
we struggle to forgive ourselves. If an earthly doctor would not blame you
for your condition, how much *more merciful* is the Great Physician? Make
a habit of celebrating God's unwavering grace, and false condemnation will
gradually fade away beneath the light of his unfailing love.

But what if you are like Dakota and made choices that contributed
to your condition? God's prescription is much the same: forgive yourself
because he has forgiven you. Romans 8:1 does *not* say, "there is now no *false
condemnation* for those who are in Christ Jesus." It says, "there is now no
condemnation for those who are in Christ Jesus." *No condemnation.* Period.

"But there is a valid reason for my guilt," you may argue. It doesn't matter. "I don't deserve forgiveness because I am still struggling to overcome
unhealthy habits," your mind protests. It makes no difference. God does not
give us what we deserve; he gave us his most beloved son. If you believe in
Jesus, you are in a *constant* state of grace (Rom 8:10, 1 Cor 1:30).

Your challenge is to keep guilty feelings about past mistakes from
paralyzing you in the present. This too is false condemnation. Instead, focus
on the transformative power of Christ's mercies which are new every morning (Lam 3:23 NLT). Jesus is calling you forward and a future vibrant with
promise awaits you. His love will inspire and strengthen you to make the

changes you need to become more like him this day. That is the heart of godly sorrow.

For if, by the trespass of the one man, death reigned through that one man, how much more will those who receive God's abundant provision of grace and of the gift of righteousness reign in life through the one man, Jesus Christ! —Rom 5:17

Chapter 9

Respond to Accusations of "Not Enough Faith"

Now faith is confidence in what we hope for and assurance about what we do not see. —Heb 11:1

GUILT AND FALSE CONDEMNATION have one last wicked relative to look out for: an ugly step sister who wags her finger at you accusing, "If you had enough faith, you would be healed." For short, we will call her *Faith Fail*.

Faith Fail is a diabolical twist on guilt because—although sin did not cause your disability—you feel guilty of perpetuating it. According to *Faith Fail*, your chronic condition is "your fault" because it is what you lack that keeps you from experiencing healing. Maybe if you just tried a little harder, prayed a little longer, or believed bigger, circumstances would be different.

The hardest lies to defeat are the ones that contain a kernel of truth. Undoubtedly, Jesus teaches that anything is possible with faith (Mark 9:23). But I *am* confident that God is able to heal me. I have longed for it with all my heart and prayed for it with all my might. Heaven must be littered with my prayers.

Why then am I still sick if faith automatically guarantees healing? The merciful Father I know cannot be up in heaven waiting for me to utter some magical prayer words I haven't thought of yet. Maybe the continued presence of disability in my life is about more than my personal faith score. Are there other truths simultaneously at work that can help send *Faith Fail's* accusations packing?

TRUTH #1—HEALING DOES NOT SOLELY DEPEND ON YOU:

Mark 2:1–12 and Luke 5:17–26 recount the story of four extraordinary friends who want healing for their paralyzed pal. But they encounter a problem. Jesus is speaking to a packed house and they can't get close enough to ask for help.

The four men love their paralyzed friend too much to accept defeat. So they get "creative" and come up with plan B. With a loyalty golden retrievers would admire (albeit the subtlety of a herd of rhinos), they hoist their friend up to the roof. They dig out an unsolicited skylight and lower their friend down to Jesus—right in the middle of his sermon.

Can you just hear the gasps of the little old church ladies in the front pew? It takes guts to interrupt the Savior's sermon. But instead of being ticked, Jesus was tickled with these fearless friends. He saw the all-in devotion that made them willing to dabble in vandalism, risk personal embarrassment, and chance the possibility of braining God's Son with a ceiling chunk. Each gospel reports that Jesus healed the paralyzed man after he "saw *their* faith."

Don't skim over these simple words and miss their explosive meaning. Christ responds—not to the faith of the sick man—but to the faith of his friends. What incredibly good news! Personal faith is not a prerequisite for healing. When we feel hopelessly crushed by life, God can use the faith of our loved ones to bless us. So, take some weight off those shoulders. Your healing doesn't just depend on you.

TRUTH #2—FAITHFUL PEOPLE STILL FACE HARDSHIPS:

Faith also does not exempt us from difficulty in this life. If it did, everyone would be a Christian. Instead, the Bible teaches that, "the righteous person may have many troubles (Ps 34:19)." Many of the most faithful believers throughout history never received miraculous healing in their earthly bodies.

Paul was a New Testament superstar who healed others in the name of Jesus (Acts 28:9). He even raised a young man from the dead after an unfortunate window napping incident (Acts 20:9–12). But God gently refused to heal Paul of his own thorn (unspecified illness), explaining that it would benefit him to rely on the Lord's strength (2 Cor 12:7–9).[1]

---

1. For a deeper look at the life of Paul, see Chapter 19 "Cultivate a Balanced View on Healing."

Want a more contemporary example? Mother Teresa devoted her life to serving the poor of Calcutta, India and was declared a saint by the Catholic church. She had a heart pacemaker.[2] C. S. Lewis authored some of the most influential Christian works of the past century, yet died at age sixty-four from kidney failure.[3] The world-renowned evangelist Billy Graham spent his final years on earth with Parkinson's disease.[4]

Look to these giants of the Christian faith when *Faith Fail* knocks on your door. Their lives are evidence that earthly trouble is not an indicator of spiritual weakness. Sometimes it takes an even greater miracle of faith to keep believing in God's goodness when your prayers go unanswered. It takes courage to look beyond the disappointment of your weaknesses to value God's strength. It takes perseverance when you are worn out by suffering to keep reaching for your Father in an effort to trust his promises. The measure of your faith is not whether you receive healing—it is in how you walk with God through life's challenges.

Which means you are not a *Faith Fail*. In the midst of your battle with chronic illness, you chose to read this book because you care about your relationship with God. It doesn't matter if those feelings are hiding deep down or if you barely have the strength to read a paragraph. You made a choice to engage with the one who has never let you go. And God calls your act of reaching . . . *Faithful*.

> His master replied, "Well done, good and faithful servant! You have been faithful with a few things; I will put you in charge of many things. Come and share your master's happiness!" —Matt 25:21

ACCUSATION FROM OTHERS:

How should you respond when other people blame your sickness on sin or a lack of faith? Here are a few tips:

1. Pick your battles and have a plan:

As a disabled Christian, you will fight numerous battles daily: against physical ailments, depression, financial pressure, etc. With so many stressful forces to combat, it is important to conserve energy where you can.

2. Associated Press, "Mother Teresa," para. 1.
3. McGrath, *C. S. Lewis—A Life*, 358.
4. Ribeiro, "6 Celebrities," para. 4.

At any church, there will probably be a few curmudgeons who have an immature understanding of the gospel. My advice is not to engage with these people. Smile and try to politely walk away. If the church leadership adheres to simplistic/hurtful views on healing, find a different church where you feel loved and supported.

Occasionally you encounter this view from a person you cannot avoid (a friend, family member, or coworker). You may especially want to take time to address the issue when it is a valued relationship. Planning is key to having a positive conversation.

It is very difficult to respond clearly and without anger when you are caught off guard. If a friend approaches you with a hurtful accusation, say, "Let's schedule a time to talk about that on another day. When are you available?" Cool off and think through your talking points. This is an important conversation, so pick a place where you will not be interrupted. Listen carefully and pause to collect yourself before responding.

If you are uncomfortable, take a supportive spouse, friend, or family member with you. Explain why you found their accusation hurtful, and take time to explore biblical truths about sin/sickness together. If you are too upset for a conversation, ask them to read Chapter 7 "Deliverance from Guilt" or the two truths from this chapter addressing *Faith Fail*. Lastly, before you speak with this person, keep the following tip in mind.

2. *Consider the motivation of your accuser:*

Yes, there are always those over-zealous acquaintances who delightfully butt in to situations they cannot begin to understand. But when someone close questions your actions or faith, they are often trying to be helpful instead of hurtful. Remember that their accusations can be driven by their own brokenness. Most likely, they have prayed for you and are also wondering why God hasn't healed you. In trying to cope with their own confusion or disappointment, they may find it easier to question you than to question God.

I have also known people who struggle to accept God's grace and are always trying to earn God's favor. Being critical of themselves makes them more judgmental of others. They want to help you figure out what it is you did/haven't done to still be disabled, so that you can "fix" it.

Both behaviors are sad and hurtful. But often people are trying to help you find healing in their own misguided way. Once I realized this, it helped take the sting out of false judgments. Taking time to consider the motivation of your accuser can diffuse your anger and help you to respond lovingly.

3. Be convinced of your righteousness in Christ:

It is incredibly important for your heart to be convinced of your worth to God and your valued position within his family. Because, as my grandfather is fond of saying, "You can't make a fool see sense." Sometimes, despite our best efforts, people refuse to be persuaded. The closer the person is to you, the more likely it is to shake you. We must deliberately hold on tight to what God says about us in the Bible and give his voice first place in our hearts.

Your word is the truth. So let this truth make them completely yours.
—John 17:17 CEV

Chapter 10
Overcome Lies with God's Truth

The weapons we fight with are not the weapons of the world. On the contrary, they have divine power to demolish strongholds. We demolish arguments and every pretension that sets itself up against the knowledge of God, and we take captive every thought to make it obedient to Christ. —2 Cor 10:4–5

Win the battle in your mind and you will prevail every time. Lose the battle of the mind, and you don't stand a chance. — Dr. Matt Merrill

DISABILITY IS NOT FOR the faint of heart. Truthfully, it is like finding yourself in a war zone surrounded by enemies. Loss of independence, decimated dreams, financial insecurity, isolation, bodily discomfort, and strained relationships all simultaneously have you in their crosshairs. However, your deadliest enemy isn't the army you face on the battlefield but the espionage subtly working to weaken the defenses of your mind.

Newly disabled, I completely ignored the negativity that infiltrated my thoughts and devoted all my energy towards fighting my disease. I reasoned that improving my health would lift my depression. I soon discovered that you cannot even begin to win a war when you are sabotaged from within.

Fellow warrior, even in the midst of horrific circumstances God can give us triumph in the battle for our minds. As a twelve-year veteran of disability, I urge you not to neglect your mental health as you wait for your physical health to improve. While my doctors have helped me in many ways, my "new normal" is still nowhere near the "normal" I would like to have. For years I grieved the difference and felt like a worthless failure.

God finally showed me that my negative thought patterns were robbing me of just as much quality of life as my disabilities themselves. If I was going to have peace within my circumstances, I needed God to renew my mind.

The first step of Operation Defeat Depression[1] was learning to vigilantly monitor my thoughts to identify the lies I was believing. This is an essential strategy I continue to use to safeguard my thoughts from discouragement. *Having a healthy mind requires thinking about what you are thinking.*

How can you be on the lookout for lies? By lies, I mean any negative thought you believe about yourself, your future, or about God that is contrary to what the Bible says. One telltale sign of these thoughts is that they accomplish the purposes of Satan. He "comes only to steal and kill and destroy (John 10:10)." Lying thoughts quickly steal your peace, kill your confidence, and destroy your hope. They are accusatory, belittling, and question your identity in Christ. The closed captions from one of my internal battles with lies would read:

> *Why has God left me? Does he see me spending hours on the couch when I could be out there doing things for Him? He must be punishing me. Does he still love me? Why would he? I couldn't even get dressed today; I am so worthless. Look at that pile of dishes in the sink; I'm a terrible wife.*

Trying to refute these thoughts with my own understanding was like being trapped in an evil game of Whack-A-Mole. I would club one lie on the head saying, "That's not true," only for two of its malevolent friends to pop up and taunt me. In an attempt to escape one of these futile fights I began listening to an online sermon from Elevation Church.

Elevation's pastor, Steven Furtick, has an exceptional gift for preaching God's truth with both honesty and grace. However, that day I listened to a sermon from his equally talented wife. Holly Furtick spoke on overcoming doubts we have about ourselves. She shared a strategy of making truth cards with encouraging verses on them and keeping them readily available. That idea birthed my Lie/Truth cards.

Now before you think I am a pessimist for adding "Lie" to the label—hear me out. I chose to include "Lie" for a very simple reason: *I cannot defeat enemies that I can't identify.* Years of allowing self-abusing thoughts to enter my mind made them my default mindset. It helps me to write down thoughts like, "God doesn't love me," and clearly label it for what it is—*a*

---

1. Wondering where I stand on antidepressants? Check out *The Miracle of Modern Medicine* in Chapter 19 "Cultivate a Balanced View of Healing."

lie—so that I will always have a reminder that this thought is untrue. But proclaiming negative thoughts to be lies is not enough to keep them from coming back. So what should we do? Look to Jesus for our battle plan.

Did you know that Satan tried to infiltrate Jesus' thoughts with lies during his temptation? Please don't let that scare you. It didn't scare Jesus. He knew that "all authority in heaven and on earth (Matt 28:18)" had been given to him. It is a mistake to credit Satan with too much power, and frankly, he does not deserve our focus. While the Bible acknowledges that believers fight against the forces of darkness (Eph 6:12), 1 John 4:4 declares that, "the one who is in you is greater than the one who is in the world." God's Holy Spirit inside of you makes you more powerful than Satan, and the devil knows it.

Satan's only available play is a bluff. If he can make you question who you are as God's child, he can undermine your trust in the Father. Satan is aptly called the deceiver (2 John 1:7).

Thankfully, he is not very original. Satan's very first words to Jesus in the wilderness challenged Jesus' identity, "If you are the Son of God . . . " Two thousand years later, he is still using the same tired accusations, "If you were really one of God's chosen children, he would heal you. If he really loved you, he would answer your prayers." Believing these lies *is the temptation* that distances us from our loving Father and opens the door to anger, depression, anxiety, and fear.

Jesus shows us exactly how to slam the door on these intruders in Matthew 4 NLT. When we are tempted to believe lies, we must stop listening to Satan by focusing our thoughts on a higher voice. Jesus refuted Satan by relying on what he knew to be an inarguable source of truth: God's Holy Word (Ps 33:4). To each accusation he responded, "The Scriptures say . . . " and shot down Satan's arguments with Bible verses.

Jesus knew that lies lose power in light of truth. God's word is the only unwavering standard we have for calibrating our thoughts. So I began by writing down Bible verses that disproved the lies I had been believing. Every time a negative thought echoed in my mind, I would pull out my cards, remind myself it was a lie, and focus on God's truths.

Six months later, the transformation was astounding: my mental landscape was completely remodeled. Despair and doubt were overtaken by joy and hopeful trust. Instead of waking up dreading the day ahead, I began waking up to worship songs playing through my thoughts. God's truth accomplished what I thought healing would only ever be able to do . . . it brought my happiness back.

This process of learning to stand in God's truth is still priceless to me. It is the closest thing I have ever felt to resurrection. Scratch that. *It was resurrection* because my mind was reborn. Now when lies try to creep back into my consciousness, they do so at their peril. I know how to win this war.

Fellow warrior, there is no more worthwhile investment than learning to guard your thoughts with the truth of God's word. The battles that have the greatest power to change your life are within your mind. Triumph there, and you will be able to live victoriously in all circumstances.

Are you ready to take your own thoughts captive and make them obedient to Christ? For quick reference, I have included the Bible verses I used to supplant my own lies (listed below) in Appendix 1. Use it as a tool in moments when you need God's voice to transcend your fears and doubts. As you become comfortable with this process, I pray you are inspired to search God's word for the truths you need to conquer any lie. His word is a sure foundation.

Overcome Lies with God's Truth: (See Appendix 1)

- *God doesn't love me.*
- *When bad things happen, it means God doesn't love me.*
- *When bad things happen, it means God is punishing me.*
- *God has forgotten me.*
- *God doesn't hear my prayers.*
- *God is far away and doesn't care about my pain.*
- *God is never going to rescue me.*
- *Because I am weak, I am worthless.*
- *I am a failure.*
- *My condition makes me a burden to my spouse. I'm not a blessing.*
- *I am hoping in the Lord in vain.*
- *Circumstances will never change or get better. They will always be the same.*

Chapter 11

Curb Your Anxiety

Cast all your anxiety on him because he cares for you. —1 Pet 5:7

Note to Reader:

Anxiety is a normal reaction to disability. However, if you feel your anxiety has reached unhealthy or debilitating levels, it is important to seek professional help. There is no shame or weakness in getting counseling or in taking medication prescribed by a psychiatrist. I firmly believe that God uses doctors and medical science to heal. It takes a strong and wise individual to admit they need help and seek it out.

How else can you hit the reset button on thoughts that have become bitter, desperate, or fearful? In combination with medical therapies and counseling, here are a few other faith-based weapons that I have found helpful:

WEAPON #1—WORSHIP:

I remember a car ride with my husband when my soul felt like it was being swallowed alive by stress. I had the sensation of drowning as Parker's voice became garbled and faint. Adrenaline poured through my veins until every muscle in my body felt the desire to flee. How I wanted to run and leave the messiness of disability behind! The intensity of the impulse was frightening. I needed an outlet . . . now.

Suddenly, a thought pierced my inner chaos with dazzling clarity, "Go ahead—run. Run to me." Prayer alone wasn't going to be loud enough to silence my fears. Instead, I felt in the very depths of my heart that my only option was to worship. Parker tuned to a Christian radio station and, as we glorified God for his love and goodness, the fury of my fear began to still.

In that moment our car became a temple. I sensed the presence of God's loving kindness as surely as if he was physically wrapping his arms around me. By the time we arrived home, I was so in awe of my Father that there was no room left in my mind for worry. I felt completely exhausted but even more completely at peace.

I have been using worship as both a weapon and preventative measure against anxiety ever since that day. There is something undefinably special and unique about worship that emotionally connects us to the heart of God.

Psalm 100:4 says, "Enter his gates with thanksgiving and his courts with praise." This verse is a command—but it is also a clue. Thanksgiving and praise are passkeys to recognize (and thus "enter") God's presence. You can increase your awareness of God through worship by using thanksgiving/praise as tools to shift your attention beyond yourself. The more you choose to focus on your Father's loving face, the more your fears will begin to fade.

The nature of worship is so singular that you do not have to be a Christian (or even religious) to recognize that worship is worthwhile. I remember being stunned when a friend told me that her atheist boyfriend sang in a church choir. "Why?" I asked astounded. Her response was so remarkable I remember it a decade later:

> As a musician he loves all music, and he recognizes that there is something transcendent about worship. While he can't put his finger on what makes it special, he is intrigued by the radiance that only worship music holds. He says it is different from any other music.

Scientists are also recognizing the value of worship. Professor Marino Bruce of Vanderbilt University has been following the health trends of a group of churchgoers vs. non-churchgoers for eighteen years. His conclusion? Worship is good for your mental and physical health. He found that attending worship services was "associated with less stress and enhanced longevity."[1] In fact, it reduced mortality by 55 percent within a group of 5,449 middle-aged adults (ages 40–65).

---

1. Patterson, "Worship Is Good," para. 5.

So, when you find yourself in a cycle of worry, try worship. Set aside your fears by taking time to celebrate your Father. You may be surprised at how much they shrink in the presence of his "everlasting love (Jer 31:3)."

WEAPON #2—SHARE YOUR THOUGHTS WITH A TRUSTED FRIEND/COUNSELOR:

Once in a blue moon I get a worry into my head that I can't dislodge on my own. This can be especially true if the thought is rooted in shame or is slightly weird. (You know—those thoughts that will make you sound unhinged if you share them with someone else.)

I have come to think of these thoughts as "wild thoughts" because they behave like a trapped animal. Too ashamed to ask for help, I first try to fight them internally alone. This is a mistake. Like a caged tiger, the thought relentlessly paces my mind and becomes more agitated the longer it is cornered. But if I bring the thought out into the open, it will return to the wild and leave me in peace.

For example, even after I came to believe that God was using my disabilities for his glory, I could not shake the thought that I was also being punished for going farther than I should have with my boyfriend when I was nineteen. Ludicrous! I know Jesus loves me and has taken the punishment for my sins. And *logically*, if God gave every hormonal teenager a disability, we would be in danger of extinction as a human race. I knew the thought was absurd, but it wouldn't leave me alone.

Thank God for the gift of my husband. (My love, if I had a dollar for each time I thought this, we would give Elon Musk a run for his money.) Parker will listen to any crackpot idea that is floating around in my head without judgement. I told him what was bothering me and he sincerely replied, "That thought was sent to distract and exhaust you. It is so ridiculous; it is not even worth fighting. God loves you and would never do that to you."

His words confirmed what I already knew to be true in my spirit, and the "big bad thought" stopped bothering me because it was out in the open.

When you're taunted by a "crazy" thought, consider sharing it with a trusted friend or counselor. Pick someone who has a solid relationship with Christ and is level-headed. The ideal person for this task is able to respond without fear or judgement. There's a good chance your wild thought will vanish when it is brought into the light.

WEAPON #3—REVERSE THE *WHAT IF . . . GAME*:

If you have struggled with anxiety, you've played the merciless game of *What If*:

- *What if* my condition deteriorates and I get worse?
- *What if* the doctors don't know how to help me?
- *What if* I can't work enough to financially support my needs?
- *What if* I burn out my friends and loved ones?
- *What if* I break beneath the strain and stress of disability?

But does *what if* always have to beat you up? Or is it possible for *what if* to lift you up? During my own particularly brutal round of *what if . . .* , I felt God speak a challenge to my spirit:

> *What if* you reversed the *What If . . . Game*? Circumstances could get worse, but they could also get better. Instead of worrying about what may never come to pass, *what if* you imagined all I can do with your life. If you insist on playing *what if . . .* , let's play the positive version . . . the powerful version.

When *what ifs* invade your mind, counter them with this radically different version of the game:

- *What if* I am cared for by a God for whom "all things are possible?" —Matt 19:26
- *What if* God is turning my hurt into something helpful for others and spiritually good for me? —Rom 8:28
- *What if* God is working wonders on my behalf? —Joel 2:26
- *What if* God will provide for my physical needs? —Ps 68:10
- *What if* my God is so faithful he will never leave or forsake me? —Deut 31:8
- *What if* "I can do all things through Christ who strengthens me?" —Phil 4:13 NKJV
- *What if* "I am being transformed into his [*God's*] image with ever-increasing glory?" —2 Cor 3:18

Tips for Playing:

1. I find it powerful to anchor my *what ifs* in biblical truth because God's word is a safe place to put our hope. But you don't have to have the Bible memorized to put this idea into practice. Memorization has become difficult for me, so when I cannot recall a scripture verbatim, I voice ideas that reflect biblical themes I know to be true. (Ex. *What if* God's plans for me are more beautiful than I can imagine?)

2. Focus your *what ifs* on who God is. God's character is accurately represented in the Bible and never changes. We can always be certain of his character even when we are disappointed or confused by our circumstances.

3. When you are especially overwhelmed, speak your positive *what ifs* out loud. This helps me focus and drown out my more stubborn worries.

4. Respect the process. Like any game or sport, you have to practice to achieve noticeable results.

This can be a mental gamechanger. Now, whenever I catch my mind playing the *What If . . . Game*, I exchange the negative *what ifs* for good. When I am finished, my soul invariably feels lighter and excited about the beautiful life God has in store for me. As I make a habit of putting positive and powerful *what ifs* in my mind, anxious thoughts increasingly take a backseat.

Chapter 12
Lose the Obsession with "Normal"

If you cling to your life, you will lose it; but if you give up your life for me, you will find it. —Matt 10:39

FACEBOOK IS NOT MY friend. In fact, I rarely visit my account because it tends to make me cry. Why does a social media page make me so emotional? Because I inevitably compare my life against my peers. As I see them excel within their chosen careers, celebrate the birth of their children, and take vacations paid for by a two-income household, I find myself thinking, "I wish I were normal."

"Normal" is a double-edged desire. Wanting normalcy is positive when it drives us to do everything within our power to have healthier bodies and a better quality of life. But it can be a seductive siren call. When you have used every medical advancement at your disposal and exhausted second (or seventeenth) specialists' opinions, an unchecked desire for normalcy can be emotionally devastating.

As a disabled person, I have found that the pain of wanting to be normal can be even more damaging to my quality of life than the physical suffering I experience. There is no quicker way for me to build a mini tissue mountain than to rehash the visions I had for my life when I was healthy. When I obsess over normalcy, I can become dangerously discontented, distracted, and disconnected. Personally, it prevents me from recognizing my blessings and from moving forward into the unique story God is crafting out of my life. Can you relate?

What does it really mean to be "normal" anyway? Consider these synonyms for "normal": average, ordinary, commonplace, unexceptional. They sound pretty boring when you think about it. Under close inspection, the idol of normalcy loses some of its luster.

But the antonyms for "normal" are far more exciting: remarkable, extraordinary, memorable, unique. If I truly look into my heart, these are the words I want to echo from my life story. The only catch is, remarkable life stories don't come cheap. Instead, the stories that we find most inspiring are of the victorious underdogs, the unlikely heroes, and those who overcome against tremendous odds.

Parker is the first person to admit that he has a fuzzy long-term memory. In his own words, it takes something of truly epic for him to remember a childhood event. One of the memories he treasures is from the 1996 Summer Olympic Games.

Parker vividly remembers his family gathering around the television to watch the United States women's gymnastics team. They were neck and neck with the favored Russians—a first ever team gold medal for American women on the line. Everything came down to Kerri Strug's performance on the vault.[1]

Strug's first attempt was disastrous. She sat her landing and badly injured her ankle. Eight-year-old Parker thought the United States team was done for. But then he watched in disbelief as she approached the vaulting apparatus. She was going to attempt her second vault injured. (You can watch a clip of her vault on YouTube.) Parker remembers,

> It felt like time slowed down when she accelerated into her second run. Her execution in the air was flawless and then something astonishing happened. After briefly touching down, she stuck the landing balanced on one foot! It was so unlikely that there was a moment of shocked silence before the stadium and my family erupted into electric cheers. Later, we learned that she had jumped on a sprain—with two torn ligaments in her ankle. I'll never forget her sheer willpower and bravery. It was a guts and glory win.

The 1996 Women's Gymnastics Olympic Team was dubbed the "Magnificent Seven" in honor of the seven talented women who brought the first team gold medal home to the United States. But Parker only recalls one plucky athlete. More than twenty years later, his face still becomes animated reliving the memory.

1. Bondy, "Kerry Strug Stands Tall."

Strug's vault became iconic, not because she was an Olympic athlete, but because she jumped when she was hurt. It is the triumph, coupled with the injury, that inspired Parker and our nation. If you took away her hurt, you would rob her story of its power.

I am sure that when Kerri Strug imagined her perfect Olympic vault scenario, it did not include torn ligaments. But finding herself in a nightmare situation, she pushed through the pain and put her body at risk for her team. Because of her tenacity, her real story is far more memorable than her imagined ideal ever would have been. It takes bravery to let go of the plans we have for our lives. It also takes courage to push fear aside, in pursuit of another way.

I am working on taking that risk with God's help. I realize that I cannot be an example of Christ's ability to overcome without hardship in my life. I trust that God is not heartlessly using me as a visual aide but has a plan to redeem disability for my good too. Together we can triumph over tragedy. While disability does not make me more or less special than others, it is part of my own unique assignment. Who knows how God will use our stories to inspire those around us?

I pray that you and I are able to find balance in our desire for normalcy. That we continue to keep our ears open for medical advancements but also trust God enough to stop excessively grieving over a need to be normal. As we let go of our plans, it creates space for God to work. May we find abundant joy in the extraordinary plans of "him who is able to do immeasurably more than all we ask or imagine, according to his power that is at work within us (Eph 3:20)." Life's least expected journeys are often the most worthwhile.

> *Lord God,*
> *When our need to be normal becomes unhealthy, help us let it*
> *go. Make us aware of how you are empowering and transforming*
> *us into extraordinary instruments of your love. Amen.*

Part 3

Attitudes to Cultivate

. . . let God transform you into a new person by changing the way you think. —Rom 12:2 NLT

Introduction:

Garden Something Good

Finally, believers, whatever is true, whatever is honorable and worthy
of respect, whatever is right and confirmed by God's word, whatever
is pure and wholesome, whatever is lovely and brings peace, whatev-
er is admirable and of good repute; if there is any excellence, if there
is anything worthy of praise, think continually on these things [center
your mind on them, and implant them in your heart].
—Phil 4:8 AMP

IMAGINE YOU WANT TO create a garden from an overgrown plot. Your very first task is the back-breaking job of taking back the land from the weeds. You cut down brambles, dig up turf, and dislodge stubborn rocks. Finally, your hard work pays off . . . the upturned soil waits like a blank canvas. Time to plant something new and beautiful.

However, you must sow quickly! An empty flower bed is the only invitation weeds need to move in. If you don't provide desirable plants as competition, the weeds will soon overrun the soil you worked so hard to reclaim.

But fill your garden with sunflowers, roses, strawberries, and sweet corn and the weeds have no room. They are simply crowded out by the wanted plants. When an occasional thistle does manage to pop up amongst your flowers, it is easy to pull. Experienced gardeners consider weeding and planting a garden to be a complementary process.

Your heart and soul are like garden soil. In Part Two you began weeding out negative thoughts by taking out the trash. But letting go of harmful mindsets is most effective when it is coupled with cultivating attitudes that are healing for your heart. You need a biblical outlook that nourishes your well-being.

So put on your gardening gloves and get ready to dig in. This section is a collection of attitudes that will sow life back into your spirit. With God's help, you can keep the weeds of fear, depression, and anger at bay by encouraging the good fruits of hope, inner peace, faith, courage, and strength. Will you join me and plant for a healthy heart?

Chapter 13

Move from Fretful → Fruitful God Time

I am the vine; you are the branches. If you remain in me and I in you, you will bear much fruit; apart from me you can do nothing.
—John 15:5

WARNING: YOUR HOUSEPLANTS ARE on the move. This is not a drill. It is not science fiction. It is a natural phenomenon called phototropism.

All plants need sunlight in order to create their food (even seaweed). Phototropism is the process by which plants bend towards light in order to maximize their energy production. Sunflowers are dramatic examples. Like adoring fans, they turn their faces to follow the daily arc of the sun.

If you have a houseplant, go and take a quick look . . . , is it reaching for the light streaming through the kitchen window? Your leaf baby may be so proficient at phototropism that you have to regularly turn its pot to keep it growing straight. But what would happen if you shut your plant in a closet? Cut off from the light that gives it life, it would eventually become weak and die.

Hold this image of the houseplant in your mind. Just as all plants need sunlight, all relationships require time and effort to grow. Your relationship with God is no exception. *Setting aside time to spend with God is the most important step you can take to build a connection with him that is healthy and vibrant.*

But is your God time increasing your anxiety during this difficult season? If so, then tap the brakes and ask yourself,

How am I spending my time with God? Am I constantly on my knees pleading for healing? Have my prayers become a running list of what I need God to do for me? Has determination to pray disability away taken precedence over every other aspect of my spiritual life?

It is easy for worries to hijack our time with God when we desperately need his help. Don't get me wrong . . . Jesus cares about our broken hearts and hears our every cry. We can whimper, shout, scream, and plead with the assurance that we will never exhaust his ears. He can handle it. But how about you? *Can you afford to spend your entire God time in crisis mode?*

Personally, my sanity doesn't stretch that far. When I continuously pray about my fears, they inevitably gain momentum. My pleading does more to glorify my worries than connect me to God. The Christian author, Beth Moore, says,

> It is never the will of God for warfare to become our focus. The fastest way to lose our balance in warfare is to rebuke the devil more than we relate to God.[1]

No wonder I end up hyperventilating when all I do is pray for healing . . . I am out of balance! When I focus on the darkness to the exclusion of the light, my soul withers like a houseplant starved by shadows. If I want the time I spend with God to empower my spirit, I need to take a cue from a sunflower . . . I need to continually turn my face towards the sun/Son.

Fruitful God time is God-focused. Its primary goal is to develop a deeper relationship with Christ. Jesus refers to himself as the vine and to us as his branches (John 15:1–11). He teaches that apart from him we can do nothing, but with him all things are possible (John 15:5b, Phil 4:13). When we devote time to increasing our awareness of God's love; peace, joy, and spiritual strength are the natural byproducts. As we make much of him, our problems begin to appear more manageable. Jesus is the life source of our souls.

So I am giving my God time a phototropic makeover. Instead of letting worry run the show, I'm leaning towards the light by centering my attention on Jesus. I take two minutes to ask for help, but then I choose to believe that God has heard me. In his perfect timing, he will either answer my prayers or change my heart. The rest of my quiet time is focused on building our

---

1. Moore, *Praying God's Word*, 7.

relationship. I pray to know God more intimately, read my Bible to understand him in new ways, and praise the different aspects of his character.

The result? My worry cycles are breaking. My thoughts are far brighter. Fretful is becoming fruitful because I am valuing *connection.*

Restructuring your God time may sound daunting when you are in the middle of a difficult season. But please understand . . . this doesn't have to be something you add to your to do list—it is an exchange with an upgrade. Instead of rehashing your problems in prayer, celebrate the One who can solve them. Trade ten minutes of worried pleading for ten minutes of Bible reading. Isaiah 26:3 NLT declares, "You will keep in perfect peace all who trust in you, all whose thoughts are fixed on you (Isa 26:3 NLT)"! Notice how God's word punctuates this promise with an exclamation point. Revamping your God time to value connection shifts your focus. It fixes your thoughts on Jesus and invites God's light!

If you are unsure how to get started, begin with the Bible because it has the advantage of being concrete. When I am stressed, I find that even my most well-intentioned prayers can be easily sidetracked by worry or muddled by conflicting emotions. But the Bible offers trustworthy insight into the character of God. What better way to learn about him than from his personal love letter to you?

To help you on your way, I have included a few of my favorite Bible verses and what they teach me about our incredible God. Each promise is a seed to be planted and nurtured in your heart.

God is large and in charge:

For in him all things were created: things in heaven and on earth, visible and invisible, whether thrones or powers or rulers or authorities; all things have been created through him and for him. He is before all things, and in him all things hold together. —Col 1:16–17

God is entirely good:

God is light; in him there is no darkness at all. —1 John 1:5b

God is unlimited:

... with God all things are possible. —Matt 19:26

God's greatness cannot be challenged and he holds you in his hand:

"I give them eternal life, and they shall never perish; no one will snatch them out of my hand. My Father, who has given them to me, *is greater than all*; no one can snatch them out of my Father's hand. I and the Father are one." —John 10:28–30 *(Jesus speaking about his followers.)*

Jesus is a picture of God and his love:

The Son is the radiance of God's glory and the exact representation of his being, sustaining all things by his powerful word. —Heb 1:3

God loved you enough to sacrifice his son:

He who did not spare his own Son, but gave him up for us all—how will he not also, along with him, graciously give us all things? —Rom 8:32

God loves you just as much as he loves Jesus:

"I am in them and you are in me. May they experience such perfect unity that the world will know that you sent me and *that you love them as much as you love me.*" —John 17:23 NLT *(Jesus praying for his followers.)*

God's love is unshakeable:

For I am convinced that neither death nor life, neither angels nor demons, neither the present nor the future, nor any powers, neither height nor depth, nor anything else in all creation, will be able to separate us from the love of God that is in Christ Jesus our Lord. —Rom 8:38–39

God is trustworthy:

God is not human, that he should lie, not a human being, that he should change his mind. Does he speak and then not act? Does he promise and not fulfill? —Num 23:19

God is merciful and patient:

But you, Lord, are a compassionate and gracious God, slow to anger, abounding in love and faithfulness. —Ps 86:15

God is able to bless you within your circumstances:

And God is able to bless you abundantly, so that in all things at all times, having all that you need, you will abound in every good work. —2 Cor 9:8

DISCOVER GOD THROUGH HIS NAMES:

For "lifer" Christians looking for a new way to increase your understanding of God, pick up a name study. (I enjoy the *100 Names of God Daily Devotional* by Christopher D. Hudson.) Take thirty seconds to consider all the names you are known by and how much information each name reveals about you. I am a Christian, a wife, a daughter, a friend, a writer, a teacher, a godmother, etc. People are not one dimensional, they are diamonds; multiple facets join together to make the whole stone sparkle.

However, we will never match God for his brilliance. Did you know that there are hundreds of names referring to God and Jesus in the Bible? Many of these names appear as metaphors. Deuteronomy 4:24 says God is a "Consuming Fire," Titus 2:13 calls Christ our "Blessed Hope," and Genesis 16:13 refers to God as *El Roi* which means "The God Who Sees Me." Each name illuminates something new and beautiful about his character. The thrill of the Christian journey is that there is always more of God's goodness to explore.

The ultimate goal God has for us is not power but personal intimacy with Him. Yes, God wants to bring us healing, but more than anything, He wants us to know our Healer. —Beth Moore[2]

2. Moore, *Praying God's Word*, 6.

Chapter 14

Believe That God Is for You

"When you pass through the waters, I will be with you; and when you pass through the rivers, they will not sweep over you. When you walk through the fire, you will not be burned; the flames will not set you ablaze." —Isa 43:2

WHEN YOU HAVE A disability, it is so easy to feel like you are going it alone. This is especially true when your situation is new or unexpected. God does not promise Christians that we won't have to pass through waters, rivers, and fires (pain, divorce, unemployment, etc.) during our time on earth. Instead, he gives us a life preserving promise: *I will be with you.*

My friend, you are wading through the waters of life as part of the ultimate buddy system. You won't get stuck *in* your situation, because the King of Heaven is taking hold of your hand to pull you *through.* Joshua 23:10 says, "the Lord your God fights for you, just as he promised."

Ding. Ding. You have a prize fighter in your ring. Let's meet two Bible characters who felt alone and afraid only to realize that the champion of the universe was fighting for them. May their stories encourage you to believe in the unseen hand that holds you fast.

STORY #1—ELISHA'S SERVANT (2 KGS 6:8–23):

The king of Aram's blood pressure skyrocketed every time he thought of Israel's prophet, Elisha. How did that motormouth always know exactly where Aram's armies were mobilizing to attack Israel? It was beyond humiliating! Fine. If the king couldn't take down Israel's army . . . he could send his troops to take out a tattletale.

Picture the scene at Elisha's dwelling in Dothan. His servant awakes at dawn and steps outside to begin his morning chores. Rubbing the sleep from his eyes, he glances up to gauge the day's weather forecast and gets the shock of his life: it's raining men! (Or enemy soldiers, horses, and chariots to be exact.)

His response *is not* "hallelujah." Panicking, he cries, "Oh, sir, what will we do now? (2 Kgs 6:15)." Surely a prophet and his errand boy are no match against the army of professional warriors surrounding the city.

Elisha responds undaunted, "Don't be afraid! . . . there are more on our side than on theirs! (2 Kgs 6:16 NLT)." As the prophet prays, his servant's eyes are opened. The hills beyond the surrounded city are teeming with invisible "horses and chariots of fire (2 Kgs 6:17)." The power pulsing off this heavenly army makes the Arameans look like upstart toy soldiers. Mouth agape, the wide-eyed servant watches God strike the enemy army blind and deliver them into Elisha's hands. Do you think he was able to squeak out a "Hallelujah" after all?

I am so much like Elisha's servant. I see what is directly in front of me and quake with fear. This story reminds me that when I am afraid, I need to broaden my perspective. Beyond the source of my fears, lie the armies of heaven—waiting to turn my disaster into deliverance. The scales are tipped in my favor because I have "more on [my] side." Whatever problems I face in this life, *I always have the advantage—because God always has my back.*

Are you surrounded by trouble today? Envision your problems encircled by your Savior's even greater embrace. Like Elisha, you can trust in his strong and loving arms. May God open your spiritual eyes to see the evidence of his work on your behalf.

STORY #2—MARY MAGDALENE (JOHN 20:11–18):

Mary Magdalene owed everything to Jesus. He rescued her from the living hell of being possessed by seven demons (Luke 8:2). Jesus restored her sanity and gave her a second chance at life. Can you imagine the horror she felt as she watched her Savior being crucified?

Mary must have feared that everything good in her life would die with Jesus. I suspect she felt like a ticking time bomb—terrified that at any moment she would be thrust back into the darkness of her former days. No wonder she remained weeping at Christ's tomb after everyone else had gone. How bitter it was to have her hope restored only to have it extinguished by the finality of the grave.

Raw with grief, she doesn't have enough stamina to put on a brave face when a gardener asks who she is looking for. Desperately she begs, "If you have taken him away, tell me where you have put him, and I will go and get him (John 20:15 NLT)." The gardener answers softly, "Mary." One spoken word is enough for revelation to dawn in her soul—only her Lord speaks her name that tenderly. She looks up and gazes straight into the eyes of a miracle. The "gardener" is her beloved Jesus.

The three days between the crucifixion and resurrection must have been the loneliest, most frightening days of Mary Magdalene's life. (That's saying something considering her resumé.) Sometimes our hope is nearly unraveled before the veil is torn and we are able to see clearly that God was with us all along. In the light of the resurrection, Mary realized that God was working within her worst nightmare to make her deepest desire come true. Christ was not gone—he had simply gone to work—making a way for her to be with him forever. Mary had never been more loved, and Christ had never stopped fighting for her.

But Elisha's servant and Mary Magdalene lived thousands of years ago. Is God still fighting for us here in the twenty-first century? The answer is a resounding, *"Yes!"* Acts 17:26 GNT says that God, "fixed beforehand the exact times and the limits of the places where they (people) would live." In other words, the "when" and the "where" of your birth are no accident. You were put on this planet with a purpose.

God's intentional placement encourages me that he is actively championing my cause *now*. As a POTS sufferer, I would have died a slow death of dehydration and malnourishment if I had been born at any other time in history. POTS was not even identified as an autonomic nervous system disorder until 1993[1]—a full five years after I was born. If I lived in a country less medically advanced or financially affluent than the United States, I would have a miserable existence.

The fact that God brought the circumstances of my birth together to ensure that I would have some quality of life tells me that he has a plan for me beyond sickness. God has work for me to do. By his design, I was born a United States citizen in 1988 so that I would have the tools I need to accomplish his purposes.

I bet this is true for many of you reading this book. Take a minute to consider how your very birth may be evidence of God fighting for you. What does that mean for your life?

1. Dysautonomia International, "Postural Orthostatic Tachycardia Syndrome," para. 5.

If God is for us, who can be against us? —Rom 8:31b

Even in darkness light dawns for the upright . . . —Ps 112:4a

Chapter 15
Esteem Yourself through God's Eyes

"Do not fear, for I have redeemed you; I have summoned you by name; you are mine." —The King of Heaven from Isa 43:1b

WHEN MY DOCTOR FIRST told me I was disabled, my self-esteem tanked. Years of hopes became crushing disappointments that weighed heavily on my spirit. Unable to work in my chosen field or financially contribute to our household, I felt like a professional failure and a burden to my husband. The limitations that restricted my activities made me feel like I had little to offer as a friend. As I struggled to find energy to go to church, read my Bible, or serve others, I even felt like a disappointment to God. I just didn't have the energy to check all the boxes on a "good Christian's" to-do list.

From the outside looking in, it was hard to place much worth upon my life. I'd lost many of the abilities and dreams that mattered to me. This view of myself was so toxic; I don't even like to think about the potency of the darkness I was fighting that first year.

But even in this perpetual nighttime, God's light was at work. He kept nudging my spirit with the thought, *"You are more than what you have lost."* At the Holy Spirit's insistence, I began to realize that the only way for me to move forward was to put God in charge of my self-esteem. The only antidote strong enough to revive my poisoned sense of self was God's message about who I am in his Holy Word. Each day I spent time in the Bible seeking out God's truth about my identity in him.

Choosing to define my identity through God's love was a vital lesson. It enabled me to start reclaiming my sense of self. This took daily effort, perseverance, and time. It still takes maintenance and scriptural reminders to keep self-critical thoughts at bay. But by God's grace I can now look you in the eye and say, *"I am more because of what I have lost."* God can work this miracle in your heart too. It begins with the discovery of how precious you are to him.

Here are some of my favorite scriptures about our identity in Christ. But this is just a starter list. God's word is full of beautiful thoughts about your value to him. As you spend time in Bible Study and prayer, ask God to help you see yourself through his eyes. *You are dazzling to behold!*

You are God's child:

See what great love the Father has lavished on us, that we should be called children of God! And that is what we are! —1 John 3:1

God will never stop loving you:

I have loved you with an everlasting love; I have drawn you with unfailing kindness. —Jer 31:3

You belong to Jesus, so God loves/takes care of you even when you are messed/mixed up:

Then I realized that my heart was bitter, and I was all torn up inside. I was so foolish and ignorant — I must have seemed like a senseless animal to you. *Yet I still belong to you*; you hold my right hand. You guide me with your counsel, leading me to a glorious destiny. —Ps 73:21–24 NLT

God treasures you:

And the Lord has declared this day that you are his people, his treasured possession as he promised . . . — Deut 26:18

You are chosen and special:

But you are a chosen people, a royal priesthood, a holy nation, God's special possession, that you may declare the praises of him who called you out of darkness into his wonderful light. —1 Pet 2:9

It pleased God to make you his:

He predestined and lovingly planned for us to be adopted to Himself as [His own] children through Jesus Christ, in accordance with the kind intention and good pleasure of His will . . . —Eph 1:5 AMP

You have worth because you are made in God's image:

So God created mankind in his own image, in the image of God he created them; male and female he created them. —Gen 1:27

God delights in you:

For the Lord your God is living among you. He is a mighty Savior. He will take delight in you with gladness. With his love, he will calm all your fears. He will rejoice over you with joyful songs. —Zeph 3:17 NLT *(God sings over you because you bring him joy. Isn't that amazing?!)*

God is always thinking about you:

How precious are your thoughts about me, O God. They cannot be numbered! I can't even count them; they outnumber the grains of sand! —Ps 139:17–18a NLT

God calls you an overcomer:

You, dear children, are from God and have overcome them [*evil spirits*], because the one who is in you is greater than the one who is in the world. —1 John 4:4

Chapter 16
Practice an Attitude of Gratitude

" . . . give thanks in all circumstances; for this is God's will for you in
Christ Jesus." —1 Thess 5:18

IF I HAVE EVER had anything in common with a professional athlete on
draft day it was as a rising fifth grader at Kitty Hawk Elementary School.
With intense anticipation, the pre-teens of the Outer Banks waited for the
class lists to be released. Prayers were whispered upon the hour, fingers were
crossed until they cramped, and allowances were hopefully sunk in wishing
wells. What was the reason for all this unnatural back to school fervor? Mrs.
Hutton.

Mrs. Hutton was not just a teacher; she was a zookeeper. Landing one
of the coveted seats in her classroom meant you would share your desk with
a fish, bird, or guinea pig. If fate was particularly your friend, you might
be seated next to the crown jewel of them all: her 3-feet-long lime green
iguana.

The animals were exciting, but it was Mrs. Hutton's big personality that
cemented her celebrity status. She could have been Mrs. Frizzle stepping out
of the pages of a *Magic School Bus* book. When you crossed the threshold
into her classroom, you weren't just going to learn science, you were going
to live it.

Guess who made the cut?! That spare change corroding at the bottom
of our neighborhood fountain was well spent. On my first day of class, I was
surprised to learn that there was something Mrs. Hutton was even more
serious about than science. Atop her hot pink high heels, she stared down
at us with the presence of a linebacker. (A remarkable feat for a woman who
was barely five feet tall and 100 pounds soaking wet.) As we quieted beneath
her gaze, she directed our attention to the gigantic banner over her head.

"Attitude is Everything," she proclaimed. "When you come into this class, leave your baggage at the door. Because here, we choose to have an attitude of gratitude."

Attitude is everything became the mantra that we recited at the beginning of each class. When responding to sulky adolescent complaints or mediating between two students, Mrs. Hutton would point to the banner. She reminded us that we could better our situation simply by choosing gratefulness. It was the foundation of her classroom and an idea she planted in each of her students. Twenty years later, I found out just how genuinely Mrs. Hutton lived by her motto.

My health concerns have made it too stressful for Parker and me to consider having children at this point in our journey. Most days I struggle just to take care of myself. As a woman who wanted to have four children when she was healthy, this has been a bitter reality to accept.

During a tearful conversation with my mom, I was surprised to learn that Mrs. Hutton was also childless. As her coworker/friend of many years, my mom was able to share how Mrs. Hutton responded to her disappointment. My fifth-grade memories became infinitely more precious as my mom paraphrased her wisdom:

> When I realized I couldn't have children, I knew I had a decision to make. I could spend my life neglecting all the blessings God has given me to obsessively grieve over what he has not. Or I could cherish my wonderful husband and be a positive influence for all the children who are part of my life through teaching. God has given me so much to be grateful for. I decided to take all the love and attention I would have given a child and redirect it towards my husband and my students.

What was the result of her attitude shift? A loving marriage that has lasted over fifty years. Hundreds of former students who will never forget that *attitude is everything*. In circumstances beyond her control, she made a decision to control what she could. She reclaimed and repurposed her life with gratitude.

Wow! Who knew one of my favorite childhood teachers would still be showing me the way forward as an adult? I hope to one day embody gratitude as fully as Mrs. Hutton, but I have to admit that there are days I really struggle to be positive. Sometimes when a well-meaning friend says, "Things could be a lot worse," it's a challenge not to snap back, "Things could be a lot better too." But on my good days, I am able to recognize the truth in their advice and give thanks for the blessings of my situation.

If you find yourself struggling to find reasons to be grateful, I encourage you to keep trying. The more I choose to practice and pray for gratitude, the more natural it becomes to my spirit. Keep a daily blessings journal, start your prayers with praise, or distract yourself from worry by voicing your blessings aloud. At first it may feel forced. But over the years, what started as a coping mechanism has become my default mindset. I praise God that now my grateful days outnumber the days I feel dissatisfied with my lot.

Practicing gratitude will also help you become more aware of God's hand in your life. He works to answer our prayers in surprisingly tender ways. In 2018, Parker and I celebrated the birth of our goddaughter, Emma. Emma reminds me that God is always able to deliver on his promises.

Our best friends, Mandy and Stephen, struggled with infertility for eight years. After years of failing to conceive, Mandy found it too hurtful to continue to ask God for children and decided that it wasn't meant to be. I, on the other hand, could not accept this for my irreplaceable best friend. She possesses the loveliest of spirits, and I have never met anyone more meant to be a mother. Secretly, I kept praying that God would give her the child she desired.

Twice in my life I have experienced such a powerful surge of joy that I spontaneously laughed/sobbed at the same time: when Parker asked me to marry him and when Mandy told me she was going to be a mom. Her obstetrician is still mystified about how it happened.

Emma is the miracle I expected for my best friends, but I was completely blindsided by what God did next. Our dear friends decided to pay God's blessings forward when they told us:

> We want to share our miracle with you by making you Emma's godparents. You are our family now. With so many people to love her, Emma is going to be the most blessed little girl in the world!

I will never be able to thank Mandy enough for her generosity of spirit. In all those years of praying for her to have Emma, I had no idea that God would inspire her to also give me a daughter in return. To be chosen and invited to share in raising another person's child is an incredibly special honor.

Parker and I overflowed with gratitude as we held our goddaughter for the first time. She didn't even cry as she was transitioned from the arms of her parents into our outstretched hands. It was as if she knew she belonged there also. As I gazed at Emma's perfect face, I realized I was holding tangible proof that prayer is powerful.

Parker and I relish our role as part-time parents. While we continue to pray for my health to improve so that we can have our own child, we marvel that God has given us a child to enjoy while we wait. We have been "adopted" as parents and called into a family. The unusual way in which we acquired our daughter makes it all the more beautiful. Emma, Mandy, and Stephen: you make us sing with thankfulness.

A cheerful heart is good medicine. —Prov 17:22

P.S.   Science now appreciates what Proverbs 17 and Mrs. Hutton knew all along: gratitude is good for you. According to Harvard Health, "gratitude is strongly and consistently linked to greater happiness. Expressing gratitude helps people feel positive emotions, relish good experiences, improve their health, deal with adversity, and build strong relationships."[1]

P.P.S.   Bippity, Boppity, Boo! I'm now a godmother of two! My nephew, James, has also become my godson. Sheryl and Mike, thank you for the upgrade. Loving/being loved by a child is real life magic. The chance to be more involved in your amazing son's life is the best birthday gift I've ever received.

As for that little pumpkin: James, you are an absolute delight to me. Every day I thank God for your funny ways, kind heart, and the joy you bring to my life. I marvel that you are brave enough at three to throw a sheet over your head and let me blindly lead my friendly ghost around the house as we play "Trick-or-Treat." I can't help but think that, even though you get to keep the chocolate, I win the prize. I pray you become a mighty man of God who is as courageous and compassionate as the little boy I treasure. My cup overflows.

---

1. Miller, "In Praise of Gratitude," para 3.

Chapter 17
Be Empowered by God's Past Faithfulness

Jesus Christ is the same yesterday and today and forever. —Heb 13:8

Two prayer requests stand out with staggering frequency when I mentally scan my prayers from the last thirty years. Most recently, it has been prayers for physical healing. But after a decade of waiting for my health to improve, it is easy to grow discouraged. Will God ever answer my prayers? That is when the Holy Spirit nudges me with a reminder: God faithfully sent my sweet Parker to me after fifteen years of praying for a godly husband.

I was painfully awkward around boys as a young girl. With no brothers to teach me the ropes, I never quite got the hang of relating to guys. That didn't stop me from having a very romantic soul (my first crush was in preschool). While Jesus is the one who completes me, I always felt strongly that God intended for me to share my life with another person. The years of waiting for this prayer to be answered weren't easy. I often struggled with overwhelming loneliness. But the wait was worth it.

Why? Because God was working. He was shaping my husband and me as individuals—preparing our hearts to love one another. And at the right time, God delivered! When I met Parker in college, there was an instant connection. I recognized in his eyes a spirit I had both loved my entire life and could not wait to spend a lifetime getting to know. I had such a peaceful feeling of everything being "right" that I had never had with other boyfriends. I didn't need to spend hours seeking God's direction on whether Parker was the right man for me. My heart just knew.

As remarkable as our instant connection was, it was simply the spark that ignited a blazing testimony of God's love in my life. On our wedding day, Parker showed me the verse he inscribed in my wedding band. It read

"*Beloved* Ephesians 5:25," which instructs, "Husbands, love your wives, just as Christ loved the church and gave himself up for her."

Twelve years into our marriage, Parker daily delivers on this promise. He has shown maturity and wisdom beyond his years, cherished me when I had little to give back, and always sees my heart beyond this shell of sickness. Once after watching *The Flash*, I asked my husband, "If you could have a super power what would it be?" My Treasure thought about it and with complete sincerity answered, "I always want to be able to love you better." Ladies, can you say heart palpitations? Gentlemen, take notes.

If I searched the world over, I could not find a better fit for a spouse. Remarkably, fifteen years of prayers and thoughts about my future husband did not begin to touch the reality that God had in store. Only God could imagine a man so wonderfully fashioned to love me.

When I need inspiration to keep praying for healing, I think about the beautiful faithfulness God showed me through Parker. I remind myself that God's character does not change (Heb 13:8). The same God who completely knocked my socks off with Parker is orchestrating my future. That is incredibly exciting! The Lord has a track record of exceeding my expectations. Meditating on how completely God answered this past prayer is usually enough to refuel my hope.

If my spirits are at a critical low, I'll write out an "evidence" list detailing every example of God's faithfulness in my life. Some points are life changing like, "He gave me his son Jesus," or the example of Parker. Others represent his faithfulness on a smaller scale. For instance, "I prayed for help to get out of bed this morning and I'm up." Whether an example is big or small, each one represents a prayer or a promise that God has fulfilled. I carry the list with me and scan through it when I need strength.

Recounting God's faithfulness when you need spiritual strength is also modeled in the Bible. One of my favorite examples comes from the book of 1 Samuel when David volunteers to fight against Goliath. King Saul is less than impressed with the confidence of the young shepherd boy. What chance does a teenager stand against a giant warrior who makes Dwayne the "Rock" Johnson look shrimpy? Saul voices his concerns, but David replies:

> Your servant has been keeping his father's sheep. When a lion
> or a bear came and carried off a sheep from the flock, I went
> after it, struck it and rescued the sheep from its mouth. When
> it turned on me, I seized it by its hair, struck it and killed it . . .

The Lord who rescued me from the paw of the lion and the paw of the bear will rescue me from the hand of this Philistine.
—1 Sam 17:34–35,37

I don't think this was an off-the-cuff response. The surety that David displays when answering Saul convinces me that he had been pondering this in his heart. He remembers God delivering him from the lion. He visualizes God saving him from the bear. It is the act of remembering who God is and what he has done that gives David the faith to face down a giant. God gave him victory before, and God will do it again.

Let's follow David's example. Next time you feel your hope failing and your faith in need of a jumpstart, take time to remember how the Lord has been good to you. In celebrating God's past deliverance, you will be given strength for your present battle.

Those who are wise will take all this to heart; they will see in our history the faithful love of the Lord. —Ps 107:43

Chapter 18
Know You Win in the End

"In this world you will have trouble. But take heart! I have overcome the world." —John 16:33 (Jesus Speaking)

SONNY KAPOOR IS ONE of my favorite movie characters and the manager of *The Best Exotic Marigold Hotel* in India. His hotel is advertised as a luxury retirement home for the "elderly and beautiful." But when English retirees arrive, they find their Indian palace in a state of disarray—complete with pigeons nesting in the rooms.

Has Sonny swindled them? Sonny doesn't see it that way. He has unwavering faith that it is only a matter of time before his hotel becomes what he has envisioned. His optimism is so innocent and contagious that his guests soon begin to see the hotel in the same light of love.

Now that I have introduced you to Sonny, I would like to share the quote that fixed the film in my memory. When the retirees arrive, one hotly accuses Sonny of photoshopping the pictures in his advertisement. He responds with unflappable sincerity,

> I have offered a vision of the future . . . of course I hoped that by now it would be the present. But you know in India we have a saying, 'Everything will be alright in the end . . . so if it's not alright it is not yet the end.'[1]

What valuable insight for the disabled believer! God has given his children such bright promises for the future. But like the hotel guests, we feel cheated when his healing doesn't materialize according to our time table or expectations. We know he is capable of making us well. Yet as we struggle

---

1. Madden, *The Best Exotic Marigold Hotel*, approx. 23 minutes in.

with chronic conditions or remember lost loved ones, it is clear that many Christians are never physically healed within their earthly bodies.

The Bible supports these common-sense observations. Hebrews 11:13, 16 says,

> All these people *[Bible characters]* were still living by faith when they died. They did not receive the things promised; they only saw them and welcomed them from a distance, admitting that they were foreigners and strangers on earth. . . Instead, they were longing for a better country—a heavenly one.

Our great hope as Christians is that when our lives on earth end, a glorious new story will unfold. What promises await us in our heavenly home? Just like Sonny, God offers us a vision of the future.

Revelation tells us that when Christ returns, all things will be made new (Rev 21:5). This includes our bodies. First Corinthians 15:42–44 reveals just how glorious these new bodies will be:

> So will it be with the resurrection of the dead. The body that is sown is perishable, it is raised imperishable; it is sown in dishonor, it is raised in glory; it is sown in weakness, it is raised in power; it is sown a natural body, it is raised a spiritual body.

We will receive bodies that radiate God's image in all his intended splendor—strong bodies that will be ours forever. *Awesome*. As someone who has experienced disability here on earth, I look forward to being especially thunderstruck at the difference. Imagine the joy of the blind as they gaze into the tender mercy of the Lord's eyes. Or the delight of the deaf when they hear Jesus whisper how much he has loved them. The lame will run with the grace of gazelles and those who were unable to speak will shout God's loudest praises (Isa 35:5–6).

At our homecoming, our loving Father promises to personally wipe every tear from our eyes. We will be reborn into a life free from death, mourning, crying, or pain (Rev 21:4). Instead, "everlasting joy will crown their heads. Gladness and joy will overtake them, and sorrow and sighing will flee away (Isa 35:10)."

Hallelujah! What a magnificent future awaits us. These promises make disability easier—but also more difficult.

FIGHTING THE GOOD FIGHT:

Waiting is difficult because I long for physical transformation. However, if you are in a season of intense despair, please do not misinterpret God's comforting promise of a new heavenly body as an endorsement for suicide. It would deeply grieve both of our hearts for these words to be misused to that end. God understands how much you and I want to be well and to have the freedom of fully functioning bodies.

Our Lord inspired the Apostle Paul to write eloquently on this subject. Paul, suffering from an unnamed chronic ailment (more details in the next chapter) wrote,

> For while we are in this tent *[temporary body],* we groan and are burdened, because we do not wish to be unclothed but to be clothed instead with our heavenly dwelling *[permanent body],* so that what is mortal may be swallowed up by life. —2 Cor 5:4

Paul understood the weary longing born of suffering. But he also acknowledges:

> Do you not know that your bodies are temples of the Holy Spirit, who is in you, whom you have received from God? You are not your own; you were bought at a price. Therefore honor God with your bodies. —1 Cor 6:19–20

Our bodies belong to God and house his Holy Spirit. They deserve to be treated with respect. But how do we honor God when our bodies are broken?

Paul says that we remain here on earth to accomplish the works God has planned for us. He recognized that his life, and our lives, are valuable because of the opportunities we have to impact the lives of others (Phil 1:21–25).

Don't give up! Your life is of great worth to God. He will give you the strength and rest you need to keep fighting the good fight. It is important to persevere, "For we must all appear before the judgment seat of Christ, so that each of us may receive what is due us for the things done while in the body, whether good or bad (2 Cor 5:10)."

Fighting for abundant life within disability is a tremendous act of faithfulness. So is choosing to face another day. You are a strong warrior and will be blessed for your determination. God assures us that his heavenly rewards are priceless when compared to our earthly troubles (2 Cor 4:17). Please don't forfeit any eternal treasures by making a rash decision during a moment of desperation.

If you are having suicidal thoughts, have the courage to be truthful with your loved ones and seek professional help. Seeing a psychiatrist or counselor is not shameful but rather an indicator of wisdom and strength.

Courage, dear heart. —C.S. Lewis, The Voyage of the Dawn Treader

THE COMFORT OF THE LIGHT:

On the flip side, I hope knowing that disability is a temporary state will make your challenges more bearable. I am so thankful that I won't have narcolepsy and POTS forever. The hope of heaven means there is a light at the end of the tunnel. You and I have the promise of a resurrected body that is finished, complete, and radiant. This guarantee gives my heart the strength to keep going as I endeavor to make the most of my earthly assignment. Today we may have frustrating battles, but the war has been won.

May the knowledge of your victorious future with Christ empower you in the heat of the battle. Remember Sonny's words, "Everything will be alright in the end . . . so if it's not alright it is not yet the end." This too shall pass.

Then I saw "a new heaven and a new earth," for the first heaven and the first earth had passed away. —Rev 21:1

Chapter 19
Cultivate a Balanced View of Healing

Men suffer more from imagining too little than too much.
—Hugh Jackman as P.T. Barnum in The Greatest Showman

Do we suffer because we imagine too little of God? Specifically, in regards to healing? I would answer an emphatic, "Yes!" Many Christians adhere to the belief that God always wants to heal faithful believers immediately. This idea is dangerously close-minded because it does not allow space for the role that suffering plays in our spiritual development. It narrowly defines "healing" as physical well-being and ignores any larger purposes God may be working within our lives.

When you are desperate for a normal life, it is so easy to buy into this overly simplistic view of healing. I did. But when God didn't wave his magic wand over my failing body, I became angry and confused. Necessity drove me to regroup and ask myself, "Is there more to healing?" Over time, God showed me that he is working to heal so much more than my physical body. I needed to move beyond seeing him as my fairy godmother and see him as a ringmaster.

God is *the* Ringmaster Extraordinaire presiding over the circus of humanity. With unmatched love and skill, he orchestrates the large-scale events of history and oversees the minute details of each person's life. Why go to all that trouble?

For you. God wants heaven to be full of his children. He is passionate about you and knows just how you tick. You are so much more to him than a chronic condition; you are a heart, mind, spirit, and soul. God is invested in the complete package of you and wants to mold you into his image. So he spins every situation to your spiritual advantage. He watches over your present and carefully prepares your future. Whatever it takes, he is going to give you every opportunity to find your way home.

He is equally devoted to the people around you and is weaving lives together in meaningful ways. It's a lot to juggle! But as champion ringmaster, God ably fashions the moving pieces together to create the most stunning display of his love for us. He has an integral role for you to play and is shaping you to shine.

It is worth remembering that the sovereign eyes who watch over the entire show have a radically different perspective from the performer who is blinded by stage lights. How can we, the performers on ground level, begin to grasp what healing means to God?

By reading the script—or in this case, the scripture. No one deserved physical healing more than the Apostle Paul. He was commissioned by God to tell the Gentiles (everyone who is not Jewish) about Christ. That alone arguably makes him the greatest missionary evangelist of all time. In addition, he penned thirteen of the twenty-seven New Testament books and was martyred by Rome for his Christian teachings. Paul was the epitome of a faithful believer.

He also had a problem. In 2 Corinthians 12:7, Paul says, "in order to keep me from becoming conceited, I was given a thorn in my flesh, a messenger of Satan, to torment me." Most theologians believe this "thorn in the flesh" refers to a physical ailment. While scripture doesn't say whether Paul had a bum knee or migraine headaches, we do know his health problem was annoying and made his life more difficult. God's hand-picked messenger goes on record saying, "Three times I pleaded with the Lord to take it away from me (v. 8)."

Only desperate people plead. God's response to Paul's distress? "My grace is sufficient for you, for my power is made perfect in weakness (v. 9)." Ouch. Despite the sugar coating, that is still a hard "no." However, God was not punishing Paul (Satan caused his thorn). Nor was he unmoved by Paul's pain. Why then, did he refuse to heal his faithful servant?

The Father had a different variety of healing in mind for Paul. The stakes were higher than Paul's physical comfort. For his ministry to be effective and for him to enter into all the blessings God had in store for him, Paul's heart had to be in the right place. He needed to learn to depend on God. Paul was a man of advanced education with many resources and talents he could fall back on. Only through weakness would he learn to seek and be empowered by his Heavenly Father's strength.

The upside to constantly needing God's help is that you spend a lot of time gazing into his loving eyes. Your bond grows. God used what Satan meant for evil to strengthen Paul's relationship with Jesus and produce a harvest of godliness in the apostle's heart. Paul came to treasure this transformative process, acknowledging that, "physical training is of some value, but godliness has value for all things, holding promise for both the present life and the life to come (1 Tim 4:8)." He saw the state of his physical body as nothing compared to the "surpassing worth of knowing Christ Jesus *[our]* Lord (Phil 3:8)," and being conformed into Christ's image.

God will always prioritize our forever souls over the state of our temporary bodies. Heart healing comes first because he wants us to be whole in the ways that matter most. If you have received physical healing here on earth then I celebrate that God has worked wonders for you! Use your experience to bring him glory by encouraging others that nothing is impossible for him.

But for those who are with me in the waiting room, we face the difficult task of finding balance. I will keep believing that it is possible for God to physically heal me, but I will also search for other ways that he is "bettering" me. By including internal transformation in my definition of healing, my heart is encouraged that God is in fact with me. He is answering my prayers and remaking me into the image of his beloved Son.

What eternal gifts is God giving your spirit? Is he teaching you to trust him and follow in his footsteps? Is he freeing you from fear as you witness his strength at work in your life? Are you learning how to find joy within daunting circumstances? Neither old age, sickness, or death, will ever be able to take this deeper healing away.

THE MIRACLE OF MODERN MEDICINE:

God also heals through human hands. Some churches preach that it is wrong or a sign of doubt to take medicine. They hold fast to the belief that all healing should come from prayer/miraculous intervention. But Solomon, the wisest man, cautioned that "Whoever fears God will avoid all extremes (Eccl 7:18)." Refusing medical attention is an extremist view that has heartbreakingly prevented many people from getting the help they need. It is a belief that is dangerous, harmful, and sometimes fatal.

Imagine swimming in the ocean when a rip current pulls you out to sea. You are struggling to stay afloat far from shore. As the water threatens to claim you, you cry out, "Lord, save me!" Just then, an old fisherman happens by and offers you his gnarled hand. Would you swat it away because God didn't open the heavens and send Gabriel to rescue you? Of course not! You would reach for the fisherman's weathered palm and thank your lucky stars that your prayers had been heard.

It seems obvious in this illustration that God sent the fisherman and laughable that a drowning person would reject his help. Yet, that is exactly how many Christians awaiting healing behave. They are drowning from their disease, but they swat away the medical assistance God sends them because it hasn't come blatantly wrapped in a biblical bow.

My friend, *modern medicine is a miracle*. Of course, it isn't perfect and has side effects. But medical advancements[1] have saved and improved many lives—including my own. Medicine made writing this book possible. I absolutely believe that it is a gift from God because "Every good and perfect gift is from above, coming down from the Father (Jas 1:17)."

One good gift is that human beings are made in God's image (Gen 1:26–27). He gave us stewardship over the earth. When we use the earth's resources to advance science for the benefit of mankind, we bring glory to the creator who made us in his likeness. So, if science produces something that helps you, that too is a source of healing. It should be welcomed with thanksgiving as coming from your Father's hands because, ultimately, God is the one who inspires human ingenuity (Exod 31:1–5, Eph 2:10).

I continue to hope that God will finish the healing process my medicines have begun. Until then, I am using every resource he puts at my disposal. I am gratefully embracing the medicines, doctors, and therapies that make my condition more bearable. *And* I'm expanding my definition of healing beyond the physical.

As I broaden my perspective, I find myself increasingly thankful that God is not domesticated or caged by human constructs of healing. Friend,

---

1. I include medicines for mental health as medical advancements. It is past time for our culture to lose the stigma that clinical depression/anxiety is something you should be able to "snap" yourself out of and to recognize these conditions for the chemical imbalances they are. Diabetics need insulin for their bodies to regulate blood sugar, and people with ongoing depression need serotonin, norepinephrine, or dopamine, for their brains to function properly. While mental health can be improved by lifestyle or behavioral changes (just like diabetes and other physical disorders), these conditions are most effectively treated through an integrated medical/cognitive behavioral therapy approach.

our God is wild—capable of exploding our expectations of who he is. He is equally exciting and terrifying. Just like C.S. Lewis' magnificent lion, Aslan—who is a symbol of Jesus—God "isn't safe. But he's good."[2]

Join me in pursuit of a God who is full of surprises. Sure, it's easier to believe in a God who heals in one predictable pattern, but following an untamed God requires a much deeper level of trust in his sovereignty and character. May God give us the courage to rise to the adventure.

2. Lewis, *The Lion, the Witch, and the Wardrobe*, 86.

Begin Planting

I am the true vine, and my Father is the gardener. —John 15:1

He asked her, "Woman, why are you crying? Who is it you are looking for?" Thinking he was the gardener, she said, "Sir, if you have carried him away, tell me where you have put him, and I will get him." Jesus said to her, "Mary." —John 20:15–16a

Taking charge of your soil to plant a new garden can be daunting, so I'm closing the third part of our journey together with a few words of encouragement:

Remember that you are not alone but working under the Lord's careful tutelage. Perhaps Mary wasn't mistaken when she identified Jesus as the gardener. As the creator of the universe and caretaker of our souls, God is unquestionably a master gardener. He will help you as you begin to tenderly care for the biblical beliefs that will nourish your soul. Like any young seeds, at first cultivating these attitudes may require daily care.

But with diligent tending, the roots will reach deeper into your heart until they naturalize. What was once fragile will become a strong, fruitful, and fragrant garden. All gardens are a long-term payoff. They mature and bloom more beautifully over time. So will you. When you trust yourself into the hands of the master gardener, you are destined to become a masterpiece.

For we are God's masterpiece. He has created us anew in Christ Jesus, so we can do the good things he planned for us long ago.
—Eph 2:10 NLT

Part 4

Hope in the Rule Breaker

"For my thoughts are not your thoughts, neither are your ways my ways," declares the Lord. —Isa 55:8

Introduction:
Did You Know God Has a Rebellious Streak?

See, I am doing a new thing! Now it springs up; do you not perceive it? I am making a way in the wilderness and streams in the wasteland. —Isa 43:19

IF I EVER NEEDED hope it was in May of 2016. My digestion had slowed to a crawl, and I was barely able to eat six hundred calories a day. Liquids sat unabsorbed in my stomach or burbled back up as reflux. I literally felt like I was drowning because I was choking on my stomach contents. At the same time, I was so dehydrated that my fingertips had gone numb. I couldn't grasp toilet paper or tie my shoes. Too weak to go to my part-time preschool job, I was enduring a captive's existence on my couch.

It was during this hellish time that I received the most devastating phone call of my life. The new Duke specialist I was counting on could not see me for another ten months. How could I wait that long? I was barely staying out of the hospital. The receptionist informed me that there was no cancellation list and that unexpected openings were rare. My family, friends, and I began to pray for a miracle.

I tuned into the BBC nature documentary, *Africa*, searching for a temporary escape. Instead of a lush savannah, the Kalahari Desert came into view. *Kalahari,* means "Land of Great Thirst."[1] Water is so scarce in the vast red landscape that the ground looks like cracked bread that's been in the oven too long. "Yeah," I thought, "an arid wasteland. I can relate." Feeling abandoned by David Attenborough's normally soothing tones, I was about to switch shows when he said something remarkable.

1. Attenborough, *Africa,* episode "Kalahari."

Three hundred and thirty feet below the scorching surface of the Kalahari sands, scientists have discovered the largest underground lake in the world. Unbelievably, this water is not the result of rainfall or runoff. Instead, it is an aquatic "fossil," dating back to the time of the dinosaurs. As I pondered the paradox of a prehistoric lake preserved beneath one of the world's most formidable deserts, a thought stirred in my mind:

> *I specialize in the impossible. What is impossible for you, is not for me. I broke the laws of nature to put a lake beneath a desert, and I am going to break the rules for you. Wait and see.*

Immediately, my husband and I began to pray that God would break the rules on my behalf. *The very next day*, the doctor's office called back to say they could squeeze me in for a test the following week. If I was diagnosed with POTS, a doctor would work with me through email to help me start medication. Additionally, they scheduled me into an August cancellation— a full seven months before my original appointment. When I arrived at the clinic the doctor exclaimed, "Everything with you happened backwards. I am shocked at how quickly you got in to my office. Most people have to wait for more than a year."

To this day it inspires me to reflect on how God's hand orchestrated these events. With medication, I was able to increase my calorie intake to fifteen hundred calories. This gave me enough energy to resume more normal activities. I still have many digestive challenges, but God's timely intervention reassured me that he loved me and still had good plans for my life. I believe more than ever in his ability to move a metaphorical mountain on my behalf.

Fellow journeyer, our God is quite a rebel at heart. He delights in turning the tables on impossible situations and in challenging the status quo. During Jesus' time on earth, he challenged the Jewish expectations of a Savior, societal norms, and how people understood the Heavenly Father. With his triumphant resurrection he shattered the most permanent and unbreakable natural law—death. Christ overturned the finality of the grave and declared it to be a glorious new beginning for those who believe. He is truly a rebel king.

So be encouraged, treasured one. Jesus has already broken the power of death for you! As the creator, everything is subject to him and no law of nature or man can bind him. His thoughts surpass all human wisdom and his vision is not limited by what blinds us. You will always have hope

because the *Rule Maker* and the *Rule Breaker* is in your corner. And it absolutely delights him to establish ancient lakes beneath burning deserts!

What other ways are God's thought processes different from our own?
Can knowing his point of view help us see our hardships in a different light?
It is time to break the rules.

Chapter 20

The Least Are the Greatest

*. . . many who are the greatest now will be least important then, and
those who seem least important now will be the greatest then.*
—Matt 19:30 NLT

WHEN DID YOU START dreaming of greatness? As a child, did you ever glide
around the living room imagining you were an Olympic ice skater? Command your brother/butler to serve PB&J finger sandwiches while you sat in
plastic princess heels? Perhaps you explored other galaxies as an astronaut,
probing alien life forms that suspiciously resembled long-suffering family
pets. Or envisioned yourself as the next Monet and honored your driveway
with a sidewalk chalk installation.

Even as children we idolize greatness. It is glamorous. We dream of being important, influential, at the top of our game, or exceptionally talented
or skilled. But did you ever dream of being the least?

I sure didn't! Yet post-disability, this is the label that society has given
me. I am written off and passed over as someone who has little to offer. It is
a very difficult message to ignore, because in some ways, society is right. My
abilities *have* changed. Despite winning multiple scholarships and graduating with a teaching degree, my career ambitions are now out of reach. Hard
work is no longer enough for me to excel or even live a normal adult life. I
find myself wondering if I am a burden to my spouse, family, and friends.
Frankly, I have never felt more diminished.

Yet Jesus—two simple words that can totally shift our perspective. To Christ
we are more than the sum of our accomplishments. In his kingdom the least
can be the greatest because, "The Lord does not look at the things people

look at. People look at the outward appearance, but the Lord looks at the heart (1 Sam 16:7)." For those with health conditions, that is exceedingly good news.

To illustrate just how seriously God takes the motivations of our hearts, Jesus shared a story about a Pharisee and a tax collector (Luke 18:9-14). Before we read the passage, let's consider the mindset of Jesus' audience towards his characters.

Pharisees were powerful religious leaders within the Jewish community. They were highly educated, affluent, and respected—the rockstars of their social sphere. Young Jewish boys wistfully imagined becoming one of these mighty men. Tween maidens daydreamed about marrying one.

Tax collectors, on the other hand, were the biblical equivalents of Benedict Arnold. Israel was occupied by the Roman Empire during Jesus' lifetime and Caesar demanded taxes from his conquered territories. These taxes were collected by Jews who had turned their backs on their countrymen in order to serve the enemy. They were loathed as greedy sell-outs and considered traitors.

As soon as *The Parable of the Pharisee and Tax Collector* rolled off Jesus' lips, his audience would have mentally pegged the hero and the villain. Can you imagine the hush of anticipation and the crowd leaning in closer to hear Jesus give those weaselly tax collectors a sound verbal thrashing? Instead, Christ said . . .

> To some who were confident of their own righteousness and looked down on everyone else, Jesus told this parable: "Two men went up to the temple to pray, one a Pharisee and the other a tax collector. The Pharisee stood by himself and prayed: 'God, I thank you that I am not like other people—robbers, evildoers, adulterers—or even like this tax collector. I fast twice a week and give a tenth of all I get.'
>
> "But the tax collector stood at a distance. He would not even look up to heaven, but beat his breast and said, 'God, have mercy on me, a sinner.'
>
> "I tell you that this man, rather than the other, went home justified before God. *For all those who exalt themselves will be humbled, and those who humble themselves will be exalted.*"
> —Luke 18:9-14

This wasn't a sermon—it was a torpedo! Jesus' message shattered social stigmas and spiritual misconceptions. I hope the flies weren't bad that time of year for the sake of all the slack-jawed Jews in attendance.

The aftershocks of Christ's parable still reverberate through our souls to this day. His carefully chosen characters reveal a revolutionary truth: God sees past all outward pretenses to evaluate a person's priorities. The Lord despised the Pharisee's arrogance and celebrated the tax collector's humble heart. Jesus ends with the shocker that our heavenly status will depend more on our attitudes than achievements (v. 14). That is what I call a mic drop.

Imagine a society where patience trumps a Pulitzer, neighborly kindness beats a Nobel, and gratitude outweighs a Grammy. Heaven's hierarchy will be vastly surprising. Perhaps, prisoners will teach popes about prayer. Or a chronic pain patient will offer Thomas Edison pointers on perseverance. Maybe you'll discover that Amelia Earhart thinks *you* are an even greater example of courage. It is fun to speculate on heaven's possibilities. Meanwhile, the Bible gives us a concrete example of how God's x-ray vision played out in Christ's life.

Consider who Jesus called to be his twelve disciples. It was very important that he choose wisely. His disciples would be his closest companions, witness his ministry, and ultimately, carry the Gospel into the world. A corporate headhunter would have advised him to pick influential kings, learned priests, and men who were shining examples of piety and grace.

Instead, Jesus selected men who were decidedly rough around the edges. His disciples were a ragtag group of stinky fishermen, businessmen, and even one of the dreaded tax collectors. They had hot tempers, were dangerously impulsive, and struggled with fear and doubt. On the surface, these men seemed least qualified for the job.

However, Jesus did not see inadequacy. He saw opportunity. He perceived the passion, loyalty, and relatability that, when refined by his transforming grace, would best declare his love to the world.

How comforting I find Jesus' choices as a person with a disability. Yes, disability has stripped away many of my external trappings and markers of prestige. It has definitely emptied me beyond my own resources of strength. But being "least" in the world's eyes does not exclude me, or you, from a powerful position in the kingdom of God.

On the contrary, you have been drafted to a winning team. God uses humble circumstances to prepare his people for promotion. Membership among the "least" frees you from self-importance and distracting personal priorities. This is a compelling invitation for God to begin to work his wonders in your life. When you cry out to God and say, "I am nothing," he excitedly rolls up his sleeves and declares, "At last I can make something of you!" *For those who humble themselves will be exalted* (Luke 18:14).

Therefore judge nothing before the appointed time; wait until the Lord comes. He will bring to light what is hidden in darkness and will expose the motives of the heart. At that time each will receive their praise from God. —1 Cor 4:5

Chapter 21

Weakness Is Strength

But he [God] said to me, "My grace is sufficient for you, for my power is made perfect in weakness." Therefore I will boast all the more gladly about my weaknesses, so that Christ's power may rest on me. That is why, for Christ's sake, I delight in weaknesses, in insults, in hardships, in persecutions, in difficulties. For when I am weak, then I am strong. —2 Cor 12:9–10

HAVE YOU EVER BEEN asked the interview question, "What is your greatest weakness?" Personally, I hate that question. Does anyone answer truthfully? I have never heard an applicant volunteer, "Honestly, I'm never on time, and I sneak onto social media sites during work hours. Furthermore, I really have no clue how to do this job, but my plan is to wing it until I catch on."

Most intelligent human beings say something along the lines of, "Well, I am a bit of a perfectionist." Who would you give the job to? The hardworking perfectionist hands down.

We value people who are productive. Weakness, on the other hand, is either despised or pitied as a shameful waste. I found it difficult to escape that shame when I was adjusting to life with a disability. Fortunately, I have a godly mother-in-law who will listen to me vent:

> *I do not understand why God isn't healing me. All I want to do is serve him—to teach, go on missions, love my husband, become a mom—maybe even adopt a child. It is not like I want to go gallivanting about town!*
>
> *I feel like my life is being wasted because I have to spend so much time resting. Why would God allow that when I could be doing so much for him?*

Have you ever had similar feelings? (And yes, as a Southern woman in a huff, I did use the ridiculous phrase "gallivanting about town.") But joking aside, my struggle to overcome these feelings of inadequacy has been persistent and frustrating. It is hard not to see my weakness as a handicap to becoming the person God has called me to be. Andrew Murray phrases it like this in his book, *Abide in Christ*, "The Christian thinks his weaknesses are his greatest hindrance in the life and service of God; God tells us that it is the secret of strength and success."[1]

Hallelujah that God's thoughts are not our thoughts! Jesus redeems not only our souls—he redeems our stories. He loves to shine his light through broken people. In Christ's hands hardships can become secret weapons.

The Apostle Paul agreed that weakness is a valuable opportunity. Re-read his message from 2 Corinthians 12:9–10 (at the beginning of this chapter), followed by the excerpt from 1 Corinthians below. (A bit of context: Paul is using a metaphor to compare the people of the church to the parts of a human body.)

> The eye cannot say to the hand, "I don't need you!" And the head cannot say to the feet, "I don't need you!" *On the contrary, those parts of the body that seem to be weaker are indispensable,* and the parts that we think are less honorable we treat with special honor . . . But God has put the body together, giving greater honor to the parts that lacked it, so that there should be no division in the body, but that its parts should have equal concern for each other. —1 Cor 12:21–23a, 24b-25

We as the "weak" are such an important part of God's family that God calls us *indispensable*. Let that sink into the depths of your soul. In addition, he instructs other believers to treat us with equal concern and respect. When I feel worthless, it is a breath of resuscitating air to know that God calls me essential.

These passages from Corinthians fuel my hope that somehow God is repurposing my weaknesses to benefit both me and those around me. That hope burns brighter every time I read a Bible story featuring God at work through an unlikely hero. May one of my favorite examples ignite a spark within you.

---

1. Murray, *Abide in Christ*, 220.

EXAMPLE #1—A KINGDOM SAVED BY THE ULTIMATE UNDERDOGS (2 KGS 6:24 - 7:16):

Second Kings 6–7 chronicles a horrific chapter in Israel's history. The capital city, Samaria, has been besieged by the King of Aram. The surrounded Israelites are slowly starving to death inside a city driven mad by fear. Food is so scarce that mothers have begun to murder and eat their children.

God's people desperately need a hero. Enter a mighty warrior? No. An avenging angel? Uh-uh. Superman flying through the city gates? Wishful thinking . . . . The only people at the city gates are four lepers.

Leprosy is foreign to us in modern America. Occurrences are rare and able to be treated before the disease has time to progress. But in biblical times the condition was justifiably feared. Leprosy is a long-lasting infection that slowly maims the body by attacking nerve cells. Eventually this leads to blindness, paralysis of the hands and feet, and facial disfigurement. Unable to feel their extremities, lepers often lost fingers or toes to accidents or when unattended cuts became gangrenous. Pictures of individuals with advanced leprosy are truly grotesque with an almost alien appearance. It is easy to understand why ancient peoples thought lepers were cursed by God.

In addition to the frightening physical symptoms of their disease, biblical lepers were thrown out of their communities. The rigid social protocol in Leviticus 13 commanded lepers to live in isolation and fend for themselves. They had to wear torn clothes, cover their faces, and keep unkempt hair as a warning to others that they shouldn't approach. If anyone accidentally got too close, they had to shout out "unclean!"

The lepers of 2 Kings had truly lost everything: their jobs, their status, and their families. How could they possibly help the starving city? As we approach the city gates, let's eavesdrop on their conversation. Spoiler alert: it's depressing.

> Leper 1: I can't take this anymore . . . I'm starving!

> Leper 2: Me too. Forget the rules. Let's see if we can find food in the city.

> Leper 3: Man, you know they don't have food either. Even if they did, do you honestly think they'd share it with us?

> Leper 4: I know, I know. But we'll die if we just sit here. Should we ask the Arameans for food? At least if they kill us, it will be quicker than starving. What do you guys think?

The lepers take a chance that God might show them mercy in an unlikely place and walk towards the enemy camp. They think they are headed towards surrender. But in response to this mustard seed of faith, God prepares the way for victory.

The Lord causes the Arameans to hear the sounds of a great army approaching: rushing hooves, the rumble of chariots, and fierce war cries split the air. Fearing an ambush, the Arameans shout "They've hired the Hittites and Egyptians to attack us! Run for your lives!"

The Aramean camp empties out faster than a convention of introverts. In their haste, Israel's enemies leave behind all of their belongings: food, horses, and tents. The lepers arrive to find a deserted camp full of loot. This is their opportunity! Before them is the means to meet their immediate needs and to secure their futures. If the lepers keep these treasures for themselves, they could live out their remaining days in comfort.

However, in this moment of great temptation, something absolutely astonishing happens. It doesn't have the blockbuster oomph of an invisible chariot army, but it is the true miracle of the story. The lepers agree, "This is a day of good news and we are keeping it to ourselves. If we wait until daylight, punishment will overtake us. Let's go at once and report this to the royal palace (2 Kgs 7:9)."

Wait a minute. The lepers have every right to be bitter and angry. How can they go back for the people who abandoned them in their greatest hour of need?

Perhaps, the lepers can be gracious to the people of Samaria because they have a profound understanding of pain. They know *exactly what it is like* to face an agonizingly slow death. Of course, they consider that they could be punished. Like all humans they have mixed motives. But they also express deep concern for their community. Ultimately, they choose to overlook the way others have let them down. In a superhuman act of forgiveness the lepers return to the starving city and announce the Lord's salvation.

Only God can birth a compassion that is stronger than a thousand hurts. It is his strength that enables us to bless those who have betrayed us—and by doing so the lepers prove that God is powerfully present in their hearts. The outcasts that the people of Samaria will not let live with them, are the very people they cannot live without.

Reflect on God's choice of such unlikely heroes. His salvation comes through weak outcasts—unexpected saviors who choose remarkable forgiveness in order to restore life to the people who have despised and rejected them. To me, this sounds like Jesus. God saves the Israelites through the lepers and they become part of a loving narrative he is weaving through the Old Testament to point to his Son. The lepers' weakness allows us to more clearly see the Father's love.

Did Samaria welcome the lepers back as heroes? Did God reward their selflessness with earthly healing? The Bible doesn't say what happened to them. Where is their happily ever after? I was feeling let down when a story from Luke caught my eye.

Every gospel includes an account of Jesus healing a single leper. But Luke alone records a miracle which demands our attention by its sheer magnitude—*Jesus simultaneously heals ten lepers* (Luke 17:11–19). Such an unprecedented number of healings indicates a hidden secret. Guess where this miracle took place?

Samaria. Jesus dramatically heals ten lepers on the outskirts of a city which owed its survival to the four lepers of long ago. Is this a coincidence?

Not a chance. I believe Christ always acts with authority and purpose. To me, Jesus' standout miracle on Samaritan soil is a neon blinking sign proclaiming that God did not forget the Old Testament lepers. Your guess is as good as mine as to how God rewarded them. But I suspect that these four men who were once defined by weakness, are now among the most vibrant princes of heaven.

For those of you who feel like a leper—forgotten, pushed aside, or unwanted—know that your Heavenly Father will never forget you. Even when people fail to see your worth or treat you with respect; God always sees the real you. He takes note of all your hurts, collecting each one of your tears (Ps 56:8). He knows the difficult choices you make to persevere and remembers every sacrifice that goes unacknowledged by others. On days when you wonder if God will ever tip the scales in your favor, look to the ten lepers. They stand healed and whole in Samaria to remind us that God rewards every act of faithfulness in his time.

EXAMPLE #2—JONI EARECKSON TADA—A MODERN MODEL OF GOD'S STRENGTH:

Does God still display his power through unlikely sources today? You bet. When I catch myself feeling like my disabilities are a hindrance to my calling, I think about the life of one of my heroes, Joni Eareckson Tada.

Joni enjoyed a normal life until 1967. But at the age of seventeen, she became a quadriplegic when a diving accident left her paralyzed from the neck down. It is hard to get more "broken" in body. At first, Joni grieved, battled depression, and wrestled with doubt and anger. But God had something else in mind. As Joni learned to live in her unresponsive body, God began to call to her beautifully responsive heart. Over the past fifty years, God has molded Joni into so much more than a victim of tragic circumstances. Take a look at some of the names she is known by now:[2]

- *Founder and CEO of Joni and Friends International Disability Center*: Joni's foundation is dedicated to serving disabled people with Christ's love. The foundation has delivered over 200,000 wheelchairs and Bibles around the globe, hosts family respite retreats, and has a response team to encourage and support disabled individuals.

- *Visionary*: Joni and Friends saw a need for church leadership to be educated in disability ministry. The Christian Institute on Disability was born. In 2016, they published the *Beyond Suffering Bible*.[3] This Bible comes with notes that pay special attention to disability themes and promises for those who suffer. It was crafted with such care that it feels like a personalized love letter from God to Christians with chronic conditions. Every disabled believer should have a copy of this precious Bible edition.

- *Political Reformer*: Joni has served on the National Council on Disability and the Disability Advisory Committee for the U.S. State Department. She advocated for the Americans with Disabilities Act which protects the rights of disabled people to work.

- *Television Show Host*: Joni hosts a segment which features inspirational stories from disabled people.

- *Radio Broadcaster*: Her radio program has been broadcasting for over forty years and has more than one million listeners.

- *Artist*: Joni paints detailed nature scenes—with her teeth!

- *Author*: Joni has written over fifty books encouraging readers with the truth of God's love. Her first book has been translated into thirty-eight languages.

2. Joni and Friends, "Our History."

3. The *Beyond Suffering Bible* NLT is available through Tyndale House Publishers, Inc.

It is impossible to know what Joni's life would have looked like if she had done a cannonball into the Chesapeake Bay all those years ago. Perhaps it would have been normal as she shared Christ's love with her husband, kids, co-workers, and community. I'm sure it would have been a perfectly "good" life by any Christian standards. But it never would have been the same life that she has now. After all, no one in their right mind would choose such an arduous path.

But this is what Joni says about her disability, "My weakness, that is, my quadriplegia, is my greatest asset because it forces me into the arms of Christ every single morning when I get up."[4] And within Jesus' arms, Joni's life has become a remarkable testimony. She powerfully demonstrates Christ's ability to transform our worst disaster into an extraordinary destiny. Only God knows under what circumstances our lives can have the most powerful impact for his kingdom.

That being said, let me be very clear: God never heartlessly uses you as a visual aid for his glory. He is not in the business of causing suffering; he is on a mission to redeem your pain. When God turns your weakness into strength, he displays his love to others. But he also proves his love and faithfulness towards you.

Neither Joni nor the lepers had the lives they expected. But through their weaknesses, they became attuned to Christ's power. This dependency on God changed them on the inside. Then God used them to change their communities.

Today, take a second glance at your weaknesses through Jesus' eyes— could they be strengths waiting to be born?

"For I know the plans I have for you," declares the Lord, "plans to prosper you and not to harm you, plans to give you hope and a future." —Jer 29:11

It is not the strength of the body that counts, but the strength of the spirit. —J.R.R. Tolkien

---

4. Sun, "Joni Eareckson Tada on Wilberforce Award," para. 10.

Chapter 22

Redeemed for Good

And we know that in all things God works for the good of those who love him, who have been called according to his purpose. —Rom 8:28

I HAVE ALWAYS BEEN fascinated by butterflies. As a child, I thought of them as living fairy tales: fanciful creatures metamorphosized by real-life magic. My admiration for this insect has only increased as I've grown—because now I know what *actually happens* in a chrysalis.

A butterfly's chrysalis is less magician's box and more torture chamber. Confined within its dark enclosure, enzymes begin to tear apart the caterpillar's body. The caterpillar literally liquifies until only special cells, called imaginal discs, remain intact. These imaginal discs utilize the protein from the dissolved tissues to regenerate into an entirely different form.[1]

When the metamorphosis is complete, the butterfly must break out of the chrysalis. It emerges exhausted from the struggle. Its first act of freedom is to rest and stretch its new body. Only then does the caterpillar realize that, within the darkness, it was being transformed. It has been given wings to fly.

If God intervenes to resurrect a caterpillar from its prison, he will do the same for you. Victory might not come in the form you expect, but as a believer, the hardships you face will never be in vain (Rom 8:28). God's love overshadows all of your circumstances and is working to overturn them for your spiritual good. He can use the destruction wreaked by disability to usher your soul into vibrant new wells of his strength.

I want to emphasize that practicing a biblical belief in Romans 8:28 goes far deeper than an "every cloud has a silver lining" philosophy. Some

1. Jabr, "How Does a Caterpillar Turn into a Butterfly."

Christians project false optimism because they are afraid of being "bad Christians" if they don't find the good in everything. That attitude is harmful and does not allow a safe space for us to bring grief to God. Instead, believing that God is working everything for our good begins when we are able to look at the darker moments of our past with genuine gratitude—because we recognize the fruit of God's redemptive hand.

I know this is incredibly difficult when you are being undone in the chrysalis. If that is where you find yourself today, that is okay. I want you to know that God is present in your mourning. Your hurts deeply grieve his heart. *He embraces you and understands all of your emotions.* So be patient with yourself. Like butterflies, we often need distance or rest from our problems to perceive the beauty God birthed from our brokenness. It is a gift from God. It cannot be forced.

So how can we know God is working all things together for our good? Personally, I still have a lot of questions about the "big picture" purposes of my disabilities. But I do see God at work within the daily challenges that my disorders bring. Over and over, he works miracles within my small heartaches. One of these "small" miracles was a miniature schnauzer named Penny.

When I began teaching preschool part-time, I really struggled with loneliness on my days off. My husband was working and I was too tired to invite friends over or leave the apartment. I craved contact. I wanted a cat, but my husband is allergic to feline fur. Instead, Parker suggested a dog. My *first* dog.

One look into Penny's adoring eyes and strains of Toy Story's "You've Got a Friend in Me" filled my mind. Sold. We brought her home and discovered she was a natural fetcher. As a ten-week-old pup, she bounded through piles of leaves in gleeful pursuit of her tennis ball. She even successfully returned it, wiggling in anticipation of the next throw.

Penny was also good at keeping secrets. When Parker would leave for work, I'd sneak her into the "people" bed for forbidden snuggles. She was an exceptional puppy in my completely unbiased opinion. But even exceptional puppies are a lot of work.

2:00 AM potty jaunts, puppy shots, grooming, training, walking, and the attention needed by a young puppy began wearing me out. Anything that interrupts your sleep schedule spells disaster for someone with narcolepsy and POTS. My body was crashing under the strain. I held onto Penny for three months, but it was a losing battle.

The day Parker looked at me and said, "We have to find another home for Penny," I started to cry because I knew it was true. If I couldn't take care of her, then it wasn't fair to put the responsibility on him. He was working so hard to provide for us and take care of me. But it also broke my heart because I wanted to be able to take care of the puppy I loved. I felt utterly inadequate.

At the time, finding another home for Penny seemed like a tragedy. But I no longer see it that way. Instead, letting her go was an answer to prayer:

My symptoms manifested during my senior year of college and I was married the summer after I graduated. As a result, I didn't really live with my parents after I became disabled. My parents are outstanding people who are devoted to me and to God. But they were baffled by the sudden onset of the disease and found it difficult to understand my new limitations. I still looked young and healthy—where was their vibrant and active daughter? How could I only be capable of working part-time, when I had won $75,000 worth of college scholarships?

My parents were as confused as I was. I was still learning what to expect from these complex conditions and had difficulty explaining how my daily life would be different now. It was all too fresh. I couldn't talk with them about my disabilities without inflicting pain on them or succumbing to my own grief. No one wanted to accept my new reality.

They started to question me, "Are you really pushing yourself hard enough? Can't you work to take some of the pressure off of Parker? Why can't you come visit us more often? What is so hard about cleaning a small apartment?"

I was hurt by their questions. Overwhelmed by my own pain, I couldn't see that they were trying to understand. Instead of recognizing our shared denial in the face of grievous change, I wrongfully assumed they were questioning my character. Didn't they know me at all? I was the same daughter who was an all-A student and who had her first job at the age of twelve. I was working harder than ever just to get through the day, except now I had little to show for it. Couldn't they see that I was still me, that my character hadn't changed?

I couldn't handle what I perceived as disappointment and was distancing myself from my parents when Penny arrived. But when she left, I called them heartbroken. I told them that I had to find a new home for Penny because I couldn't take care of her.

That confession struck home like lightning—and my parents finally began to understand how difficult my life had become. Only a disease with enormous ramifications could force their animal-loving daughter to let go of the puppy who had stolen her heart.

It was a turning point in our relationship. I wasn't asked again if I was pushing myself hard enough. Three years into my disability we were finally beginning to understand my new circumstances and each other.

What truly amazes me is that I have never felt lonely on my days off again. I am happy with my own company and the creative outlets God has given me. I can only conclude that God stirred that loneliness in my heart to bring Penny into my life. Yes, it was bad and difficult to have to say goodbye to my sweet dog. But God used her leaving to begin a work of healing within my family. And that is even better.[2]

This is just one story from a mounting catalogue of evidence of how I've seen God reclaim difficult circumstances for my good. Each small miracle adds to my trust. It is becoming easier to believe that one day I will be able to see the big miracles he has worked through my health struggles.

If you find yourself uncertain about the "big picture," search for ways that the Lord has been faithful to you today. Because even when we don't know the outcome, we can trust in his process. Through God's transformative love, our hardships can shape us into stronger, wiser, and more compassionate people. Our wounds can become wings.

---

2. *A Note About My Parents:*
     I want my parents to read this book with the assurance that I love them dearly. They are one of God's greatest gifts to me, and I would not have survived disability without them teaching me how to be a strong Christian. If anyone judges them based on my writing, (*most especially if you judge yourselves, Mom and Dad*), it will deeply undermine the purpose of this work. We are all works in progress and I am privileged to be able to progress through life with two people I hold in the highest regard. I love you both.

Chapter 23
History Is Not Set in Stone

"I am the Alpha and the Omega, the First and the Last, the Beginning and the End." —Rev 22:13

IF YOU THINK THE show isn't over until the fat lady sings—*Bazinga*—you are in for a surprise. *God always has the final word.* He is the ultimate authority and his judgement carries the day. Because you are his creation, he has the power to intervene in and change your circumstances.

A doctor may deliver a grim prognosis, a judge may label you "disabled," or your own fears may shout that you are destined for a lifetime of suffering. But these words are faint whispers compared to God's glorious proclamation that "no human mind has conceived — the things God has prepared for those who love him (1 Cor 2:9)." Below are two biblical examples of God intervening with the last word. Discover how our rebel God radically changes the outcome.

EXAMPLE #1—A CURSE IS TURNED INTO A BLESSING (NUM 22–24):

The Israelites have brushed off Egypt's dust and are making tracks for the promised land. The King of Moab is terrified by the sheer number of Hebrews coming towards his borders. What is a scared king to do? Hire a sorcerer.

King Balak and Balaam (the sorcerer) attempt to curse God's chosen people from three separate locations. Here is the CliffsNotes version on the success of their partnership: the duo plays a losing game of musical chairs because God has other ideas. The king sums it up best when he screams at

Balaam in outrage, "I brought you here to curse my enemies, but you have done nothing but bless them (Num 23:11)!"

Yep. You heard right—God causes all three curse attempts to backfire into a blessing.

The Numbers account reads like a comical farce. But Balaam was actually a renowned practitioner of the dark arts. He was skilled enough to be commissioned by royalty. However, the sorcerer readily acknowledges that his power is nothing next to God's. Balaam defends the blessings he spoke over the Israelites, saying to the King of Moab, "I could not do anything of my own accord, good or bad, to go beyond the command of the Lord (Num 24:13)."

You, my friend, belong to Jesus. That makes you just like an Israelite—God's chosen child. Nothing can compromise this identity. Whatever your "curse" is: a disability, a divorce, or a pink slip . . . God can command it to become a blessing. Because when all is said and done, no force on earth is strong enough to stand against those whom God has chosen to be blessed. He always champions his children.

EXAMPLE #2—IT IS NEVER TOO LATE FOR GOD'S PROMISES TO COME TRUE (ROM 4:13–25):

These verses are one of my favorite passages of scripture. With the resonance of a victory ballad, they chronicle the life of the Old Testament patriarch, Abraham. God promised Abraham that he would be the father of nations and kings (Gen 17:4–6). But at one hundred, he and his elderly wife were still childless. Undeterred, Abraham remained "fully persuaded that God had power to do what he had promised (Rom 4:21)."

Is Abraham delusional? Experiencing a textbook case of denial? As a centenarian, he cannot even see his fertile years in the rearview mirror. But Romans 4:19 acknowledges that Abraham, "faced the fact that his body was as good as dead . . . and that Sarah's womb was also dead."

Abraham was very aware of his age. He saw the wrinkles and felt the aches in his joints. He knew his body's limitations but believed in a God who is limitless. He would have a son because he believed in "God who gives life to the dead and calls things that are not as though they were (Rom 4:17)."

Take a moment to reflect on what these words say about our rule breaking God. Not only can God reverse the natural order of life to bring a baby from an elderly womb, but he "calls things that are not as though they were." Examine this phrase closely. Do you notice anything grammatically peculiar in this statement? The Bible does not say that God "calls things that are not as though *they are*" (present tense), but as though *"they were"* (past tense). Holy Cannolis! This means that God is not only capable of changing our present and future—but of changing our past.

I get chills every time I read this verse. It makes me aware that I am loved by a God whose greatness and goodness is beyond my comprehension. I am not sure it is humanly possible to fully understand the details of what God is promising in this scripture. But I believe it contains promises for our lives here and in heaven. Because when I view my life through the filtered lens of Romans 4:17, I find to my astonishment that God is already rewriting my past.

What I mean is this: when I am overwhelmed by pain and frustration during a season of suffering, I often struggle to believe and find God's purposes within my circumstances. This rule applies both to when I was in the middle of yesteryear's difficulties and to my current "now." But as time passes, I am able to look back and recognize God's presence triumphing over my struggle.

Through narcolepsy, the Lord led me to teach my beloved preschoolers. With my POTS diagnosis, he lit in me a desire to help others learn how to cope with chronic conditions. This new purpose is a gift—one that I never imagined for myself. Somehow God has taught me how to have joy within circumstances I formerly considered impossible. In the process he has trained my mind and prepared me to relate more meaningfully to others. I have come to greatly value these blessings which are a direct result of my brokenness.

In this sense, Christ has already altered my story—because my perception of the same period of time has changed. When I feared I was alone, I now see he held me closest. What I mourned as a waste, I now rejoice over as part of his plan. Then I cried over the parts of myself I thought I had lost, now I marvel at the new strengths I've found. Regardless of what awaits me in heaven, God has already changed my past here on earth. *My history is not set in stone.*

Take a minute to look back on how God has done this in your life. Isn't it astounding?

As for our futures in heaven, I can't wait to see what *"things that are not,"* God calls, *"as though they were."* Only God knows the truth about how this will unfold, but I have a feeling the stories of our lives will look radically different when viewed through his eyes.

Consider Abraham. He was overjoyed to finally have his promised son on Earth. But can you imagine the overwhelming joy be felt when God showed him the impact of his life from heaven? Abraham's faithfulness was recorded in the Bible to encourage generations of believers. He was the father of God's chosen nation: Israel.

But the cherry on the cake? No, the whole cake itself? Jesus Christ came from his family tree. Abraham's great-great-great . . . grandson brought salvation to the entire world. Like a mother who forgets the pain of childbirth when she holds her precious newborn, Abraham's years of childlessness must have faded into the recesses of his mind the moment he looked into the eyes of Jesus and saw Isaac. This was worth the wait. God had been indescribably good.

Author J.R.R. Tolkien captured the heart of Romans 4:17 when he said, "The birth, death, and resurrection of Jesus means that one day everything sad will come untrue." Let those words sink in. Every hurt, every fear, and every loss will be undone. All emptiness will be filled and every unmet desire realized. Can you imagine it? When God has the last "edit" on the story of your life, what surprises will he have in store for you?

Additional Examples of God's Ability to Break the Rules and Accomplish the Impossible:

- Houdini, who? God is the greatest escape artist of all time! —Exod 14
- A donkey finds his voice. —Num 22:21–41
- Trumpets tumble the mighty walls of Jericho. —Josh 6
- God stops the orbit of the sun so that the Israelites can win a battle. —Josh 10:1–15
- God confuses Israel's enemies causing them to turn their swords on one another. —Judg 7
- A shepherd is victorious over a famous warrior of gigantic proportions. —1 Sam 17
- Hungry lions turn into gentle housecats. —Dan 6
- Jesus takes a shortcut . . . across a lake. —Matt 14:22–33
- Miraculously fast-food feeds five thousand. —Matt 14:13–21
- No ear? No problem! —Luke 22:49–51
- Jesus = lawbreaker of the Old Testament. This is not a misprint! —John 8:1–11

Part 5

Principles of Positive Prayer

Look to the LORD and his strength; seek his face always.
—1 Chr 16:11

Introduction:

Healthy Homes

Therefore everyone who hears these words of mine and puts them into practice is like a wise man who built his house on the rock. The rain came down, the streams rose, and the winds blew and beat against that house; yet it did not fall, because it had its foundation on the rock. —Matt 7:24–25

GOOD COMMUNICATION IS THE life's blood of any relationship—even your relationship with God. When you spend time listening and talking to God through prayer, your connection deepens. God doesn't need your prayers to validate his worth or to make him aware of needs he already knows you have. Instead, we pray because we desperately need our Father.

In his portrayal of C.S. Lewis in the movie *Shadowlands*, Anthony Hopkins explains,

> I pray because I can't help myself. I pray because I am helpless. I pray because the need flows out of me all the time, waking and sleeping. It doesn't change God. It changes me.[1]

Your prayers change your perspective. And if they are not, it is time to take a close look at how you are relating to God.

There isn't a right/wrong way to pray moment by moment. Your prayers do not have to be perfect because they are heard by a God who is. To the Lord, imperfect cries of despair are the holiest of prayers. However, permanent negativity is a problem.

My prayer patterns significantly impact my view of God as well as my own spiritual and mental health. When my prayers are consistently negative,

---

1. Attenborough, *Shadowlands*.

I feel consumed by my circumstances. But when my prayers trend towards positivity, I am revived by God's strength. Patterns are powerful.

Dutch Catholic Priest, Henri Nouwen, taught that, "Prayer is the most concrete way to make our home in God."[2] What is life like in your spiritual home? Is it an encouraging and peaceful place to be? Or is it filled with repressed anger and fear? If that's you, take some advice from another fixer-upper: call on the carpenter.

Welcome to the Master's class on laying a positive foundation for prayer. God has given me so much comfort during my journey through chronic illness—but learning an emotionally healthy and positive way to communicate with him has been the most transformative.

So, pay attention to your prayers. Choose one principle from the coming pages to put into practice every time you speak with God. As they become habit, I pray you experience the same miracle I did: that even if your circumstances do not change, your thoughts and attitudes are reborn.

2. Nouwen, *Lifesigns*, 27.

Chapter 24
Tell God the Truth

We must lay before him what is in us; not what ought to be in us.
—C.S. Lewis, *Letters to Malcolm: Chiefly on Prayer*

The Lord detests lying lips, but he delights in those who tell the truth.
—Prov 12:22

Have you told God how being disabled makes you feel? Or have ideas of "acceptable" Christian prayers kept you from being honest? Personally, I used to think that being a "good" Christian meant I could never complain in prayer, question God's judgement, or be vulnerable about my despair. So, I buried my doubts and frustrations. I was afraid that airing them would be tantamount to a confession that I didn't believe in or love the Lord.

It took four years of disability for me to own up to the fact that I was angry with God: four years of playing mind games and offering hollow prayers that left me feeling more anxious and alone. I was like some sort of maniac cheerleader shouting "Come on God, you can do this." Maybe if I waved my "good" Christian pom-poms hard enough, I could ignore my doubts and the Lord would answer my prayers. Instead, all the fake smiles left me feeling further and further away from him.

Then God called me out on it. My spirit was in turmoil as I offered "acceptable" prayers in place of what I truly felt—priming me for an explosion. So when God's gentle whisper invited "Tell me the truth," I let him have it.

> *Alright, you want the truth? Here it is! God, I am really angry at you. I have always loved you and tried to do my best for you. Yet you let me become disabled and my dreams be taken away. Meanwhile, people who couldn't care less about you are enjoying*

their careers and kids. It stinks! I thought those were the things you had for my life. Why are you punishing me?

And why are you ignoring me? You are supposed to be there for me. For four years I have prayed my heart out, asking you to heal me in every way imaginable. I know you could fix this if you wanted to, God, but you haven't. And that makes me furious! Don't you love me? I do not even know what to say to you anymore. What is the point of even trying to please you?

As the dam finally burst, it was like a fist unclenched in my stomach. The fear of failing God that had been strangling my heart was released. I felt more peace than I had in years. Most surprising, I sensed God smiling at me. Why in the world would he be smiling at me? Wasn't he angry that I had just shouted at him?

Softly God spoke to my heart, "Thank you for finally being honest. Because now we can work together to move forward."

It turns out that I hadn't been fooling the God who knows my every thought (Ps 139:2). I had only been lying to myself (and creating a lot of stress in the process). I needed to be real with God so that we could approach the problem of disability together as a united team.

I know now that a healthy relationship with God requires complete honesty. My prayer life has been revolutionized because of it. The more honest I am in sharing my doubts and negative emotions with him, the closer we become. Vulnerability invites intimacy.

While this occasionally backfires with people, your relationship with God is always a safe place to bare your struggles. In the words of one of my most trusted pastors, Steven Furtick: "The presence of God is not a place to bypass your emotions—It's a place to process them." Once we stop ignoring our problems, God can help us solve them. Transparency puts you on the same page.

Feeling skeptical of my proclamation to always be honest with God? Good. Don't just take my word for it. It is always important to make sure our own ideas are supported by scripture. Take a look at these two Bible characters who were brutally honest with God:

EXAMPLE #1—JOB:

Job's story made me intensely uncomfortable for years. He was a kind person who passionately loved God. But Job was plagued by undeserved hardship when Satan asks God for permission to test him. Job's family is killed, he is financially ruined, and his body is infected with sores. He becomes a homeless outcast. It was the type of sermon material that made me want to hurdle over pews of sweet old ladies and bolt for the nearest exit.

Now, I find Job to be a surprising source of comfort because in his emotions I see my own struggles. Many of Job's words mirror my own mental battles or go even further. Listen to what Job had to say to or about God:

- "What strength do I have, that I should still hope? What prospects, that I should be patient?" —Job 6:11

- "I prefer strangling and death, rather than this body of mine. I despise my life; I would not live forever. Let me alone; my days have no meaning." —Job 7:15–16

- "Why have you made me your target? Have I become a burden to you?" —Job 7:20

- "God has wronged me . . . " —Job 19:6

Wow! It takes some stones to directly accuse God of wronging you. But that is exactly what is so encouraging about Job's story. If you keep reading, God forgives Job when he repents of the words he spoke in sorrow. The Lord blesses him with more than he had before his hardships: giving Job twice as much wealth and a beautiful new family. Despite Job's harsh words, God still loved him and wanted to bless him. Their relationship was unbroken.

EXAMPLE #2—KING DAVID:

Many of King David's prayers are recorded in the book of Psalms. Did you know that God called David, "a man after his own heart (1 Sam 13:14)"? Considering that accolade, it is surprising that David's psalms are such an emotional rollercoaster. Take a look at just a few of the emotions that David expressed in his prayers:

- *Abandonment and Anger:* "How long, Lord? Will you forget me forever? How long will you hide your face from me?" —Ps 13:1

- *Despair:* "I am feeble and utterly crushed; I groan in anguish of heart." —Ps 38:8

- *Guilt and Fear:* "For troubles without number surround me; my sins have overtaken me, and I cannot see. They are more than the hairs of my head, and my heart fails within me." —Ps 40:12

David was entirely open with God. He was a spiritual heavyweight who questioned God's presence in his life and struggled with fear when he wanted to trust. This gives me hope because God was undoubtedly with David. His hand of blessing is evident in David's life—from shepherd boy to giant slayer to king. David shared his toughest feelings and yet God saw him as a man after his own heart.

You too are safe in the Father's love. Safe to be yourself, *your entire self.* God wants all of you—not just the presentable parts but the worst bits too. So take the filter off your prayers and start being real in his presence. Bring him your rage, your ugly thoughts, your jealousy, and your doubts. Stop hiding your "unchristian" attitudes so that Jesus can help you overcome them.

Honesty is your first step in the right direction. *However, it must be coupled with the next principle if you want your prayers to gain positive momentum.*

Chapter 25
Shift Your Focus to God's Promises

If you want to change the direction of your life, change the declaration of your lips. —Pastor Steven Furtick

LIFE IS ALL ABOUT balance. Just ask a tightrope walker and he'll tell you: lean too far towards either side and you will fall. When I began exercising my newfound freedom to be honest with God, all my fears and anxieties came gushing out—for months. What started as a good thing became toxic. I found myself fixating on my problems and caught up in worry cycles:

> *God,*
>
> *I am so afraid and tired. Why is this happening to me? Help me! Please . . . What am I going to do if my body continues to deteriorate? My life has already become unbearably hard. How can I keep holding myself together? I have lost so much and I am afraid of losing what I have left. Oh God, I couldn't stand it if that happened. Please, please help me!*

I developed a dangerous pattern when I couldn't move past these prayers. They haunted my waking hours on a repeat reel.

Have you been there? Knees bent in prayer but anxiety crashing over you in unrelenting waves? Heart rate and blood pressure climbing? Does it feel like your heart and your prayers are sick?

Then it is time to take a second look at King David's psalms. When prayer escalates our anxiety, it is an indicator that something needs to change. If you pay close attention to the psalms, David consistently shifts his attention away from his problems to the God who can solve them. He was a master at changing his focus. His prayers were honest, but they were coupled with worship. Aha! Praise is the second step.

I tried following King David's example. But frankly, my own praises rang hollow with disappointment. After finally being real with God, I did not want to step back into the prison of fake prayers. How could I genuinely praise God and continue to be honest about my hurt/fears?

For the first time in months, I prayed something new:

Father,
> *My prayers are making me so anxious. I know I need to praise you, but praising you will only bring me peace if I can do it authentically. What should I be doing differently?*

I will never forget the sensation of God reaching down to rescue me in that moment. The uncontrolled anxiety drowning out his voice receded as he pulled me to the surface with this life-preserving thought:

> *Pray my promises.*

Turn my thoughts to God by praying his biblical promises for me? I could do that. Even when I struggle to praise God in my own voice, I believe that his word represents truth. I can genuinely pray God's words, knowing that my prayers have a sincere source.

The day I started praying God's promises marked a momentous shift in my thought life. Even though my problems didn't change, this new pattern powerfully changed my perspective. Instead of wallowing in my fears, I used Bible verses to redirect my thoughts to the one whose "perfect love drives out fear (1 John 4:18)." Deep depression gave way to hope.

HOW TO PRAY GOD'S PROMISES:

By God's promises, I am referring to any Bible verse that contains a blessing for God's people. The Bible is full of them. Better still? Every single one of God's loving promises are yours (Gal 3:29). Through Christ you have inherited the Fatherload.

When searching for promises to pray, look for verses that are God or Christ-centric. Promises wrestle your thoughts from earthly troubles and concentrate them on what your Heavenly Father can do. Many well-known scriptures contain God's promises for you:

- For God so loved the world that he gave his one and only Son, that whoever believes in him shall not perish but have eternal life. —John 3:16

- I can do all things through Christ who strengthens me. —Phil 4:13 NKJV

- And we know that in all things God works for the good of those who love him, who have been called according to his purpose. —Rom 8:28

Notice that in these verses it is God who gave his Son and saved you through him; God who strengthens you; and God who works for your spiritual good. They challenge us to view our problems through the lens of God's love. Our most heartbreaking sorrows seem less daunting when we remember we are pursued by a God whose love for us is stronger than the death of his only Son. Pray verses that draw your attention to the Father.

If you are wondering how to locate God's promises for you, Psalms is an excellent place to start. Or if you are trying to unearth a promise for a specific topic, check to see if your Bible has an index, concordance, or dictionary. All of these tools group verses by subject or keywords.

Are you new to navigating the Bible or feeling daunted at the prospect of a scavenger hunt? Go to a Christian bookstore and ask for a reference book that organizes verses by topic. Choose a book that includes the actual verses and not just the citation. This can be an invaluable reference tool when you need a promise quickly. (I like *The Bible Promise Book: One Thousand Promises from God's Word*—New Life Version, which is published by Barbour Books).

After locating promises that resonate with you, start to pray them from your point of view. I first learned how to reword scripture into personal prayers by reading *Praying God's Word*, by Beth Moore.[1] If you would like additional guidance on how to pray scriptures, I highly recommend picking up her book. It remains the most influential book in my Christian walk other than the Bible. While Beth Moore focuses on praying scriptures over spiritual problem areas, once you learn the process you can apply it to any Bible verse or promise.

Below I have included verses that have personal meaning for me and how I would pray them. Start by being truthful with God about your situation, but then shift your thoughts to who God is and his love for you. Praying God's promises should be positive.

A Promise for My Future:

"For I know the plans I have for you,' declares the Lord, 'plans to prosper you and not to harm you, plans to give you hope and a future." —Jer 29:11

1. See "Bibliography" for book details.

God,
> *I am afraid of what the future holds, but you know the plans you have for me. Thank you that nothing catches you by surprise. I don't understand why this is happening, but I believe you have plans to prosper me and not to harm me. You are giving me a hope and a future. My life is safe in your hands.*

A Promise to Be Near:

For He has not turned away from the suffering of the one in pain or trouble. He has not hidden His face from him. But He has heard his cry for help. —Ps 22:24 NLV

Lord,
> *I am crying out to you day and night, but you feel so far away. It feels like you don't care. But I thank you that you have promised not to turn away from my suffering when I am in pain or trouble. You will not hide your face from me. You hear my cry for help. Thank you for being with me, and help me to feel your presence.*

A Promise for When I Am Afraid:

The Lord is my light and the One Who saves me. Whom should I fear? The Lord is the strength of my life. Of whom should I be afraid? —Ps 27:1 NLV

Jesus,
> *I feel weak and helpless and that frightens me. But you are my light and the One Who saves me. So I do not need to fear. You are the strength of my life. I don't need to be afraid. Help me to trust in you.*

A Promise of Joy:

Restore our fortunes, Lord, as streams renew the desert. Those who plant in tears will harvest with shouts of joy. —Ps 126:4–5 NLT

God,
> *I have cried so many tears, sometimes it feels like my sorrow will never end. Restore my fortunes, Lord, renew my spirit as streams renew the desert. Thank you for your promise that those*

who plant in tears will harvest with shouts of joy. You have seen my tears and will not let my sadness last forever. I will shout for joy again. Bring it quickly, Lord Jesus.

A Promise to Make a Way:

"These are the words of him who is holy and true, who holds the key of David. What he opens no one can shut, and what he shuts no one can open. I know your deeds. See, I have placed before you an open door that no one can shut." —Rev 3:7–8a

> *God,*
>
> *My doctors don't know what is causing my symptoms or how to help me. I feel trapped and do not know how to move forward. But your words are holy and true, and I can trust them. What you open no one can shut, and what you shut no one can open. Lord Jesus, place before me an open door that no one can shut. I thank you for your promise to make a way for me. Help me to recognize the doors that you open.*

As you begin praying God's promises—persevere. Have you ever heard of the magic relationship ratio?[2] It takes five positive interactions with someone to cancel out the effects of just one negative encounter. Likewise, when your prayers have been continually negative, it requires dedicated positive repetition to overcome harmful thought patterns. *But if you are picking which battles to fight, I urge you to choose this one.*

Why would I fight this battle above all others? After all, I am still disabled. But when I made praying God's promises my new pattern, I became less and less disabled by despair. As God's blessings seeped into my soul, my joy reawakened and a new sense of purpose was born. God's promises brought my spirit back to life.

Begin taking back your prayers today. Shift your focus from your problems to God's promises. Immerse yourself in who he is and in his loving promises for you. Rinse. Repeat. And in his perfect timing, your hope, peace, and joy will be reborn.

Such things were written in the Scriptures long ago to teach us. And the Scriptures give us hope and encouragement as we wait patiently for God's promises to be fulfilled. —Rom 15:4 NLT

2. Benson, "Magic Relationship Ratio."

Chapter 26
Pray God's Promises with Power

For God has not given us a spirit of fear, but of power and of love and of a sound mind. —2 Tim 1:7 NKJV

INTENSE SPIRITUAL WARFARE OFTEN accompanies a new pattern that has the power to be life-changing. Satan is a sore loser. He wants to either distract you or make you give up before you make significant progress. As you begin praying God's promises, you may find yourself bombarded with doubts. *Is God's word really powerful? Do my prayers actually make a difference? Why would God listen to me?*

Don't let this assault intimidate you. When Satan attempts to shake your confidence, it is because he knows you are a force to be reckoned with. Remember that the Bible declares that you "are from God and have overcome them [spiritual forces of darkness], because the one who is in you is greater than the one who is in the world (1 John 4:4)." God's Holy Spirit resides within you and gives you the upper hand over evil. Take spiritual warfare as a sign you are on the right track and forge ahead.

You can do all things through Christ who gives you strength (Phil 4:13). As God's child, it is your right to pray his promises with power. The key to overcoming doubts about the effectiveness of prayer is to inspect the foundation your prayers are built upon.

I learned the value of foundations growing up around my dad's construction sites. A foundation is the supporting platform for the rest of a house, so it is essential to build it right. My dad would point out cracks in walls or stress buckles in ceilings and explain that a weak foundation threatens the integrity of an entire structure. But if you take the time to build a secure foundation, your home will have lasting strength—even against the legendary hurricanes of the Outer Banks.

There is only one course of action when gale force winds threaten your prayers: shore up your foundation. You can pray any biblical promise from a position of strength when you support it with these three foundational beliefs:

POSITIVE PRAYER PLATFORM:

1. *God's Word is Powerful.*
2. *Prayer is Powerful.*
3. *You have the Attention of Heaven.*

These truths are the bedrock beliefs of positive prayer. Assemble your positive prayer platform brick by brick—or Bible verse by Bible verse—so that it is solid. Below I provide Bible verses that are the building blocks of these three foundational beliefs. For your convenience, the verses are printed out in their entirety in "Appendix 2: Principles of Positive Prayer."

I can confidently pray God's promises from this platform because my foundational prayer beliefs are constructed out of the reliable material of his word. When an occasional doubt arises, I revisit what grounds me. I reread these Bible verses and remind myself that God's word is powerful, prayer is powerful, and that God has promised me his attention. May these three principles provide you with a positive platform on which to build your prayers. Go forward in his strength.

Positive Prayer Principle #1—God's Word Is Powerful Because . . .

- *God's words/promises are true:* Ps 18:30 NLT, Ps 33:4
- *God's word has authority:* Ps 33:6–9 NLT
- *God's word is alive and accomplishes his will:* Heb 4:12, Isa 55:10–11
- *It is flawless, permanent, and invincible:* Prov 30:5, Isa 40:8, Luke 1:37 NLT
- *God's word is life giving. It sustains, heals, and fuels us:* Matt 4:4, Heb 1:3, 1 Pet 1:23 NLT, Isa 50:4, Ps 107:20, Ps 119:50
- *His word protects us and is a victorious weapon against evil:* Ps 91:4 NLT, Eph 6:17, 1 John 2:14 NLT

- *God's word prepares us to do his work:* 2 Tim 3:16–17

Positive Prayer Principle #2—Prayer Is Powerful Because . . .

- *Prayer pleases God:* Prov 15:8, Acts 10:4, 1 Tim 2:1–3
- *Jesus valued prayer:* Heb 5:7, Luke 5:16
- *Prayer helps us communicate and connect with God:* Phil 4:6, Jer 29:12, Matt 18:19–20
- *Prayer gives us strength to fight temptation:* Matt 26:41 NLT
- *Prayer invites God's favor:* Matt 6:6, 2 Cor 1:11
- *Our prayers can work together with God's will to affect change:* 2 Cor 1:10, Phil 1:19, Jas 5:15–16[3], 1 John 5:14–15

Positive Prayer Principle #3—You Have God's Attention:

- *God's promises are for you. You are his child and an heir through Christ:* Eph 3:6, Gal 4:7, Rom 8:17, Titus 3:7, Eph 1:18–19, 2 Pet 1:3–4
- *Because Christ is your righteousness, you can confidently ask for help* Heb 4:15–16, 1 Cor 1:30
- *God is watching over you 24/7:* 1 Pet 3:12, Ps 121:3–4
- *No detail of your life is beneath God's notice:* Ps 37:23 NLT, Luke 12:6–7

3. See *A Word of Caution* in Appendix 2.

Chapter 27

Practice a Self-last Prayer Structure

Instead of getting on your knees and telling God how big your problem is, get on your knees and tell your problem how big your God is.
—*Pastor Steven Furtick*

HOW MUCH TIME DO you spend praying about your own needs? In the early years of my disabilities, crying out for help composed 95 percent of my prayers. Prayers for others and praise were tacked on as exhausted afterthoughts. While this wasn't "wrong," such an intense focus on my problems was harmful to my mental health.

I hope you have begun to reclaim the content of your prayers by praying God's promises. But is your anxiety also being driven by the way your prayers are structured?

If you are looking to shake off sorrows when you pray, give this a try: prioritize God and others first. Looking up to praise your Father and out to the needs of others puts your problems into perspective. I have found this is the fastest way to hit the refresh button on prayers that have begun slipping back into negativity. Use the following prayer order when you need a jumpstart in a positive direction. It works best when you give the first three steps equal—or more—attention than prayers for your own needs.

SELF-LAST PRAYERS:

1. *Praise*

2. *Thanksgiving*

3. *Pray for Others*

4. *Pray for Yourself*

1. PRAISE:

Begin your prayer by glorifying God for who he is. This type of praise differs from thanksgiving because it has a relational focus. Celebrate who God is to the world and to you. Praise his character and attributes. Most of us are accustomed to this type of praise in worship music but are unused to speaking it. If you find it awkward at first, don't worry—I did too. Keep practicing. Now, praise is my favorite of the four steps because I feel my spirit coming to life.

To help you get started, think about the names/titles given to God/Christ in the Bible. God is your Savior, Deliverer, Healer, Wonderful Counselor, and Help in Times of Trouble—to name a few. The name that God used to identify himself to Moses was *Yahweh*, which means "I AM WHO I AM (Exod 3:14)." What a gloriously open-ended name full of possibilities!

So think about it . . . who is God to you? Use his name "I AM" in your prayers by reversing it to address him as "You are." Then fill in the blank. Here is an example of how I may start my prayer with praise:

> *God,*
>
> *You are the creator of the whole world, my Savior, and my best friend. How marvelous this is to me! You are completely good. You are my comforter and warrior: you hold me in your hands and never stop fighting for me.*
>
> *You are the one who sees me for who I am beyond disability and who calls light forth from darkness. All the goodness in me is because of you. You watch over my life and are with me every step of the way.*
>
> *You are the song of my spirit and the strength of my life. You are my way maker; nothing is impossible for you. You are the King of Heaven and the King of my heart.*

2. THANKSGIVING:

Continue praising God by thanking him for your blessings. Thank him for the gift of his son Jesus and for making a way for you to live in heaven with him forever. Thank him for your loved ones, for his provision of strength, for material blessings, for nature, and for the ways your body does work. By acknowledging the many blessings God has given you, you will be reassured of his goodness. Gratitude builds trust.[1]

3. PRAY FOR OTHERS:

One of my greatest challenges with disability is that it makes me very self-centered. I spend a lot of time thinking about my medicine schedule, how to eat/space my food, how to structure my day to get the most of my energy, etc. Mentally it is exhausting and leaves little time to think about others. I am so focused on what I need to do that I quickly get thrown off or miss opportunities when the unexpected happens. It is even easier to get caught up in my troubles and live in my own little bubble when my fatigue is overwhelming.

But no one, I repeat *no one*, has a perfect life. Everyone around us has a need: whether it is physical, spiritual, emotional, financial, relational, etc. Intercessory prayer is a practical way to please God and serve our communities. It can be done anytime, anywhere, and without any prep work.

Praying for others is vitally important to my well-being because it pulls me out of my own circumstances. It reminds me that I am not the only one suffering—therefore, I am not alone in experiencing trouble. One of my heroes, Corrie Ten Boom, says it like this:

> I kept on praying to dispel my fear, until suddenly—and I do not know how the idea came to me—I began to pray for others. I prayed for everyone who came into my thoughts, people with whom I had traveled, those who had been in prison with me, my school friends of years ago. I do not know how long I continued in prayer, but this I do know, my fear was gone. Interceding for others had released me.[2]

Praying for the hardships of others also highlights the areas of your life God *has* blessed. Everyone has a blessing that is someone else's place of hurt. For example, I have a friend who I secretly suspect is genetically engineered because she is so healthy. I would love to have her energy. She wants to get married and start a family more than anything. The only problem is that she hasn't met the right man.

Meanwhile, God has given me a husband that could not be more wonderful if he had walked straight out of my dreams. Whenever I pray for my

---

1. For more on how gratitude builds trust, see Chapter 17 "Be Empowered by God's Past Faithfulness."

2. Ten Boom, *Amazing Love*, 61–62.

friend to find the partner she deserves, I am reminded of how thankful I am for my own marriage. I realize that I wouldn't trade Parker for her health in a million years.

Our problems are put into perspective when we broaden our prayers to include others. We are reminded of the many blessings we have from God. We become aware that there are others suffering worse difficulties. Suddenly, our own struggles seem much smaller.

4. PRAY FOR YOURSELF:

By the time I reach this fourth step, my heart is reassured that God is in control of my life, he cares deeply for my needs, and I am not alone in suffering. It surprises me how what could have been a marathon prayer of despair and fearful tangents becomes a few succinct requests. Problems that seemed unbearable then appear manageable—and I can pray about them from a perspective of peace. I am able to leave my worries in God's capable hands and work towards his purpose for me this day.

Take a step in a positive direction. Pray for yourself last.

Chapter 28
Quickly Connect Throughout Your Day

"Rejoice always, pray continually, give thanks in all circumstances;
for this is God's will for you in Christ Jesus." —1 Thess 5:16–18

GOD'S COMMAND TO PRAY continually is not the impossible standard of a tyrannical egotist. It is an invitation to live deeply connected to him. Jesus says, "I am the vine; you are the branches. If you remain in me and I in you, you will bear much fruit; apart from me you can do nothing (John 15:5)."

Humans need connection to God. Like the vine that feeds the branches, Jesus is our source of life and strength. When you draw close to him, you benefit from his presence.

If I am being honest, the Bible's command to "pray continually" used to really stress me out. How could anyone satisfy this standard without setting aside the demands of daily life to live a monk-like existence? Such a goal felt equally impractical and unattainable.

Post-disability I'm increasingly aware of how much I need God. I need him to give me the strength to get out of bed in the morning; to help me swallow, wash laundry, and have the courage to push past my frustrations. Being so dependent on God's help minute by minute has taught me an important lesson: *praying continually does not have to be complicated.* It can be as simple as returning your thoughts to Him.

Quick, one-line prayers are a practical way to include God in your daily life. They are appropriate at any time or in any situation. They are feasible whether you are in a bathroom, boardroom, or on a bus. Here are a few examples to get you started:

- *May revelation of your perfect love cast out my fears.*
- *God, come hold me in your arms.*

- *Jesus, help me to know you well—I want to be your friend.*
- *Thank you for sending someone to help me today.*
- *Help me walk to the kitchen and prepare my lunch.*
- *God, thank you for giving me the strength to go to work today.*
- *Father, may your peace help me rise above my frustrations right now.*
- *Lord, help me to love my life again.*
- *Holy Spirit, help me develop good habits so that you can make the most of my life.*
- *God, thank you for giving me enough energy to make love to my husband.*
- *Jesus, come tell me how much you love me and the promises you have for me.*
- *Lord, I'm so tired—help me not sound dumb when I am speaking to this person.*
- *God, may my eyes be fixed on you and not my troubles.*
- *Control my thoughts, Lord Jesus.*
- *Thank you that I was able to go to church today.*
- *Holy Spirit, protect me against being distracted from God's purpose for me in this day.*
- *I trust myself to your love, Lord Jesus.*

The possibilities are endless. God is always with you, but it delights him to be invited into the details of your life. Choosing to journey together through your daily struggles and triumphs will strengthen your connection to the one true vine.

So invite him into your frustrations. Give him a shout-out with each small victory. Include him in your daily routine. Such a friendship with Jesus is priceless and easier than you think.

Here is a closing one-liner I love from the historical romance novel, *Love's Fortune:*[1]

> *"For all that Thy love has yet in store for me, O God, I give thee gracious thanks." —Laura Frantz*

---

1. Frantz, *Love's Fortune*, 290.

Chapter 29

Discerning God's Voice
in Times of Stress

*Then a great and powerful wind tore the mountains apart and
shattered the rocks before the Lord, but the Lord was not in the wind.
After the wind there was an earthquake, but the Lord was not in the
earthquake. After the earthquake came a fire, but the Lord was not
in the fire. And after the fire came a gentle whisper.*
—1 Kgs 19:11b-12

PRAYER IS A CONVERSATION with God. Successful conversations require give
and take. You have to share *and listen* if you want to connect with another
person. Likewise, listening is an essential part of prayer for every Christian
who wants to know the Father. It takes a quiet mind and expectant silences
so that he may reveal himself to your heart.

When I say God "speaks" to me, it is not in an audible James Earl Jones
voice. While God is absolutely capable of speaking aloud, I think he is aware
that the majority of people would wet themselves if Mufasa suddenly thun-
dered in their ear. To me, God's voice has always been the gentle whisper
from 1 Kings. What I "hear" comes in the form of a comforting thought, an
impression he puts on my heart, or a Bible verse that particularly resonates
with me.

But discerning which thoughts are from God can be difficult when
your own fears or ideas are vying for your attention. How can you be sure
you are hearing God's voice? Here is a framework that helps me sift through
which thoughts are from God when my mind is overwhelmed. Always complete the first two steps and follow-up with the additional measures when
applicable.

TO DISCERN GOD'S VOICE IN TIMES OF STRESS:

1. *Listen to the voice that gives you peace.*

2. *Bring it to the Bible. Check that what you are hearing is consistent with the heart of God's word. Ask yourself)*

   A) *Am I interpreting this (thought or verse) in the context of Christ? and*

   B) *Am I aligned with what God values most?*

*ADDITIONAL MEASURES FOR MAKING MAJOR DECISIONS:

1. *Include others.*

2. *When appropriate, pray for God to shut doors.*

1. Listen to the Voice That Gives You Peace:

Have you ever been told, "I know something is wrong with you, but I'm not sure what is causing your symptoms, how to treat them, or where to refer you to next"? I have lived that nightmare. I spent four years stumping a string of the nation's top specialists before I was diagnosed with POTS. Meanwhile, eating had become unbearable and I was losing weight with alarming speed.

My desperation grew with every unfruitful doctor's appointment. I spent hours researching medical conditions and asking God to show me which path to take. It became increasingly difficult to identify God's voice as my mind scrambled for a solution:

> *Maybe I have Ehlers-Danlos syndrome. Could it be myasthenia gravis? Maybe I should make an appointment with a specialist at John Hopkins. Would the Mayo Clinic be able to help? God, please give me an answer on the next website.*

Following internet rabbit holes to worst case scenarios will make you prematurely gray. At the same time, I knew God did not want me to give up. But how could I tell whether an idea came from him or from fear? Finally, I prayed, "God, how can I identify your voice?"

The thought "Listen to the voice that brings you peace" cut through my inner chaos like a beam of light. As I considered what would bring me peace, I realized that my feverish internet search was being driven by a desperate need for control. *I had* to be in charge of finding answers because I was afraid that, like the perplexed doctors, God wouldn't help me.

God's way of peace challenged me to make a choice of trust. Practically, this meant asking my husband to research for me (and not hovering over his shoulder while he did it). He could remain more objective and research within time limits. God would help us find the right doctor and diagnosis. For the sake of my sanity, I needed to take a more hands off approach.

As fear faded to the background I was able to tune back in to the Lord's peaceful whisper. I felt God encouraging me to tell *all* of my specialists about my stomach symptoms. I thought that was strange, but it was a relief not to have to find another gastroenterologist. A few weeks later, my sleep specialist recognized a pattern in my symptoms and sent me to be tested for POTS.

Listen to the voice that brings you peace. This simple rule is a priceless tool when your mind is swamped by fear. Thoughts and actions motivated by fear, anxiety, stress, or hopelessness are not from God. His voice stills your heart instead of stirring up turmoil in your spirit.

That does not mean what God asks of you is always easy. But his voice will always lead the way to more: more of his peace, more of his strength, more of his courage, and more of his kindness. However, before you take action, *always* check that your thought is consistent with God's word.

The words that I have spoken to you are spirit and life. —John 6:63b

2. God's Voice Is Consistent with the Heart of His Word:

Do not conform to the pattern of this world, but be transformed by the renewing of your mind. Then you will be able to test and approve what God's will is—his good, pleasing and perfect will. —Rom 12:2

Would you equate Albert Einstein's genius to the brain power of an amoeba? No way! Their minds are worlds apart. The chasm between God's thoughts and ours is infinitely more staggering. Where does that leave those of us who think *string theory* is the name of a yo-yo shop? In need of a higher mindset.

Thankfully, God gave us an instruction manual to help us recognize his voice. Second Timothy 3:16 says that, "All scripture is breathed out by

God." We can get to know God's character and align our thoughts with his by studying his word. The Bible is a reliable window into the Lord's thoughts.

It is worth remembering that—while God's word is flawless—the human beings who interpret the Bible are not. Historically, many people have justified their own selfish actions by taking God's word out of context. The Bible was wrongfully interpreted to condone the killing of non-Christians during the crusades, the African slave trade, and Nazi persecution of the Jews.

These extreme examples caution us to be careful. Misinterpreting God's word for yourself may have a smaller ripple effect, but it can still rob you of your peace, efficacy, or compassion. So when you evaluate thoughts you believe to be from God against a biblical standard, avoid being too narrow in your focus. The Bible should always be taken into consideration as a whole. Check that these two criteria apply:

A) Am I interpreting this verse in the context of Christ?

Bible hopping (randomly flipping open the Bible hoping for a quick verse of encouragement) is attractive when you want an instant word from God. The problem with this strategy is that out-of-context verses should not always be taken at face value. To have a balanced understanding of the Bible's core messages, you need to read it with intentionality.

For example, once I asked God, "What do I need to do to be well?" I opened my Bible to a verse accusing "Your own conduct and actions have brought this on you. This is your punishment. How bitter it is! How it pierces to the heart (Jer 4:18)!"

I crumpled in defeat. *Was this all my fault? Was I getting worse because I still struggled with anger and doubt? Was there a sin I needed to repent of?*

Gathering me in his arms, Parker looked me straight in the eye and said:

> Remember that Satan used a Bible verse to try and misdirect Jesus during Christ's temptation. This was meant to distract and upset you. God sees you through Christ's righteousness. Jesus loves you and is not cruelly condemning you for a sin you can't identify. *You must put this in the context of Christ.*

So must you. We are a resurrection people living in the triumphant wake of our risen Lord. When striving to identify God's voice, you and I should ask ourselves, "Are these thoughts consistent with the Bible's message about Jesus' love and mercy? Do they speak to my identity as God's precious child? Do they invite me to leave my past behind as Jesus beckons me forward into a brighter future with him?"

Love is the reason Christ came, and his voice *always* resounds with it.

B) Am I aligned with what God values most?

When seeking God's guidance, you may find yourself needing to choose between several biblical truths. Jesus faced a similar choice when the devil dared him to jump off the temple to prove he was God's Son. Satan tried to manipulate Jesus by taunting:

> For the Scriptures say, "He will order his angels to protect you. And they will hold you up with their hands so you won't even hurt your foot on a stone." —Matt 4:6 NLT

Jesus couldn't care less about Lucifer's double dog dare. He doesn't need to swan-dive off the temple to prove himself to anyone. He already has the approval of the only person who counts: his Father. Christ overturns Satan's challenge with another Bible verse, "*The Scriptures also say, 'You must not test the LORD your God (Matt 4:7 NLT).'*"

Oh snap! It is a Bible showdown and Satan just got shown who is boss. Jesus entered the ring with the more valuable truth.

Alternatively, look to the life of Rahab. "You must not lie (Exod 20:16 TLB)" is pretty much Sunday School 101. But this gutsy woman lied to protect two Israelite spies. James 2:25 commends her saying, Rahab "was shown to be right with God by her actions when she hid those messengers and sent them safely away by a different road." Saving two lives was more important than a lie.

The danger of holding unswervingly to an obscure Bible verse is that you can undermine an even greater truth. Align your priorities with what God values most by considering the key messages that make up the heart of his word: love, selflessness, and trust. As you open your eyes to the big picture, one truth may transcend the others to light your way forward.

*ADDITIONAL MEASURES FOR MAKING MAJOR DECISIONS:

Use special care when seeking God's direction for major decisions. Some examples of major decisions include evaluating surgical options, filing for disability, considering parenthood as a disabled adult, or changing your career/

living situation in response to your health. These two additional safeguards can help you proceed thoughtfully.

1. Include Others:

Prov 15:22 teaches that, "Plans fail for lack of counsel, but with many advisers they succeed." Including others in your decision-making process is especially important when you're stressed because a strong desire to get well can give you tunnel vision. Others may recognize pitfalls you are unable to see or be able to suggest alternative options.

Talk through the pros and cons of your situation with family members, godly friends, and your trusted spiritual mentors. Ask them to pray for guidance on your behalf and allow them enough time to prayerfully consider God's direction.

You may also have doctors, therapists, or lawyers invested in your care. These professionals can give very valuable advice. Before any doctor's appointment, my husband and I pray, "Lord, give the doctors your wisdom and direction. Speak through them, and help us to know which words are from you." Don't be afraid to ask your doctor, "What would you do in my situation?" Seeking advice from trustworthy spiritual mentors and professionals will help you make educated/well-rounded decisions.

2. Pray for God to Shut Doors:

What he opens no one can shut, and what he shuts no one can open.
I know your deeds. See, I have placed before you an open door that
no one can shut. —Rev 3:7b-8a

I want God to be specific when I ask for directions. Making decisions would be so much easier if he would hand me detailed objective check-lists and color-coded timelines. But God rarely works that way and I often find myself trying to choose between multiple open doors.

How do I discern which open door to walk through? Is one better than the other? How do I avoid stressing myself out when I am straining to hear God's voice?

If thinking about how to choose between multiple possibilities makes you break out into a cold sweat, then try something different the next time you need to discern which way to go: *Ask God to shut the doors he does not want you to walk though instead.*

This prayer has set me free from hours of paralyzing indecision! I don't view it as spiritual laziness but as a declaration of trust. When you ask God to shut doors you effectively say:

> *I am giving up my need to agonize over the agenda. I'm trusting that you are watching over my life and my future. I believe you will faithfully keep me from wrong paths because you know it is my desire to follow you. I trust that if a door remains open I can walk through it knowing you are with me.*

The beauty of such a prayer is that it lets you begin to take action; trusting more in God's ability to direct your steps than in your need to know.

How have these additional measures played out in my decision-making process? Over the last few years, I have had to make complex decisions about two stomach surgeries. My combination of disorders is so rare that I often find myself considering treatment options that are new and innovative.

Translation? I am the guinea pig. There was no research data supporting whether these surgeries could ease gastroparesis caused by POTS. Both procedures had the potential to either help or hurt my quality of life.

The first surgery I considered was a pyloroplasty—a procedure opening the sphincter between my stomach and small intestine to give stagnating foods/liquids an exit. Three out of my four doctors opposed the idea because the therapy had not been proven for POTS patients. Was God shutting the door?

Friends, when I ask God to shut a door, I expect him to slam it shut. The violent coughing from reflux, bloating, and starvation are so miserable that I will not give up a therapy without a fight. The surgeon was the only doctor who had actually performed the procedure and he had helped over three hundred patients eat more normally. He felt 90 percent confident that it would not make me worse. I trusted that he was concerned about my welfare because he answered all my questions over multiple appointments without pushing me to have the procedure. My husband, family, friends, spiritual mentors, and I all prayed over the decision. Despite the concerns of my other doctors, we felt unanimously peaceful about it.

The pyloroplasty was a roaring success and one of the best decisions I have ever made. It took care of the nausea and bloating and allowed me to return to a normal weight. I am woman enough to admit that I cried joyful tears at the first spoonful of salted caramel gelato I'd had in three years. Oh Lord, may there be ice cream in heaven!

Although I am much better, the reflux and cough still interfere with my sleep. The same surgeon and I cautiously approached the idea of a stomach bypass. If it worked, I would be free of the reflux. But if it failed, my ability to eat could be permanently jeopardized.

This time God slammed the door, nailed it shut, and bricked it over. Three diagnostic tests revealed that I would continue to have problems with cough because of a weak esophagus. As a result, all of my doctors (including the surgeon) advised against it. My prayer team also unanimously agreed that a bypass was a terrible idea.

I have reached the limit of what medical science can do for my digestion at this time. Now I need to be thankful for the many ways in which I am better and let the rest go. I can do so gracefully, knowing that I pursued every avenue towards normalcy.

Disability is full of decisions that are multifaceted and muddled. Take the pressure off yourself and place your stress on God's strong shoulders. He is not intimidated by your complexities or deterred by your messiness. Pursue his will with due diligence, but then trust him to prepare the way before you. You can rest peacefully in his care.

When my spirit grows faint within me, it is you who watch over my way. —Ps 142:3

Part 6

Prayers for Specific Needs

Ask and it will be given to you; seek and you will find; knock and the door will be opened to you. —Matt 7:7

Introduction:
If the Shoe Fits . . .

*To everything there is a season, A time for every purpose under
heaven . . . —Eccl 3:1 NKJV*

PARKER LOVES PLANNING A good surprise. I love his surprises. But when we
were first dating his commitment to absolute secrecy led to some snafus. I
showed up to more than one date in a cute dress and ballet flats to find him
in full hiking gear. Some blisters and a few ruined pairs of footwear later, I
set a ground rule: He could surprise me to his heart's content, as long as he
told me what shoes to wear.

Heels are great on a dance floor. They aren't the best choice for a hay-
ride. Just as we need shoes that are appropriate to different situations, it can
be helpful to have prayers that match specific concerns.

Consider this section your prayer closet. As you rummage through,
you'll find prayers that have been tremendously freeing to me at different
times during my chronic illness journey. Some prayers I regularly revisit.
Others carried me through a particular season. Both have value. Tune into
your inner Cinderella or Cinderfella, and wear the prayer that fits!

Chapter 30

Prayers for the Dark Night of the Soul

The Lord is close to the brokenhearted and saves those who are crushed in spirit. —Ps 34:18

IMPORTANT NOTE:
This prayer is for moments when you are overwhelmed by despair. But if you are having suicidal thoughts—or intend to hurt yourself—call 911. If this is not the case, it is still important to have a trusted and responsible person with you at this time. It is not safe to be alone when extreme levels of grief are clouding your judgement.

"Something is obviously wrong. But I don't know how to help you or where to send you next." The specialist shrugged nonchalantly and walked out of the examining room.

I wanted to slap the man. How dare he be so indifferent? I was desperate—and this was one unhelpful doctor's appointment too many. The world felt unnaturally quiet as Parker and I drove back to our hotel. Three steps inside the door an angry buzzing sound filled my head. It was all the warning I had before I became completely undone.

For the first time in a six-year health struggle, I wasn't sure if I could keep believing in God and his goodness. I felt utterly abandoned. The thought that my faith was in jeopardy terrified me for a very real reason: If I lost faith in God, I would have no hope. The fight would be lost. To keep going with God was difficult. Without him, I would go insane from sorrow.

My enemies were too strong for me. I was so worn out by battle fatigue that I didn't know if I had the ability to hold onto God anymore. My despair was at a tipping point. I opened my Bible in a last-ditch effort to find God. Mercifully, he found me:

He [*God*] will keep you strong to the end, so that you will be blameless on the day of our Lord Jesus Christ. God who has called you into fellowship with his Son Jesus Christ our Lord is faithful. —1 Cor 1:8–9

These verses birthed the "Hail Mary" prayer. It is a prayer for the dark night of the soul.

THE "HAIL MARY" PRAYER:

I am using the term "Hail Mary" in the athletic sense—as it refers to a last-second attempt to score or make a goal. (Parker, please note that you have succeeded in teaching your unathletic wife some sports vocabulary over the years. Mission accomplished.) This is the prayer I pray when all my other resources are exhausted. That night, I clung to God's promise in 1 Corinthians 1:8–9 and prayed:

> *God,*
>
> *I have done my best, but I just cannot fight anymore. This is too much for me to handle. I don't have any strength left. I am not sure that I can keep believing in you or in your goodness. But the thought of losing my faith in you frightens me more than anything. Because without you, I am nothing. All that is good in me would die.*
>
> *God, listen to me. Regardless of what I say or do in the future, hear and honor the desire of my heart now. Don't let me lose faith in you, Lord Jesus. This verse says that you will keep me strong and blameless until the end. I ask you to do that for me today, God, because I don't know if I can hold on to you. Do not ever let me stop believing in your love or loving you. This verse promises that you will be faithful. Be faithful to me now. Hold on to me and never let me go.*

This prayer brought me back from the brink. Admittedly, I was still struggling to believe. But I also sensed that there was something very powerful about a request for God to preserve my faith: something that delighted and honored him.

It was time to stop striving and let God be the one to keep my world together. I could relax and lean into his strength. When I couldn't take care of myself, he would take care of me. An inkling of peace invaded my chaos and murmured that I was going to survive this.

God answered my prayer that day. I did not lose my faith. Instead, it noticeably grew as he held me close and soothed my soul. It was a wonder to watch God do what I could not. To witness the resurrection of my spirit as my love, faith, hope, and peace were reborn. To realize I had been rescued from an existence of feeling dead inside—not through my own effort—but by his mercy. To me this is a miracle: to be so chosen.

You too have been called into a relationship with a God who loves you beyond your understanding. He holds you through every dark day and night. *When you come to the end of your own resources or feel your faith failing, ask God to make good on his promise to keep you strong.* Appendix 3 has a list of verses you can pray when you need him to be your champion. God will faithfully keep you forever in his hand.

> *My sheep listen to my voice; I know them, and they follow me. I give them eternal life, and they shall never perish; no one will snatch them out of my hand. My Father, who has given them to me, is greater than all; no one can snatch them out of my Father's hand.*
> *—John 10:27–29*

GIVE A GROAN:

Some news leaves us speechless with sorrow. It cuts us to the core and involves too many complex feelings for us to give voice to our tangled emotions. Did you know that God has you covered, even when you can't find the words to pray? He is fluent in groan.

Romans 8:26 AMP says, "In the same way the Spirit [comes to us and] helps us in our weakness. We do not know what prayer to offer or how to offer it as we should, but the Spirit Himself [knows our need and at the right time] intercedes on our behalf with sighs and groanings too deep for words." When the Israelites were enslaved by the Egyptians, the Bible says it was their groans that got God's attention (Exod 2:23–24).

God still hears the cries of his people. His Holy Spirit resides inside you and knows your every thought. He steps in to communicate with God on your behalf when your hurts are too painful to put into words (Rom 8:27). So sigh, groan, cry, whimper, moan, or harrumph, and let the Holy Spirit translate. You don't need to speak for your message to be received.

> *Groanings which cannot be uttered are often prayers which cannot be refused. —Charles H. Spurgeon*

USING YOUR SANCTIFIED IMAGINATION:

Many counselors and psychologists use a cognitive behavioral therapy tool called positive visualization. They talk patients through meditation exercises to help them let go of stress or think about desirable outcomes. Here is an example from a counseling session I attended:

> Imagine you are standing by a crystal-clear stream. The surrounding forest is alive with the colors of autumn and leaves are drifting down to rest on the water. Place your problem on the leaf. Watch it float downstream out of sight.

While this was relaxing, I found myself feeling a little irritated with the counselor. Some problems are just too big for floating leaves!

In times of intense stress, I prefer using my sanctified imagination. This is using your imagination to visualize positive interactions with God. It differs from positive visualization because it is informed by biblical truths. Your thoughts should always be based on the character of God or Jesus as they are represented in the Bible. I find this to be a more effective form of visualization because it is anchored in the strength of God's love. While leaves may sink beneath the weight of my disabilities, I know that God is capable of handling all of my problems.

I will lead you through an example of what I imagine when I'm having a dark night of the soul. First, find a quiet and safe place where you will not be distracted. Remember to have a reliable loved one with you if you are extremely upset. Let's begin:

> *Imagine yourself curled up in God's arms. You are safe and secure. His strong arms surround you, providing a place of shelter and rest. You feel protected in his embrace and lay your head in the crook of his elbow. Warmth radiates from his arms enveloping you in a sense of belonging. The very air around you is alive with his love.*
>
> *With every breath, you breathe in the knowledge that you are unconditionally loved—just as you are in this moment. There is no need for pretenses within this love that is unfailing and everlasting. As you exhale, you release all your sorrows, worries for the future, and pain to your kind Father. Right now, your only job is to relax in his embrace.*
>
> *God comforts you like a parent soothing a small child. He gently strokes your hair and whispers that everything is going to be alright. You can see the exquisite tenderness and care in his eyes. He tells you that you are beautiful and strong. He says that he is proud of you. He softly begins to sing of his love for you.*

As his lullaby floods your soul with peace, he places his hand on your heart. He draws out all of your sadness, anger, and fear. He takes these dark poisons into himself, where they are instantly eclipsed by his goodness and gone forever.

Love like sunbeams travels through his fingers infusing into your heart. A soft glow illuminates your chest as he replaces your hurt with his light. It grows brighter and stronger by the minute, spreading outward through your entire body. You feel calm, secure, and hopeful.

He lifts your head to meet his gaze. "My child," he says, "your troubles are in my hands, and I promise to take care of you. You do not need to worry or be afraid. I am your champion, and I will always fight for you. You are not alone now, nor will you ever be. You are mine and my love for you will last forever."

Can you see how biblically-based visualization is incredibly comforting? This is just one of many scenarios you could imagine to remind yourself of God's love. As you journey into your sanctified imagination, here are a few questions to get you started:

1. In your imagined interaction with God, what is he doing? (Wiping your tears, binding your wounds, picking you up?)

2. What does his facial expression communicate to you?

3. What encouraging words is God speaking to you?

4. Imagine that you are looking at yourself through God's eyes of love and forgiveness. How does he see you? What qualities shine through?

5. How do you feel in God's presence?

Chapter 31
Ask for an Attitude Adjustment

*This is the confidence we have in approaching God: that if we ask
anything according to his will, he hears us.* — *1 John 5:14*

SOMETIMES I WISH THAT God was more like a magician—a couple of magic
words, a flash of smoke, some jazz hands for good measure, and *presto!* Narcoleptic no more. I prayed constantly for God to change my circumstances
during my first few years of disability. But eventually I took the hint: my
disorders were not doing a disappearing act.

What were my other options? Bribery? I'd lost my last bargaining chip
when he refused my offer to become a missionary. Nor would the nuns have
me since I said "I do" to Parker. Blackmail? Not enough leverage. But something had to give—before I gave into anger.

Jokes aside, I was becoming someone on the inside I didn't like. I responded by praying even harder for healing. When God healed me, wouldn't
the negative emotions bullying me go away too? But as my frustration with
not being healed grew, so did the tyrants of anger, fear, and despair.

Eventually, I realized these feelings were robbing me of more joy
and peace than my disabilities themselves. I only had one option left . . .
if God was not going to change my position, perhaps he would change my
perspective.

My friend, if you want God to answer your prayers, try asking him for an
attitude adjustment. Because every single time I've asked God to change my
outlook, he has shown up with the reliability of a German bus. The process
of letting go of my anger began with this prayer:

God,

> *I have tried not to be angry about the fact that you haven't healed me. I've ignored my angry thoughts and redirected my mind towards your goodness. I have done everything within my power to willfully shake off my resentment. But this situation just hurts too much. The anger is still there. It is hard to face the fact that I may have to live the rest of my life with these conditions when I know you could make me healthy again.*
>
> *I'm also sure I cannot do this without you. Deep down I know that I love you. I truly do not want to be angry with you anymore. I hate what this anger is doing to my spirit. But frankly, I don't know how not to feel angry with you right now. Will you please help me? Will you take my anger towards you away?*

Little by little my anger began to fade. A few months later, I suddenly realized it was gone. To me this is magic because I cannot tell you what stopped my anger. God in his mercy simply washed it away.

Now, whenever I am faced with overwhelming emotions of fear, doubt, depression, or flare-ups of anger, I admit it is too strong for me. I give my attitudes into God's waiting hands and try to go on with life. To this day, he has never left a prayer for an attitude change unanswered.

Why are these prayers, above all others, so effective? Reread the verse from 1 John 5:14 at the beginning of this chapter. God's will for the events/circumstances of every person's life is different. When we ask God to change our situation, it can be difficult to know whether we are praying in accordance with his will. We want short term comfort but God sees big picture outcomes. It could very well be God's will to heal you now. But he also may allow you to wait, while he redeems your situation for your spiritual growth and his glory (Jas 1:2–4, John 9:3).

However, you can be confident that it is always God's will for you to become more like Jesus. The Bible says you should throw off your old self by letting the "Spirit renew your thoughts and attitudes. *[This is how you]* Put on your new nature, created to be like God—truly righteous and holy (Eph 4:23–24 NLT)."

When you ask for the fruit of the Holy Spirit (love, joy, peace, forbearance, kindness, goodness, faithfulness, gentleness, and self-control)[1] you align yourself with God's priorities. It is a request that delights him. God is much more interested in lasting inner transformation than in instant miracles.

---

1. Gal 5:22b–23a

So if you find your situation unbearable, ask God for an attitude adjustment. He has made it possible for me to have a fulfilling life even with a broken body. A healed outlook is the most important ingredient to rediscovering joy.

Chapter 32

Pray for What You *Really*
Want from Healing

*When Jesus saw him lying there and learned that he had been in this
condition for a long time, he asked him, "Do you want to get well?"*
—John 5:6

IF JESUS EVER POSED a seemingly dumb question, it was when he asked a
man who had been paralyzed for thirty-eight years if he wanted to get well
(John 5:1–15). Can't you see the human resource team squirming? Come
on, Jesus! Exercise a little tact. But since we know Jesus always has our best
intentions at heart, there must be hidden value in his question. What was
Jesus trying to uncover?

Take a moment to consider *why* you want to be healed. If this seems
insensitive, remember that I also long to be well. Healing is a no-brainer!
Living without the discomfort and inconveniences of disability would be as
glorious as a lifelong vacation in Tahiti. But let's dive deeper. Beyond feeling
better, what do you want healing to accomplish? Why is it so important for
you to be healed? Here are my answers:

- *I want to be healed so that I can have my joy and peace back.*
- *I want to be healed so that I can be a better wife. I want to help my
  husband more and love him without hindrance.*
- *I want to be healed so that I can invest more in my relationships and
  spend more time with people.*
- *I want to be healed so I can enjoy life without having to push so hard.*
- *I want to have enough energy for Parker and I to be parents.*

- *I want to be healed so that I can use my God-given gifts. I want my life to have purpose again.*

List made, Jesus asked my heart this question, "How many of these goals actually rely on physical healing?"

My jaw dropped on the floor. These are the desires that drive my relentless pursuit of healing. Yet many of these goals can be achieved fully (or in part) without me being healed.

Jesus can teach me how to be joyful in suffering. Instead of the fragile peace produced by an easy situation, I can have a powerful peace that transcends my circumstances. I can be a better wife now by putting away the clean dishes before Parker gets home from work. I can invest more in my relationships today by making a phone call and deepening a friendship. It will always be frustrating to have to push hard on a daily basis. But if I spend less time mourning my losses and more time tuning into how God is working in me, he will increase my enjoyment of life. Disability has been so difficult, surely God would only allow it if he was going to do something indescribably good.

Some longings do require a measure of physical healing to be realized—like my desire to be a mother. Without my energy improving, it would be selfish of me to ask Parker to essentially be a single parent. But God gave me a special love for and ability to connect with children. He has enabled me to push through my personal pain and be a positive influence in the lives of my godchildren, nephews, and friends' children. No, it is not the same as having my own child. But I have children who call me to tell me they love me, a fridge covered in handprint artwork, and a growing catalogue of memories that make me smile. I would be poorer if I turned away from this source of joy because it is not what I had envisioned.

As God helps me find creative ways to love my husband, family, friends, and invest in the children around me, I am checking the box beside my last goal. I am using my God given gifts. Jesus has reawakened my sense of purpose and ignited new dreams in my heart.

It was a game changing revelation for me to realize that I can still have many of the things I most want out of life. I can hope for a better today because my goals are not on pause until my health improves. Of course, I still believe in and ask for healing, but I am much more focused on how God can meet the desires of my heart within my current situation.

Take another look at why you want to be healed. Physical healing is ideal, but is it a requirement for all of your desires to be met? Are some goals available to you now—at least to a degree? Proverbs 13:12b encourages that "a longing fulfilled is a tree of life." Pray for the outcomes you want to see from physical healing, and you may make the joyful discovery that God can fulfill many of your longings just as you are. May his blessings flow.

> Lord Jesus,
>
> I thank you for the revelation that I do not necessarily have to be healed to get most of what I want out of life. Help me to love and enjoy my life now. Teach me to connect to your joy and peace through all circumstances. Even in this time of suffering, give me a purpose that motivates me to get up every morning. Show me how to make small choices that strengthen my relationships and allow me to be present for my loved ones. Thank you for making many of the things I truly want available to me in all seasons. Amen.

Chapter 33
Peace That Passes Understanding

Do not be anxious about anything, but in every situation, by prayer and petition, with thanksgiving, present your requests to God. And the peace of God, which transcends all understanding, will guard your hearts and your minds in Christ Jesus. —Phil 4:6–7

DID YOU EVER SING "I've Got the Joy, Joy, Joy, Joy," in Sunday School? My favorite verse was, "I've got the peace that passes understanding down in my heart!" I did not have a clue what it meant, but I loved the challenge of singing it. My classmates and I would eyeball one another in unspoken competition. We all sang that particular verse a little louder with our backs straightened and chests puffed out. Victory was yours if you could make it to the end without getting tongue-tied.

What comes to mind when you think of peace? For most of my life, I thought of the twenty-third Psalm, "He makes me to lie down in green pastures; He leads me beside the still waters. He restores my soul (v. 2–3a)." I equated peace with the gentle moments of life. Peace was cloud gazing in wildflower meadows or sitting with my family around a cozy winter fire. It was moments of natural happiness and contentment—when all was right with the world.

Disability has forced me to up my game. A passive peace just won't cut it anymore. I need to be able to harness peace even when it does not make sense. I need a peace that can withstand adversity and help me live victoriously when everything is going wrong. I want a next level peace that is powerful. *I need peace that passes understanding.*

What does this version of peace look like? Peace that passes under-standing (PPU) enables you to reach beyond the parts of your story you don't understand and rely on God's character. It is remaining calm when the doctor says, "You have cancer," because you know that your Father is going into battle with you. It is facing day after day of chronic pain in dependence on the Lord's strength. PPU is being able to sleep at night when your medi-cal bills are piling up, sure that God will provide a way. It is believing that the Lord is for you when all the test results are against you. It's electing to hope, when you are at the end of your own problem-solving abilities, in God's promise for a better tomorrow. Peace that passes understanding fuels you forward.

Reread Philippians 4:6–7. These verses outline healthy habits that can help us develop this transcendent form of peace. First, we are instructed to bring *all* our requests to God when we're anxious. Tell him about your backache, heartbreak, or how hard it is to find a palatable gluten-free birthday cake. No worrisome thought is too small or embarrassing to bring to his notice. You can never burn him out, nor will he tire of you (Jer 31:3). Your Heavenly Father cares about your entire well-being—attending to every detail of your life as if you were the only person in his universe.

Secondly, peace that passes understanding is promised to us when we present our requests to the Lord with *thanksgiving*. Praise is counterintuitive when we are laying raw hurts at God's feet. But give it a try. Reach out in trust. There is something in your situation to be thankful for, even if it is only that God is in control of it. Express wonder that his love is more power-ful than any problem you encounter. Thank him for sending his son so that you don't have to walk through this alone. Or voice gratitude for the gift of his Holy Spirit who inhabits you and gives you strength.

In addition to applying these peace-inducing practices, I specifically ask God to give me peace that passes understanding. Because as hard as I have tried to improve my habits over time, I still struggle with anxious thoughts. Thankfully, God meets me where my efforts fall short. He gladly gives PPU when I ask for it. This gift proves his presence in my life, because my own efforts are not strong enough to manufacture such an unshakeable peace in my spirit.

Peace that passes understanding is God's gift to you too. Ask him to ground you. "He will keep in perfect peace all those who trust in him (Isa 26:3 TLB)."

God,

I need your help this day. My life feels like it is spinning out of control, and I don't know how to get the help I need. But you know all of my needs and you see a way for me. Thank you that my life is in your hands and that you are by my side. May your peace eclipse the facts and fears of my situation. Please give me your peace that passes understanding. Amen.

Chapter 34
Mustard Seed Faith

. . . Truly I tell you, if you have faith as small as a mustard seed, you can say to this mountain, 'Move from here to there,' and it will move. Nothing will be impossible for you. —Matt 17:20

SCRIPTURE DESCRIBES FAITH AS "being sure of what we hope for and certain of what we do not see (Heb 11:1)." The eleventh chapter of Hebrews is a crash course on faith and gives a running account of how God worked through the lives of his people. My favorite verse features Moses who "persevered because he saw him who is invisible (Heb 11:27)."

To me, this is the root of faith, seeing beyond our circumstances as we look to the one we know to be faithful. Sometimes our hearts perceive what our eyes cannot see. I long for this type of living faith—a faith that trusts in God's goodness, even when life has confiscated my dreams and I can't find a way out of trouble. But trusting in God can be difficult when you feel broken beyond repair.

Good news waits at the grocery store. The next time your faith feels a little wobbly, hunt down some mustard seeds. Take a look at one of those suckers. It is tiny—no bigger than a pinhead. Yet Jesus said we only need faith the size of a mustard seed to move a mountain.

God can do a lot with a little. I am convinced that when we pray and ask God to help us believe in him, he sees it as an act of faith. It is a small step, but it still takes trust.

Travel with me to Mark 9:14–29 to meet a desperate father: a man whose son has been demon possessed since childhood. Pay attention to the father's words. He is breaking beneath the strain of keeping his son from self-harm.

Continual suffering has nearly extinguished his hope. Can you hear the weariness in this father's request? (*Context added.*)

> (*My son has been demon-possessed*) "Since he was a little boy. The spirit often throws him into the fire or into water, trying to kill him. Have mercy on us and help us, if you can."

> "What do you mean, 'If I can'?" Jesus asked. "Anything is possible if a person believes."

> The father instantly cried out, "I do believe, but help me overcome my unbelief!" —Mark 9:21b-24 NLT

The father readily admits to Jesus that he has doubts. It has crushed him to watch his son be tormented for so many years. He asks Jesus to help him believe with his last flicker of faith. Will this half-hearted request be enough?

Absolutely! Jesus knows how much misery this man and his family have been through; yet the father has not given up. If the man truly believed nothing could be done for his son not even his desperation would drive him to Jesus. Yet he shows up. He asks for help. And Jesus heals the boy in response to his father's mustard seed of faith.

Like the worn-out father, we do not always *feel* like we have faith. Sometimes life has just been too hard. But biblical faith is not an emotion . . . it is taking action to demonstrate your trust in God. Notice that every person commended in Hebrews 11 proved their faith through actions: Noah *built* an ark, Abraham *followed* God into the unknown, Moses' parents *hid* him, the Israelites *marched* around Jericho, Rahab *welcomed* the spies etc. However, if we dive into the stories of these heroes, they all experienced moments of fear, failure, or doubt. They used their mustard seed of faith to help them transcend their feelings.

Nevertheless, there is one important difference between these "Hall of Faith" heroes and the boy's father:

> All these people were still living by faith when they died. They did not receive the things promised; they only saw them and welcomed them from a distance, admitting that they were foreigners and strangers on earth . . . Instead, they were longing for a better country—a heavenly one. —Heb 11:13, 16a

The boy's father had the joy of seeing his son made whole, but many faithful Bible heroes died before seeing the entire fulfillment of God's plan.

I truly hope and pray that God heals you in your lifetime. But if you continue to struggle with sickness, it does not mean that your faith is weak. It takes an even greater faith to persevere after God's promises when you have endured a long wait. That is the faith of champions.

If you are clinging to faith by your fingertips, pray and ask Jesus for a mustard seed of faith. Give voice to the words of the boy's father, "I do believe, but help me overcome my unbelief (Mark 9:24)!" This simple request is a stand of faith. It is an action that honors God. He will nurture your mustard seed of faith until, like its namesake, it grows into a strong and vibrant tree.

It is like a mustard seed, which is the smallest of all seeds on earth.
Yet when planted, it grows and becomes the largest of all garden
plants, with such big branches that the birds can perch in its shade.
—Mark 4:31–32

Chapter 35
Revelation of God's Love

And I pray that you, being rooted and established in love, may have power, together with all the Lord's holy people, to grasp how wide and long and high and deep is the love of Christ, and to know this love that surpasses knowledge—that you may be filled to the measure of all the fullness of God. —Eph 3:17b-19

CAN YOU IMAGINE THE God of the universe showing up genie style to grant you one wish? That is exactly what happened when Solomon became the King of Israel (1 Kgs 3:1–15). God comes to the new king in a dream and offers to give Solomon anything his heart desires. What a coronation gift! God is pleased when Solomon asks for wisdom to lead his people. What would you request?

My first instinct is to cry out, "healing!" But the longer I've fought this battle in my body, the more I have considered this question. In order to live my life abundantly for God, there is something I need at an even deeper level. I need to be free from fear.

Can you visualize a life without fear? I am not talking about a fearlessness that is reckless, but rather a boldness that is rooted in an unshakeable confidence in God. Imagine having no concerns about the needs of today or stress about your to-do list. Envision never losing sleep over what you could lose or how you might miss out. What would it be like to have no anxiety about the future? To never feel insecure about your identity or unreasonably worried about disappointing others? What if you could try anything because you were not afraid of embarrassment or personal failure. Is such a life possible?

1 John 4:18 says, "There is no fear in love. But perfect love drives out fear, because fear has to do with punishment. The one who fears is not made perfect in love." *The secret ingredient of a fearless life is ever-increasing revelation of God's perfect love.*

So I am praying for revelation of who I am in the eyes of God—that he helps me see myself radiantly clothed in robes of Christ's righteousness (Isa 61:10). I am asking the Lord to increase my understanding of how he will withhold no good gift from me, because he has already loved me with an intensity that nailed his One and Only Son to the cross (Rom 8:32).

I am issuing an invitation to the Holy Spirit to help me wrap my heart around a Heavenly Father who knows all my shameful secrets, yet has chosen me to be his child anyway. I want my friendship with the Lord to be more real than the air I breathe or the food I eat. Therefore, I am praying for a continual revelation of God's love—so complete—that it changes my perspective on hardships and gives me the courage to embrace every opportunity the Lord brings.

How paradigm shifting would such intimate knowledge of God's love be? If I could grasp how deeply the Father loves me, it would be like being given wings to soar. I'd have absolute freedom. I would be unstoppable.

The thought of truly seeing God—by knowing him for all he is and growing to better understand his limitless love . . . leaves me breathless. Sometimes I wonder if this is even possible on earth or if this revelation is in itself heaven. But if God ever shows up to grant me one wish, I am requesting an ever-increasing awareness of his perfect love. Scratch that. I'm asking for revelation of God's love anyway. Will you join me? For a life unhindered by fear would surely be paradise.

> *Jesus,*
>   *Continually reveal your perfect love to me. Help my heart to grow in understanding of your love every day of my life—until I am absolutely fearless. Amen.*

Chapter 36

The Benjamin Button Prayer

Even youths grow tired and weary, and young men stumble and fall;
but those who hope in the Lord will renew their strength.
—Isa 40:30–31

IF YOU DEVELOPED YOUR health condition at a young age, the Benjamin Button Prayer is a prayer of encouragement especially for you. Grab some popcorn and raid the pantry for your candy of choice—you and I are going to the movies.

The Curious Case of Benjamin Button is a fictional tale about a man who is born old. Benjamin begins his life as an eighty-year-old child and ages backwards through adulthood until he dies as an infant.[1] It is hands down one of the strangest movies I have ever seen. Brad Pitt and Cate Blanchett give impressive performances, but I left the theater in 2008 hoping to forget the image of a wrinkly old kid.

Fourteen years later, I am still thinking about "young" Ben with his elderly exterior. I relate to the character now. Since my disabilities began when I was in my early twenties, I often feel like I am missing out on my youth. Most people my age are starting their first jobs, taking trips with their spouses, and planning their future families. I am being told I can apply for disability, traveling to see out-of-state doctors, and taking it one day at a time. I should be in the prime of my life, but I feel like an old woman. It is just not fair!

One truth helps me cope . . . the Bible is full of Benjamin Buttons. Many of the Lord's chosen instruments faced years of adversity as young or middle-aged adults. Every time I learn about a new Bible character who falls into this pattern, I feel less cheated by the present and more hopeful about

---

1. Fincher, *The Curious Case of Benjamin Button.*

177

my future. Check out these Bible bigwigs and the hardships they endured *before* God did a significant work in their lives:

- *Sarah (Abraham's Wife)*: Despite God's vow to bring forth his chosen nation from Sarah and Abraham, she was barren. Years after God's promise (menopause too for that matter) Sarah gives birth to Isaac at ninety! (Gen 17:17)

- *Joseph*: Joseph's brothers stage his death in order to sell him into slavery. Then he is falsely accused of rape. Mercifully, an encounter in prison paves the way for Joseph to become Pharaoh's second in command. His rapid ascent allows him to save Egypt (and the family who betrayed him) from famine. (Gen 37–46)

- *Moses*: Commits murder and leaves his life as an adopted Egyptian prince behind. He flees into the desert and works as a shepherd for forty years. Moses is eighty years old when God sends him back to Egypt to rescue the Hebrews. (Exod 7:7)

- *Ruth (The Moabite)*: Leaves her homeland to follow her mother-in-law to Israel after both of their husbands die. With no men to farm their land, the widows face an uncertain future dependent on the kindness of others. But God provides a kinsman redeemer to marry Ruth. Their son was the grandfather of King David. (Ruth 1–4)

- *David*: Samuel anoints David the future King of Israel as a teenager, but King Saul refuses to accept that he has been fired by God. For many years, David hides in the wilderness to escape Saul's persecution. Then he fights a civil war against Saul's son for the throne. He is thirty-seven years old when he finally becomes the King of Israel and Judah. (2 Sam 5:4–5)

You and I are in good company if our lives have not started out well. For God's people, prolonged hardship regularly comes before a unique calling. Lamentations 3:27 NIrV says that, "It is good for a man to carry a heavy load of suffering while he is young."

Our calamities can be a classroom and place of preparation—they are the advanced course. God allows our limits to be challenged so that we will look to our teacher for wisdom and strength. As we problem-solve with him he equips us for special vocations. The students with the most promising futures go through the most rigorous training.

This is good news for those of us who have struggled at a young age. While many people mourn the passing of their youth, we have something to anticipate. The heart of the Benjamin Button Prayer is believing that your life is on a unique course with the best yet to come. It is taking a stand to say that you are not going to miss out because—like quality wine—God is making you better with age. May we one day describe ourselves with the same words the Bible uses to describe Job, "The Lord blessed the latter part of Job's life more than the former part (Job 42:12)."[2] Let us pray:

> *Oh Father,*
>
> *It is incredibly difficult to suffer during what should be the best years of my life. So I pray that the prime of my life is still ahead. Grant me my youth! I thank you that you can alter the natural course of life for your children. As I grow older, may my life bloom with health, joy, purpose, and fulfillment. May I be increasingly astonished by your goodness. Amen.*

For "young at heart" readers who are wondering if there is anything to look forward to in your twilight years, Job has an encouraging word for you too. Job 33:4 says, "The Spirit of God has made me; the breath of the Almighty gives me life." Every breath you take is made possible by the grace *and gift* of God. As long as you are breathing, God has a plan and a purpose for you. His goodness is a reason to believe in a brighter tomorrow.

Regardless of the date on your birth certificate, fix your hope on Christ by asking him to renew your strength. It may not come in the package you would prefer. Sometimes God increases our physical stamina: other times he revives our spiritual strength. But one way or another Jesus has promised to empower you. May you find that—in the words of my most recent P.F. Chang's fortune cookie— "What you once thought was impossible, will be possible."

Jesus looked at them intently and said, "Humanly speaking, it is impossible. But with God everything is possible." —Matt 19:26 NLT

---

2. Job is an Old Testament character who is known for his suffering. The book of Job chronicles his hardships and God's eventual deliverance from them.

Chapter 37
Pray for Fulfilled Desires

[God] satisfies your desires with good things so that your youth is renewed like the eagle's.—Ps 103:5

THINK BACK TO YOUR childhood. What did you want to be when you grew up? In my earliest years I bounced between aspiring to be an artist, ballerina, or mermaid (Disney's *The Little Mermaid* was released the year after I was born. Under the sea seemed good to me). Around age ten, I traded in my mermaid tail to follow in my mom's footsteps. I wanted to be a public-school teacher.

I never lost that conviction. I threw myself into tutoring, babysitting, camp counseling, children's church, and peer health education to get practical experience with children. I loved relating to kids and seeing the light turn on when they learned something new. Supervisors and parents repeatedly reaffirmed my dream by telling me that I had a natural gift with children. Yes! This was my purpose. Teaching was what God made me to do.

Narcolepsy symptoms appeared my senior year of college. The shift was dramatic. My energy plummeted and I spent nights terrified by vivid dreams. I would wake up unable to move (a narcolepsy symptom called sleep paralysis). My heart raced without warning (POTS). I battled dizzy spells and struggled to stand as I sporadically lost feeling in my legs. Student teaching was a nightmare but it was too late to switch majors. When I was diagnosed a year later, I knew that my dream job was out of reach.

How could God allow this to happen? Hadn't he nurtured this desire? Why would he take my purpose away?

Nothing has ever shattered me like coming to terms with the reality that I could not teach full-time. After six months of treatment, I was well enough to take a part-time job. I started teaching the four-year-old preschool class at our church—three hours a day, three days a week.

I am ashamed to admit that at first, I felt like the job was a waste of my education. (In my Elementary Education major, preschool teachers were considered glorified childcare workers rather than educators. How ignorant we were.) I accepted the position to spend time with children and to help ease the financial burden on Parker's shoulders. My part-time salary only came to four hundred dollars a month, but at least it was something. I went into the job feeling like it was a substitute for what I really wanted and like my dreams had been downgraded.

Praise God, I have never been more wrong. I quickly realized that I had *way* underestimated preschool teachers. Single-handedly wrangling eight four-year-olds gave me the challenge I longed for. It took intelligence to solve multiple problems at once, the stage presence of an entertainer, and lots of Paw Patrol stickers to keep everyone learning. My little tadpoles (I had the frog- themed classroom) were a breath of fresh air and gave me a renewed sense of purpose.

I blossomed in my new role and fell in love with teaching preschool. Surprisingly, it was a much more appropriate fit for my natural abilities and personality. At preschool I could unleash my creativity and connect with students on a more personal level. We sang the Penguin Hokey Pokey, played twister to learn body parts, and colored with our toes on Dr. Seuss Wacky Wednesday. I loved that I could teach the way I wanted to and didn't have to worry about being fired for hugging a student. I even went to birthday parties and met families at the zoo during the summer.

Best of all, I could tell these children about God. We acted out memory verses, read Bible stories, and prayed. Every day I told them how special they were to Jesus: that they were smart, funny, beautiful, talented, and irreplaceable in his eyes. The opportunity to sow these seeds of God's love has been the greatest honor of my life. I pray that these truths are cemented in the hearts of my students always.

Putting my classroom to bed that first summer, God reminded me that I had once told a friend, "I wish there was a job where you could just love people." Ironically, developing narcolepsy gave me that gift. I never would have considered preschool as an option before illness struck. Yet here I was, investing in the spiritual lives of my students and sharing more love than I ever would have been able to as a public-school teacher.

Seeing God turn my biggest disaster into a pathway for fulfilling the desires of my heart lifted so much of the weight of disability. Yes, I still have bad

days. I still get frustrated with my body's limitations. I absolutely hope that
God will heal me one day. But the beautiful outcome of seeing your desires
fulfilled is that even when your body is struggling, your heart can still be
light.

Pray and ask God to fulfill your desires. Then keep your eyes wide
open, because he may not do it in the way you expect. God knows you and
me better than we know ourselves. Now, if I had the choice between public
school and preschool . . . I would choose preschool every time.

> *Good Father,*
>
> *You see and know the desires of my heart. The hardest part
> about sickness is that it makes my desires feel out of reach. But
> nothing is out of reach for you. You made my heart and put these
> good desires in me. Make a way for my desires to be fulfilled and
> lead me in the path you have prepared for me. Amen.*

Chapter 38
Ask for a New Dream

See, I am doing a new thing! Now it springs up; do you not perceive it? I am making a way in the wilderness and streams in the waste-land. —Isa 43:19

IN THE MARTHA vs. Mary debate, I am a Martha through and through.[1] I would rather work than rest (a continual challenge since my body also thinks I am Sleeping Beauty). My mental gears are always busy mapping out the day (let's get real . . . the next ten years of my life). And nothing makes my Martha-self thrive like working towards an objective. Goals are essential to my mental health.

Five years into my marriage, I began to wonder, "What now?" Pre-disability my timeline read "Babies!" (Complete with woodland nursery graphics and a list of essential children's books.) Now there was just a big blank. I felt lost without a goal to invest in.

Psalm 37:4 teaches, "Take delight in the Lord, and he will give you the desires of your heart." This verse is both a reassuring promise and an invitation into the unknown. God can "give us the desires of our hearts" by answering a long-treasured yearning. (For example, when he used preschool to fulfill my desire to teach.) But at other times, God "gives us the desires of our hearts" by teaching us to want something new. Did I trust God enough to ask him to shake things up? Would he respond by planting a new dream in my spirit that matched his will for my life?

---

1. Luke 10:38–42: Mary and Martha were sisters whom Jesus visited. Martha was stressed out about everything she wanted to do to serve Jesus. Mary chose to spend time with Jesus. Jesus said Mary made the better choice. "Martha" is sometimes used as a term for someone who is hardworking and driven.

It was worth a shot. I cried out to the one who made me with all my Martha tendencies:

God, if it is not time for me to be a mom, I need a new mission. Please give me a new dream!

Remarkably, something new was born. God began urgently pressing my heart to write down all the comfort he had given me in my struggles. It wasn't much to go on, but I threw a notebook in my purse. I jotted down ideas in parks, in the grocery store parking lot, and at doctor's offices. I even slept with a pad of paper by the bed to scribble down thoughts that popped into my head as I dozed off.

I gathered my notes a year later. What the heck did God want me to do with them? I openly wept in amazement as the revelation hit home: God had given me the means to write the book I once searched for.

As I pen these words, I still do not know what will become of this work or how it will get into the hands of others. But I have faith that God's plan is incredibly good. Already this new dream has breathed life back into my spirit and taught me so much about Christ's love. It blows my mind how much God has changed me through adversity and how many tools he has provided to see me through this season. Every page is a reminder of how faithful he has been to me.

The writing itself is a beautiful mystery. I don't understand how a single creative thought comes out of my brain fog or how God's peace transcends the cheese grater moments of trying to put his thoughts into words. I marvel that he chose such a weak vessel for this deeply personal partnership which has made Jesus so real to me. The sense of Christ's strength enabling the work is unlike anything I have ever known. If it took me five years to write anything else, I would have given up *long* ago. Yet, God keeps building excitement for this dream in my heart.

It is my dearest hope that this book validates my struggles by helping millions of disabled readers live victoriously in Jesus. I want everyone who fights an exhausting battle against a health condition to know that their life has worth and value to God. What a redemption story that would be! But regardless of the form the end product takes, I have been incredibly blessed by the process.

Has your chronic condition limited your options? If you find yourself wondering what to do with the blanks in your timeline, then start praying for a new dream. Pay attention to the fresh desires that begin to take root in your heart. Ask God to open your eyes to the plan he envisions for your life.

What has he dreamed for you? By adopting God's desires, you invite the more exciting future—because he dreams in colors you have never dared to imagine.

> *Lord Jesus,*
> *Give my heart an exciting new dream to cherish. Thank you that your plans for me are good and that your dreams always exceed my own. May I catch your vision. Amen.*

P.S.   When a desire is unmet, it does not necessarily mean that it is not part of God's plan for your life. Often God just puts a desire on hold. So while you are waiting, don't let an unbalanced focus on the future rob you of God's plans for you this day. He can give you purpose and joy in your current season.

Chapter 39
When You're Ready—Pray Big

The measure of God's abilities will always surpass the measure of our
audacity. No prayer is too big for our God.
—Pastor Steven Furtick, Sun Stand Still

PRAYING BIG IS DIFFICULT when your heart is discouraged. During my first few years of disability, there came a point when I couldn't pray for healing anymore. Every unanswered prayer was a letdown. Alternating between high hopes and intense disappointment slowly crushed my spirit. It was just too painful. The healing prayers were fueling my anger with God and my frustration with life. So, I switched gears out of necessity and began praying for God to help me in the midst of suffering.

If the rollercoaster of disappointed hopes has made you too heartsick to pray big prayers today, please know that God understands your pain. His word acknowledges that "Hope deferred makes the heart sick (Prov 13:12a)." God also promises that he is "close to the brokenhearted and saves those who are crushed in spirit (Ps 34:18)." If survival prayers are all you are capable of praying right now, Jesus is full of compassion for your distress.

Now that I have a decade of disability under my belt, may I encourage you? The time will come when your pain is less raw and when you have learned to cope within your limitations. As unbelievable as it sounds, the time may even come when you begin to recognize ways that God has blessed and strengthened you through your disability. But for this conviction to be genuine, it cannot be premature or rushed. There is truth in the cliché that "time heals many wounds." Once you find acceptance, you will be able to revisit the scale of your prayers.

My friend Amanda (a Type-1 Diabetic) recently inspired me to reexamine my prayers when she shared:

When I pray, I don't just ask God to heal my diabetes. I ask him to send a cure for all diabetics. You have been fighting complex medical issues for years. When I pray for you, I pray for a miracle.

What a stunning and selfless faith. It had been three years since I prayed for healing, and her words were a powerful call to arms. Was I ready to pray "big" again? Did I still need a strict diet of "survival prayers only" to safeguard my heart? Would praying for healing hurt if God didn't deliver? The only way to find out was to try.

So I prayed for a miracle. I prayed for a cure. I prayed for God to wipe all disability from the face of the earth. I prayed to wake up tomorrow morning to find myself transformed into the human Energizer Bunny. And I felt . . . peaceful.

Time has given me the gift of perspective and trust. During those years of being unable to pray for healing, I learned that God could give me abundant life in the midst of suffering. Now that certainty enables me to ask God to work miracles on my behalf without fear of how he is going to follow through. Because whether God chooses to heal my condition or change my mental mindset towards disability—*either way he is working a miracle.* He will bless my life if I am healed. But he will also bless my life if I am not.

Looking to God for survival moved the knowledge of his love from my head to my heart. Jesus is my safety net. Even if I am chronically ill for my entire life, he will redeem my suffering for good. This sets me free to hope in healing without risking huge emotional fallout. I can make bold requests for my future while finding contentment and purpose in my present. His love gives me the strength to hold onto these two co-existing truths. Because in either possibility, Jesus is waiting.

> *Blessed Jesus,*
> *I pray that there comes a day when we all are able to pray "big" prayers. When the security of your love frees us from fear of disappointed hopes. And as we see your love in all of our future scenarios, may this assurance allow us to boldly approach your throne. Amen.*

Now to him who is able to do immeasurably more than all we ask or imagine, according to his power that is at work within us, to him be glory in the church and in Christ Jesus throughout all generations, for ever and ever! Amen. —Eph 3:20–21

P.S.   Reverend Mark Mofield once heard someone say to a hurting friend, "Let me believe in God's promises enough for both of us until you are ready to believe in them yourself." One of the most valuable acts of friendship or caregiving is to lift up another person's place of hurt. True friends faithfully step into the breach and offer prayers that have become too painful/stressful for their loved ones to voice. Memories of God answering years of my secret prayers for others are among the most joyful moments of my life. This is a significant act of service you can offer others, regardless of disability.

But most of all, I would like to thank each and every prayer warrior who has prayed for my healing at times when Parker and I could not. Thank you for your priceless act of friendship. Your tenacity on our behalf is a gift we treasure. We look forward to the day when we can all shout for joy because of the "gracious favor granted us in answer to the prayers of many (2 Cor 1:11)."

Chapter 40

Pray to Remember Disability

Remember that you were slaves in Egypt and that the Lord your God brought you out of there with a mighty hand and an outstretched arm. —Deut 5:15a

WERE GOD'S CHOSEN PEOPLE, the biblical Israelites, just a bunch of whiny complainers? I have often thought that if I were able to see the miracles they witnessed, my faith would be unshakeable. They had a front row seat to God taking down the Egyptians in epic blockbuster style. *Kapow!* Hailstones. *Eek!* Frogs in the futon. *Shazam!* Bloody beverages. *Timm-berrr!* Cows kicking the bucket. And the grand finale? A footpath to freedom through the parted Red Sea.

It is unbelievable how in the span of one month, the Old Testament Israelites go from praising God for delivering them from slavery to accusing him of sending them into the desert to starve. How could they already take their freedom for granted? Do they have short-term memory loss? Are they blind? God is *literally* leading them with a cloud by day and pillar of fire by night (Exod 13:21). How can they question God's ability to bring them into the promised land with this visible proof of his presence right before their very eyes? Where is the gratitude? Where's the trust?

As I gain more life experience, I see that I too have the heart of an Old Testament Israelite. I spend hours praying for help only to devote seconds to my "thank you" when it comes. I quickly forget the ways God has given me freedom and take his blessings for granted again. I make idols for myself when life becomes comfortable and praise the work of my own hands. Then new challenges arise and I quake in fear because I fail to remember God's past deliverance. Oh fickle, fickle, wayward heart!

I am so thankful that God overlooks my shortcomings because of Christ's mercy. It's clear that I need his mindset to keep my present perspective in check. And when I imagine a future of improved health or complete healing, I realize that I will need balance then too. I will need the balance of remembrance.

I want to remember everything about being disabled. The unfathomable depth of grief as I came to terms with a life I did not want or choose. The lonely years I spent craving companionship when I was too exhausted to reach out to others. The feelings of complete failure as I watched the dreams of the wife, teacher, and mother I wanted to be crumble. The diminishment of having my abilities, interests, and goals stripped away and how insecure that made me.

I want to recall the bodily distress of dehydration and the terrible irony of starving while surrounded by food. The hundreds of episodes of cough a day, the mountains of tissues, and how I needed God's strength to accomplish basic household tasks. The bone weariness that sets in after years of downward spiraling health and how I was physically and emotionally driven to the brink of my endurance. The constant worry of being a burden to others and how terrible it was to wonder if I was going crazy because my symptoms were so strange. How I was so afraid and uncomfortable that I sometimes unfairly lashed out at those I love.

I want to remember all of these horrible feelings so that I never take a single one of God's blessings for granted. Every health improvement is a gift I have cried and longed for. It is easy to feel entitled to good fortune when all you know is blessing. But when you live through a hellish season, "normal or boring" suddenly looks like heaven. Comparison is a powerful motivator.

Remembering what God has brought me through makes me overflow with gratitude. My eating has improved enough in the last year to allow me to reintroduce some foods. I never thought I would say prayers of thanksgiving specifically for avocados, kidney, and lima beans. Or find myself breaking into the "Hallelujah Chorus" over a cup of popcorn. But I find myself praising God for these simple pleasures as if they are priceless treasures.

If such profound joy is the outcome of these smaller improvements, how would it feel to be completely healed? Believe me when I say . . . it would feel like being raised from the dead. Even imagining it brings tears to my eyes.

On that day, I want to remember how far into the darkness God reached for me. I want to vividly recollect how it felt to be imprisoned by my own body so that I can minister to those who are still suffering with compassionate insight. I want to encourage them with the words I most wanted to hear. If I forget how it felt to struggle, I will no longer be able to minister meaningfully.

When life becomes easier, most of all I want to remember that God did not abandon me to trouble. He stood at my side strengthening me until together we could stand against disability. May I always remember that he never let go of me in the darkness until he opened the way to the light.

Holding these memories close will give me the courage to face whatever new challenges lie ahead. Jesus is the deliverer who has rescued me time and again and he will walk with me into the promised land.

What do you want to remember when your day of healing comes?

> *Lord Jesus,*
>
> *Help me to see your redemptive mercy and goodness at work in my life this day. Enable me to joyfully focus on the present while I continue to hope for healing. Teach me to fully appreciate every improvement in my health. And if the day comes when you heal my chronic illnesses, help me never forget my years of struggle.*
>
> *I pray for remembrance: so that I may truly value your blessings, find contentment in all circumstances, effectively serve those still hurting, and courageously follow wherever you lead. You are my Savior both now and forever. Amen.*

Part 7

Seeking God When You Are Suffering

One thing I ask from the Lord, this only do I seek: that I may dwell in the house of the Lord all the days of my life, to gaze on the beauty of the Lord and to seek him in his temple. —Ps 27:4

Introduction:
Celebrating Chapstick Kissing Explorers

STOP! THIS SECTION OUTLINES ways to grow your relationship with God during seasons of suffering. But to be honest, I didn't have the energy to actively pursue spiritual growth during my first few years of disability. It was all I could do to keep holding on.

If you are too overwhelmed to add one more thing to your plate right now, *that is okay*. There is still good news for you. God's redemptive grace can "upcycle" your hardships and use them to spark spiritual growth (Jas 1:2–4). Adversity opens your eyes to how "God is your safe place and strength. He is always your help when you are in trouble (Ps 46:1 NLV)." God has *already* positioned you to make spiritual progress.

Respond by taking refuge in the arms of the God who has promised to never let you go (John 10:28–29). If that is all you have strength for this day . . . *it is enough*. Relax, take a breath, and come back to this part when you are ready. For now, cha-ching! You have a free pass to go to "Part 8: Transformed Through Trials." Go in peace.

Who is still with me? Congratulations! You are officially a Chapstick Kisser. Say what? You heard right—a Chapstick Kisser.

Everyone has lovable quirks. One of my husband's is that he absolutely hates the feel of Chapstick. I, on the other hand, could single handedly keep Burt's Bees in business. I try to remember to kiss Parker goodnight before I turn my lips into an oil slick, but I occasionally forget. What does my anti-Chapstick spouse do?

Parker dives under the covers and jokingly feigns sleep—but he always emerges (usually of his own accord). Instead of a reluctant grossed out peck, he wraps me in his arms and gives me a tender goodnight kiss.

These are some of Parker's most meaningful kisses. Each one tells me that he values me more than he abhors Chapstick. It is a powerful way to pucker up.

You, my friend, are a next level Chapstick kisser. You have gone way beyond Chapstick to pursue God through cancer, Parkinson's, or paralysis. Can you imagine how much God treasures your desire to push past serious obstacles to forge a deeper connection with him?

This passion should be a source of hope for you. Disability has not so thoroughly beaten you that it has snuffed out your desire to draw nearer to God. It also proves that you are his because he continues to call to your heart and give you the strength to follow his voice (John 10:3–4). Your persevering response delights him.

Cling to this truth as an anchor. Hold it tight. When my life careened into the uncharted waters of chronic illness, I felt lost at sea. I could not relate to God or spend time with him in the ways I was used to. I needed God to teach me a new way to navigate life and approach our relationship. Yet without my established routines, I struggled not to drown beneath the belief that I was disappointing God. Would seeking him in unfamiliar ways weaken our connection?

Quite the opposite! Disability made my time with God different, but it also made it more dynamic. Outside of my comfort zone, he gave me a fresh perspective on how to seek him. It is journeying into the unknown with Jesus that strengthens our understanding of who he is.

Channel your inner explorer and shake up your routines. In this section you'll discover comforting insights that will expand your definition of "God-time," flexible strategies for serving others, and tips for staying connected to the body of Christ. Try something different and fix your eyes on the horizon. Every explorer knows that you must leave behind what is familiar to discover something new. Will you adventure into the depths of God's love?

You will seek me and find me when you seek me with all your heart.
—Jer 29:13

Chapter 41
Simply Show Up

Rejoice always, pray continually, give thanks in all circumstances; for this is God's will for you in Christ Jesus. —*1 Thess 5:16–18*

WHO LOVES YOU THE most? As your strongest relationships come to mind, consider: How do you know that they love you? What evidence do you have of your bond?

God blessed me with a husband who loves me completely. I remember the day that I knew he loved me—before he ever said the words. It was actually pretty scary. In a tranquil lake date turned horror movie, we were wading to shore when we noticed our legs looked hairy. They were covered in small leeches.

Be still my heart and strike me dumb! An axe murderer may as well have jumped out of the woods. One look at all those blood sucking parasites and I was paralyzed from fear. I couldn't even scream.

Parker saw my wide eyes and jumped into action. He ignored his own leeches and stooped to gently pry over fifty leeches off my frozen form. Hell became heaven as I thought, "Sweet Lord Jesus, please let me marry this man!" It was the sexiest act of selflessness ever.

I thank the Lord for answering my lakeside prayer, because Parker has only been getting sexier. Now I tear up when I think about the birthdays that he has spent coaching me through uncomfortable medical tests and all the dinners he has made after a hectic day at the office. I marvel at the countless ways he daily lives up to the promise he etched inside my wedding ring: "Husbands, love your wives, just as Christ loved the church and gave himself up for her (Eph 5:25)."

Who comes in at the top of your list? Perhaps you are thinking about a parent who delayed retiring so that you could graduate from college debt free. Or the neighbor who uses her own sick days to drive you to doctors' appointments. Aren't the people who truly love you the ones who are always there for you? Even when you are throwing up, freaking out, or moving for the fifth time?

Love shows up. Proverbs 17:17 teaches that a "friend loves at all times." The most powerful love is present when it isn't easy or convenient. Our core relationships are founded and nourished by these moments—moments when someone chose us despite the obstacles. Sacrifice deepens relationships because we appreciate that love is an action and a choice. Our most meaningful relationships are with those we can count on to be consistent and committed.

DOES SHOWING UP *REALLY* MATTER TO GOD?

The guiding verse of this chapter says that it is God's will for us to "Rejoice *always*, pray *continually*, give thanks *in all circumstances* (1 Thess 5:16–18)." Translation? God says whether you are celebrating or disappointed, "Come, rejoice." If you feel inspired or inadequate, "Come, pray." In seasons of blessing and brokenness, "Come, give thanks." Whether you are weak, strong, fearful, hopeful, distracted, or focused, still he always calls: "Come!"

I think it is safe to assume that God wants us to show up. Some of my most precious moments with God have been the result of a decision to worship when I am weary, worried, or even confused. I've shown up—not from a legalistic fear of disappointing God—but because my need to connect with him outweighs the obstacle in my path.

Worshipping when I am weak can look radically different from my routine "God time." Sometimes all I have left in the tank is the energy to read a Bible verse or listen to a single worship song. At my absolute worst, I simply utter a one-word prayer: "Help!"

Occasionally nothing seems to happen. But I have more often been surprised by how intensely I encounter God's presence as he meets me in my smallest steps. When I rise above my feelings and point my feet towards home, God responds as the father of the prodigal son did in Jesus' parable (Luke 15:20–24). Seeing his exhausted child struggling towards him from afar, he kicks up his heels and sprints with reckless abandon to close the distance between us.

If you give God your all ~~even~~ *especially* when it's small, you send heaven a mighty message. You proclaim God as the one significant constant in your life. You acknowledge that knowing him is everything. You declare that he is more important to you than your moods or even your ability to understand the circumstances of your life.

Best of all, this wholehearted pursuit delights your Father (Deut 30:10). He celebrates your perseverance as he rejoices over you. In an ecstatic mad dash, he runs to catch you up in his loving embrace.

WHAT'S THE DIFFERENCE BETWEEN SHOWING UP AND TRYING TO EARN GOD'S LOVE?

Showing up is not about trying to win points with God. You can't score more of his love by attending every outreach event or earn extra likes by worshipping when you're worried about paying doctors' bills. Whether you spend your Saturday night partying or praying, you won't one-up your neighbor for God's affection. Nor can you memorize enough Bible verses for God to give you the extra sparkly pair of angel wings he's reserved for his favorite. If that were possible, I would clothesline you for those babies.

Earning God's love is impossible because it has already been given to you. Through the death and resurrection of his perfect son he has given you a love that is flawless. Your devotion will not increase his already limitless love and your mistakes cannot diminish what is everlasting.

I've been a Christian for over thirty years and I still have to regularly remind myself that I don't have to earn God's love. Such purity of love is foreign to the patterns of our worldly relationships where we compete for favor and recognition. Regardless of our actions, God loves all of his children. Yet it is obvious that some people share a closer connection with God than others. How can all of this be true?

It helps me to think about the relationships a caring parent has with their grown children. Good mothers and fathers love their children equally. But the relationship they have with one child may look very different from their bond with the other. It all depends on how their son or daughter responds to their love. Every relationship is a two-way street that requires investment from both parties to keep it growing healthy and strong. The degree to which a child spends time with, shares interests with, and includes their parent in their adult life will determine the depth of the connection.

Likewise, showing up is about including God. Revelation 3:20 promises:

> Here I am! I stand at the door and knock. If anyone hears my voice and opens the door, I will come in and eat with that person, and they with me.

Jesus will always be near to us. He stands knocking at the door of every heart. But it is up to us to open it.

Whenever you push past struggle to worship, pray, or seek God's guidance, you invite Christ's presence into your life. He will respond to this loving sacrifice by infusing your relationship with an unprecedented richness. In his perfect timing, you will be blessed for every small step you make towards him. So keep up the good work! Because, just in case you did not realize it, *today you showed up.*

Come near to God and he will come near to you. —Jas 4:8

Chapter 42

Focus on Being with God
vs. Doing for Him

*Love the Lord your God with all your heart and with all your soul
and with all your mind and with all your strength. —Mark 12:30*

IF I COULD HAND you a snapshot of the first twenty-one years of my Christian life you would see me owning my walk like Tyra Banks. Alright, perhaps that is a bit of an exaggeration. But I diligently tried to be a model Christian who ticked all the right boxes: I was at church every Sunday; spent fifteen to thirty minutes of God time each day; routinely volunteered for service projects; helped lead worship; and began my second read-through of the Bible all before graduating High School. At least I could have rocked some jeans in a Sears catalogue.

Now? I question whether my Christian life could even land me a spot in the background of a truck stop billboard. I am lucky if I have the energy to physically attend church once a month and I have days when I'm too tired to spend more than thirty seconds in prayer. I struggle to read my Bible through eyes blurry with fatigue, and in order to conserve energy for helping my husband with the housework, I've stopped volunteering.

The guilt of not being able to fully participate in my church activities initially shredded my identity. It also clued me in. Despite believing my service came from my love for God, deep down I had made our "relationship" a checklist. There was a part of me that still believed I had to prove myself worthy of God's love and that craved approval from other Christians. Would God still want me now that I needed to do things differently—when I was often homebound and unable to serve him like I had in the past?

Praise God that his emphatic answer is *"Absolutely yes!"* Our God is a superb paradox. We are nonessential to his existence. He tells us that "he is not served by human hands, as if he needed anything. Rather, he himself gives everyone life and breath and everything else (Acts 17:25)." Yet, he wants us just the same. Through the intensity of Jesus' love, we are highly prized as God's children and treasures (1 John 3:1, 1 Pet 2:9 TPT).

Discouraged doers, do you know what this means? The pressure is off. God doesn't need you to *do anything* for him because he has already *done everything* for you. When Jesus made us right with God, worship, prayer, Bible study, and service were transformed from *obligations* to *invitations*.

I began this chapter with a verse known as the greatest commandment. But as you reread Mark 12:30, I challenge you to think of it as your greatest invitation. What type of relationship does Jesus want to have with you? What visuals does this caliber of love and commitment bring to mind?

I hear Christ calling us to a love that is all consuming. He is inviting us to fall in love with him. What would that be like? Perhaps you've been blessed enough to find true love on earth through a spouse or a child. If so, you know that thoughts of your loved one are always on your mind. They trump and influence all other thoughts. In the presence of your loved one even the most mundane task can bring you joy. (I remember being thrilled to spend time with Parker when he needed help cleaning his college apartment for a move-out inspection. There is zero doubt you have fallen in love if you are excited to scrub a bachelor's bathroom.)

As years pass and true love matures, you face life together. Your love has your back in trouble, shares the honor of your successes, and comforts you simply by his/her presence in times of sorrow. You make important decisions together. And when making everyday choices, you consider the preferences of your beloved. Love transforms two individuals into a united team.

This is the type of relationship God wants you to have with him. A steadfast bond that encompasses every part of your being as you fall forever deeper for the lover of your soul. Defining Christian identity as "doing for God" cannot create this type of bond. Religion simply isn't a substitute for relationship. It takes the time investment of being with someone, sharing life's experiences and challenges, allowing them access to your vulnerabilities and dreams, and going all in to forge this kind of lasting love. Even *before* Jesus became our sin offering, he agreed that a vibrant relationship with God "is more important than all burnt offerings and sacrifices (Mark 12:33)."

That is the best piece of news I've received since Croissant and Doughnut mailed a baby announcement for Lil' Cronut—especially since chronic illness has put a decided crimp in my Christian activities. In finding myself less "busy" for God, I began "being" with God. I started seeking him in chaos, in quietness, in loneliness, while watching tv—including him in my entire day. I am sharing my thoughts with him, listening for his voice, and inviting his presence whether I am singing praises or doing dishes.

The impact of finding Jesus with me—even elbow deep in suds—can only be summed up with one word: *revolutionary*. I spent twenty-one years doing for God and calling him "Father." But now that I have stopped *doing for him* long enough to actually *be with him*, I am finally able to call him "Friend."

If you have too much pain to endure the car ride to a church service, can't sing his praises without choking on reflux, or skip communion due to Celiac disease, know this: the most important part of being a Christian is for your relationship with God to be your highest priority. Holy habits, patterns, and routines are tools for entering God's presence, but Jesus himself advocated for "nurturing relationship before doing what religious ritual requires (Matt 5:23–24)."[1] It can be appropriate to make adjustments in difficult seasons.

God has unlimited creative potential to nourish your relationship despite any limitations life throws at you. Exchange doing *for* Jesus to do life *with* him. He is your safe harbor. Spend time quietly in his presence. Ask him to teach you about who he is. Pray that you learn something new about his character every time you read his word or take a walk outside. Establish being with God as the defining factor of your relationship. Because above all else, he wants to be with you too.

For God so greatly loved and dearly prized the world that He [even] gave up His only begotten (unique) Son, so that whoever believes in (trusts in, clings to, relies on) Him shall not perish (come to destruction, be lost) but have eternal (everlasting) life. —John 3:16 AMPC

---

1. Reverend Mark Mofield

Chapter 43

Place Importance on Internal Transformation

Though outwardly we are wasting away, yet inwardly we are being renewed day by day. —2 Cor 4:16

I WAS FINALLY LEARNING how to walk in God's grace as a chronically ill Christian. I was simply showing up to invest in my relationship with God and that was all good. But just when I felt tentatively prepared to give myself a timid pat on the back, I ran into the Great Commission.

"Go into all the world and preach the Good News to everyone (Mark 16:15 NLT)." This is our Christian mission. (Not to mention Jesus' final instructions before ascending into heaven.) It has always been my privilege to partner with God in advancing his kingdom. But as I considered Jesus' command in context of disability . . . *thwump!* Like a guillotine, guilt severed my newfound peace. My head began rolling with questions. Have you ever thought . . . ?

> *How will I share the gospel when I am mostly homebound? How can I build relationships with non-Christians when my social circle is shrinking with my limitations? God, I want you to use me as an instrument of your love. So why have you benched me? Have I produced anything worthwhile during this season or has chronic illness been a giant waste? How can I be fruitful in suffering?*

If you are worried about how you are going to spread the gospel when you're suffering, take three calming breaths. Three breaths to remind you that Sir Isaac Newton's third law of motion states, "For every action there is an *equal and opposite reaction.*" (Thanks Mom, all those years of watching you prep science experiments for your fifth graders paid off.)

Hidden within Newton's scientific principle is a spiritual application: *when you cannot see God working outwardly through you, he may be accomplishing an equally important work inside of you.* If it is not your season for winning converts, it may be your season of inner conversion.

For me, chronic illness felt like someone violently stripping me naked of the outward markers of my identity. It takes time to surface after such an assault. But God has gradually shown me that more than my body is changing. Outwardly I face many hardships, but inwardly God is connecting me to stores of hope, perseverance, and trust that I did not know he'd put in my heart. As my strength fails, I learn to look to God for his. When I can't reach others for God, he is reaching into me to teach me about the depths of his love, the unfailing nature of his promises, and that nothing is beyond the scope of his resurrection power. It is during this season of marked physical inactivity that God has most actively changed my character.

Are you in the middle of this frustratingly fabulous metamorphosis? It's frustrating because we tend to value external evidence of how God is working through our lives over internal transformation. We like what we can measure. We can track the hours we have spent witnessing, tally up our tithe, and record the quarts of soup we've made for a homeless shelter. These easily recognizable indicators reassure us that we are playing an important role in God's plan.

But is there a measuring cup for hope? How can we quantify perseverance or gauge resiliency? Where can we find scales to weigh growing faith? Our inner progress is difficult to see when compared against outreach. It has a decidedly less glamorous production value, which is why many of us have trouble recognizing our own inner transformation as an equally significant work from God.

God's values are different. First Samuel 16:17 teaches that "People look at the outward appearance, but the Lord looks at the heart." God sees past our outer pretenses to our innermost hearts. Here's how much he cares about the character he finds there:

> "I the Lord search the heart and examine the mind, to reward each person according to their conduct, according to what their deeds deserve." —Jer 17:10

Our character is so important to God that he examines our hidden motives and agendas *before* we are rewarded for our actions. *Yikes!* If you have attended church long enough, you've heard a sermon about how faith without action is dead (based on the principles found in James 2). But the reverse is also true: actions performed in poor faith (bad motives) are cheap and self-serving. Take a minute to read and consider the outcomes from these two Bible stories:

- Gen 4:1–7: Cain and Abel
- Acts 5:1–11: Ananias and Sapphira

At first glance, it appears the actions of both parties are worthy of respect. Who doesn't love a giant fruit basket? Or would thumb their nose at a generous church donation? But Cain, Ananias, and Sapphira's gifts were spoiled by the pride eating away at their cores.

Scripture doesn't specify the motive behind their actions, but we can make an educated guess from our knowledge of human nature. Perhaps Cain reasoned that he should keep the best fruits for himself. Surely his crops were more the result of his own toil instead of God's blessing. Ananias and Sapphira were probably more concerned with impressing their friends with a veneer of generosity, than actually cultivating charity in their hearts.

God was displeased with both offerings because they were marred by the motives of the givers. Their gestures were hollow because their hearts were not in it. Jesus doesn't want self-serving "sacrifices"; he desires our wholehearted devotion and actions prompted by genuine faith.

Inner transformation comes first. It is being remade in the image of Christ that empowers us to reflect him to the world. Second Peter 1:4 tells us that if we want to "participate in *[God's]* divine nature" we should,

> . . . make every effort to add to your faith goodness; and to goodness, knowledge; and to knowledge, self-control; and to self-control, perseverance; and to perseverance, godliness; and to godliness, mutual affection; and to mutual affection, love. For if you possess these qualities in increasing measure, they will keep you from being ineffective and unproductive in your knowledge of our Lord Jesus Christ. —2 Pet 1:5–8

God wants your spirit to be fully stocked with the fruit of his Holy Spirit so that his kingdom can advance. These qualities are essential to your arsenal and his mission. It's worth learning how to wield these wonderful weapons because an army is only as strong as its soldiers. The time a soldier spends training, developing skill, and honing strength and stamina becomes an advantage on the battlefield.

Do not belittle the importance of the internal. God is doing valuable work in this significant season of your life. He will use the patience, compassion, and trust you are gaining now to enable you to bless others at the next level. Internal transformation absolutely supports the Great Commission of your Commander and Chief.

But the fruit of the Spirit is love, joy, peace, forbearance, kindness, goodness, faithfulness, gentleness and self-control. Against such things there is no law. —Gal 5:22–23

Chapter 44

Tools to Increase Your Awareness
of God's Presence

*You make known to me the path of life; you will fill me with joy in
your presence, with eternal pleasures at your right hand. —Ps 16:11*

THESE HABITS HELP ME connect to God's presence and lift my thoughts to
his. I present them to you as tools to bring you joy, not as a to-do list that
you are being judged against. Sometimes all I can manage is #4, *Rest with
God.* Pick and choose your tools according to your daily needs, and remember that the possibilities for connecting with God are endless. This list is
simply a starting point. My prayer is that it inspires you to come up with
your own ideas to become more aware of Jesus.

1. KICKSTART YOUR DAY—PROCLAIM WHO GOD IS
AND WHO YOU ARE IN HIM:

Give this a try if you need a pick-me-up to face your day. Proclaiming who
God is, and who you are as his child, packs a more powerful punch than
anything you can percolate in your Keurig. This is an essential practice for
those mornings when you dread opening your eyes to the hard day ahead.

The proclamations I find most reassuring and effective spring from
biblical truths. Take ownership of God's word, speak it from a first-person
point of view, and use it to inspire your own praises. It is your birthright to
claim biblical truths because they are God's promises for you. Here are a few
examples of how to adapt a verse into a proclamation: *(*Denotes the Bible
verse that inspired each example.)*

The Lord is my light and my salvation. I will not be afraid. The Lord is the stronghold of my life. I am safe in his embrace. I can confidently tackle anything that comes my way today because he is by my side. (*Ps 27:1)

God has made this day, and he made me, his beloved child. My Father has good things waiting for me today. I will rejoice and be glad in it! (*Ps 118:24 NLT)

I delight greatly in the Lord; my soul rejoices in God. What's more? I know God delights in me because he has clothed me with garments of salvation and arrayed me in a robe of Jesus' righteousness. God sees me through eyes of perfect love, like I am a bride adorned with jewels. He says that I am beautiful, strong, capable, loved, and wanted. That is who I am! (*Isa 61:10)

I will admit, at first this felt halfhearted and forced. But as I continued to make this a practice, I gradually internalized these thoughts. One morning I woke up to find that my mind resounded with thoughts of faith instead of the usual paralyzing fears.

My mind may still flit to the challenges I'll be facing, but it has become much easier to reel it back in. Because underneath any frustration is the established conviction that—whatever awaits me today—God will also be waiting. He is my strength and has good plans for me. I rarely need to make these proclamations aloud anymore because they echo in my heart as my default mode. In repetition they became part of my identity.

Get your day off to a positive start by proclaiming God's awesome power and unending love for you. Then take this tool to-go! Use it anytime you are bombarded by negative thoughts to redirect your thoughts to God's truth. If you don't have a Bible with you, then speak biblical themes you know to be true. Developing intentional habits to center your thoughts on who God is and what he says about you matters more than precision. May speaking become believing.

2. MAKE SPECIFIC PRAYER REQUESTS WITH MEASURABLE GOALS:

Pray and ask God for help with small things that you want to accomplish or have happen today. For example:

- *God, give me a good belly laugh today.*
- *Jesus, help me to have the strength to go to work this morning.*

- *God, give me the energy to go for a walk outside.*

By "measurable goals," I mean that you want to be able to look back at your day and say with certainty, "God did that." Having a laugh, going to work, or walking outside are all actions. It is easy to tell whether or not God answered your prayer. Every answered prayer is valuable because it provides evidence of God's faithfulness towards you. Use these prayers as a training exercise for trust. It becomes easier to have faith that God is working on your behalf to answer more challenging/abstract requests (health, joy, peace, etc.) when you regularly watch him help you accomplish measurable goals.

3. TALK TO GOD THROUGHOUT YOUR DAY:

God is interested in your smallest concerns and finds you fascinating in your most mundane moments (Ps 37:23 NLT). Include him in your day by turning your thoughts to him often. Send up a quick word of thanks or a request for help. It doesn't have to be eloquent or time consuming. It can be as simple as, "God, your creation is beautiful," or "Please help me get the lid off this baby food jar." Consistently turn your focus towards God and you will become more aware of the intensity of his loving gaze upon you.[1]

4. REST WITH GOD:

On days that I am just too tired to actively spend time with God, I say this prayer:

> God,
>   *I am exhausted, but I miss you. Please come hold me here on the sofa and watch a movie with me. I know you are always with me, but I want you to know that you are invited.*

Wow . . . I could feel God's smile as I typed that simple childlike prayer. It delights him to know that his children want him. We all want to be included in the lives of those we love. God is no exception.

With those whom we love most, we want an all-access pass to their lives. (Even for the behind-the-scenes boring bits.) When you say "I want you here, even when I have nothing to give," it is a powerful proclamation of your belief in God's unshakeable love.

---

1. For additional ideas, revisit Chapter 28 "Quickly Connect Throughout Your Day."

So invite your Father into your weariness, beloved one. Rest peacefully in his arms.

Let the beloved of the Lord rest secure in him, for he shields him all day long, and the one the Lord loves rests between his shoulders.
—Deut 33:12

5. END YOUR DAY WITH THANKFULNESS:

Count your blessings if you want to be blessed. Every positive in your life is a reminder of God's love, protection, provision, and consideration. When I list my blessings in prayer or by writing in a journal, it reassures my soul that God is active on my behalf. I am able to fall asleep in peace as my fears retreat before this confirmation of God's tender care.

If you are having trouble thinking of blessings to count, remember you can always thank God for the blessings of his character. Thank him for sending Jesus and for the gift of salvation. Thank him for caring about you and for always being near. Even when you feel like you are scraping the bottom of the blessings barrel in your own life, you can praise God that the blessing of who he is never changes. His love is a constant to be thankful for.

Try making thankfulness a bedtime habit. Not only is it a positive way to end your day, but it is a practice with a promise for tomorrow. Thankfulness primes your mind to wake to hopeful thoughts. When your last thoughts are grateful, it is a strong ending *and* a secure beginning.

It is good to praise the Lord and make music to your name, O Most High, proclaiming your love in the morning and your faithfulness at night . . . —Ps 92:1–2

Chapter 45
Tips for Serving with Disability

"Instead, whoever wants to become great among you must be your servant, and whoever wants to be first must be your slave— just as the Son of Man did not come to be served, but to serve, and to give his life as a ransom for many." —Matt 20:26–28

SERVICE IS AN INTEGRAL and undeniable aspect of a fruitful Christian's life. Jesus was the King of Kings yet he considered service to be his greatest purpose. And he calls us, the heirs to his kingdom, to take up his cause.

Mine was always the first hand up when someone asked for a volunteer. I was a "can-do" kind of girl. But once I was on the side of needing help, I was shocked to discover that accepting assistance is by far the more difficult challenge for me. It is uncomfortable and deflating. It has been an exercise in humility to both admit my weaknesses and learn to graciously accept help from others.

I much prefer the euphoria that rewards the person who lends a hand. But helpers can only exist with someone to serve. It takes two for one person to experience that golden glow.

As fallible and fragile human beings, our lives are all a collection of moments when we are able to help others and when we need to receive help. The trick is being able to adjust to the role that your season demands of you. When you become disabled, it is tempting to think you have nothing to give. Don't buy into that lie. Being dependent on others does not exclude you from serving. You just have to get creative.

It can be a tremendous act of service towards your loved ones to focus on not falling apart (been there, done that — and let me tell you, it took a

Herculean effort). Or to refrain from biting the head off a team of nurses when it has taken over an hour to get an IV into your dehydrated veins. It's service when you choose to be uncomfortable with a substitute in order to give your caregiver respite time. In your intense seasons, God is honored when you simply choose to keep moving forward one moment at a time.

Don't be stressed or ashamed if adding one more commitment to your schedule is going to threaten your sanity. You are serving in the way you are able.

However, if you have achieved relative stability—if not normalcy—I encourage you to find a way to serve. Not only does it please God, but it is essential to your mental health. For me, serving others takes my mind off my own problems and boosts my self-esteem as I realize that I still have something valuable to give. We all need to feel like our lives have purpose.

But I have to serve differently as a disabled individual. The unpredictability of my symptoms makes it difficult for me to be involved in anything that requires a regular or reliable commitment. You too will have to learn to work within your body's limitations in order to serve smart. This takes trial and error, but I hope to save you a few bumps with tips I've gleaned from my own bruises. May they help you find ways to serve within your struggle.

1. GOD VALUES SERVICE WITHIN THE CHRISTIAN FAMILY:

Disability rapidly shrank my circle of friends and acquaintances. My ability to work, socialize, or even run errands is a fraction of what I was capable of as a healthy individual. Now I rarely interact with nonbelievers in my day-to-day life. Sure, I share the good news of Jesus with my preschoolers—but they mostly come from Christian families.

I began feeling ashamed that I wasn't making a difference in the lives of the lost. Yet how could I possibly take on more responsibility when it is a constant balancing act to have enough energy for Parker and my part-time job?

Thank goodness for the tender heart of God who encourages us through his word. Galatians 6:9–10 calmed my anxiety with a timely reminder that I was doing something worthwhile (*emphasis added*):

> Let us not become weary in doing good, for at the proper time
> we will reap a harvest if we do not give up. Therefore, as we have

opportunity, let us do good to all people, *especially to those who belong to the family of believers.* —Gal 6:9–10

Christ absolutely cares for the lost. But he *especially* values his family. Service on behalf of our brothers and sisters in Christ is significant. Each seed of godly truth I sow into my preschoolers' hearts strengthens God's family and contributes to the overall health of the church body.

Likewise, for the church to thrive as a strong spiritual family, it must be made up of strong nuclear families:

> When Jesus was asked what the greatest commandment is, he cited two: Love God, and love your neighbor. The closest neighbor you have is the spouse you sleep next to or the people in the bedrooms down the hall. —Rev. Mark Mofield

If the best you can do right now is supporting your spouse, that is the perfect place to start serving. You and I owe the quality of our lives to our caregivers. They deserve our best efforts because they daily sacrifice their own desires to selflessly provide for our needs. Every choice you make to help your immediate family protects their strength by lending them yours. Now they have a little extra in the tank for that moment when they need to reflect Jesus.

When we treat our spiritual and immediate families well, we show the world that God's family is a family like no other. We build God's kingdom by creating a vibrant, caring, and committed community that others want to be a part of.

By this everyone will know that you are my disciples, if you love one another. —John 13:35

If you want to change the world, go home and love your family. —Mother Teresa

2. PRACTICE INTERCESSORY PRAYER:

Simply put, intercessory prayer is praying to God on behalf of others. You are "interceding" for another by voicing their needs to God. Praying for others may not be a flashy way to serve, but it is powerful. Paul counseled Timothy (and by extension us):

> I urge, then, first of all, that petitions, prayers, intercession and thanksgiving be made for all people— for kings and all those in

authority, that we may live peaceful and quiet lives in all godliness and holiness. This is good, and pleases God our Savior, who
wants all people to be saved and to come to a knowledge of the
truth. —1 Tim 2:1–4

Intercessory prayer has a lot of points in its favor. Pleases God? Paul
says so. Changes the lives of those around us? Yep; blesses others with a little
peace and quiet. And for those of us who are trying to figure out how to
serve others during a season of personal suffering, intercessory prayer has
one major advantage: *it is extremely flexible.*

You can intercede for others anytime and anywhere. You can pray
whether you're wearing Prada, rocking a power suit, or still in pj's. It does
not matter whether you call on God from a car, chapel, or commode. You
can pray in a snatched 30 seconds or for a devoted 30 minutes. You don't
have to be part of a team or undergo any special training. No topics are off
limits. You can pray for governments, family members, non-believers, social
reform issues, or your Facebook friend's sick cat.

Prayers change our planet. You can impact the world simply by being
aware of the needs of others and intentionally praying on their behalf.[1]

3. SERVE SMART—TAKE ADVANTAGE OF YOUR GOOD DAYS:

My biggest hurdle to serving again was accepting the fact that I was no
longer reliable. I can regulate my body to an extent with medication, hydration, nutrition, and good sleep hygiene, but I still have unexpected flare-ups.
While I can make an educated guess, I never really know what a day will
hold until the moment arrives.

Smart service for me means getting creative to take advantage of times
when I am feeling good. I brainstorm on how I can serve as an individual
instead of relying on a team set up by my church. Planning ahead allows
me to give much more of myself because I can accomplish goals on my own
time table. Here are a few ideas to get you started:

- Many churches have call lists of people who are homebound or in need
  of encouragement. We understand this better than most people. Call
  and encourage someone who is lonely during your spare time.

---

1. For Bible verses about how prayers change our planet, see "Positive Prayer Principle #2—Prayer is Powerful Because . . . " in Appendix 2.

- Join a card ministry. Church card ministries send sympathy cards, cards of encouragement, and birthday cards. You can write a comforting or celebratory message ahead of time to have it ready and waiting.

- Do you spend a lot of time resting on the couch watching TV? Put that time to good use by asking your children's pastor if you can help cut out shapes for Sunday School or VBS. They will probably hug you. As a preschool teacher, I spend at least an hour a week pre-cutting.

- Cook a meal when you have the energy and freeze it. It will be ready to go when your neighbor is in the hospital or new parents need nourishment.

- Do you like putting together a shoebox for Operation Christmas Child? Put one together and wrap it at leisure in July. When holiday craziness rolls around, you only need to take it to church.

- If your hobby is painting or gardening, make someone's life more beautiful. Donate a piece of art or some flowers to a nursing home. By planning ahead, you can ask if there is a patient who doesn't get many visitors or who has a room that needs brightening up. Tailor something specifically to their interest.

    Keep in mind that the nursing home must protect patient privacy. Don't be offended if you cannot deliver your surprise. However, staff can often provide an idea of what a patient would like without compromising personal information.

4. TIPS FOR JOINING A TEAM:

I encourage you to start with one-time commitments. It is easier to complete these successfully because you can rearrange the rest of your week to optimize your chances of feeling good that day. It's much harder to work around a regular commitment.

However, if your heart is set on a permanent team, an honest approach will help you find the *appropriate* fit. You should be truthful and realistic with your team (and yourself) about your limitations from day one. Discuss how you can be an asset when you are able to participate.

In addition, trouble shoot to be prepared for times when your symptoms appear without warning. Create an easy back-up plan or choose to fill a role where the show can go on seamlessly without you. These measures demonstrate respect for your team and will help everyone have a positive experience.

Sometimes a team needs someone more reliable and that is ok! It is better for them to be honest with you from the beginning. Try not to internalize this as rejection—it just wasn't the right fit. Move on to find something more flexible.

The only way for me to finish this book was by leaving preschool. I needed more time to devote to the new dream that God had planted in my heart. But writing is solitary work. For my own sanity, I thought I should schedule something to get me out of the house and keep my teaching skills fresh.

At my mom's suggestion, I contacted the elementary school near my home about volunteering with a kindergarten class. I gave them my credentials and experience. I set the expectation that, due to health issues, I was hoping to volunteer for an hour a week on a flexible schedule.

The school paired me with the angelic Mrs. McMullen. I use the term "angelic" in all sincerity: Mrs. McMullen's easy-going nature allows me to share my teaching gifts without the stress of a teaching position. If I am feeling well, I come in and pull students who are falling behind for one-on-one practice. On bad days, I send her a text that I will see her next week. This doesn't disrupt the classroom flow because she has set me up as a support, not a necessity. In her own words, "You are a gift . . . I try not to expect you, but every time you are here it is a wonderful surprise."

Not many teachers can pull this off. But Mrs. McMullen's personality is the ideal fit for someone in my situation. She gains support for her struggling students and I experience the fulfillment of teaching without the pressure. When you find the appropriate opportunity, both parties will mutually benefit.

Chapter 46

Church and Community

We should think about each other to see how we can encourage each other to show love and do good works. We must not quit meeting together, as some are doing. No, we need to keep on encouraging each other. This becomes more and more important as you see the Day getting closer. —Heb 10:24–26 ERV

OFTEN SUNDAY ROLLS AROUND and I am too exhausted to attend church. However, being stuck at home doesn't mean you have to miss out on God. Technology has worked wonders for bringing church experiences to the homebound. Many churches make their sermons available online, but if you need a recommendation, I have included some of my best-loved pastors and worship bands in Appendix 4, "My Favorites."

Sermons and worship songs are not just for Sundays—use them whenever your spirit needs a boost. Download a sermon on your iPad or smartphone to listen to later in the car or while you are waiting for a doctor's appointment. Stream worship songs as background music for prayer or as an encouraging accompaniment while you do chores.

Appendix 4 also includes Bible study tools and my favorite devotionals for personal growth. They have all been a peaceful balm: inspiring me to hope at times when my spirit has been troubled. Many of the resources I list are written by authors who have my deepest respect because of their firsthand experience with disability or chronic illness. May God use them to comfort and encourage you.

I am grateful we can listen to sermons and worship online when we need it. That being said, I urge you to use them as additional resources and handle them with care because . . .

The church is a body of believers (1 Cor 12:12–31). While you may be able to find great content online, there is no substitute for in-person community. God made us to be sociable creatures. Even in the garden of Eden, God recognized that "It is not good for the man [*Adam*] to be alone. I will make a helper suitable for him (Gen 2:18)." We are designed for community, and Christian connections are crucial to our mental/spiritual health. I strongly advise you to join a local church and attend when your health allows it.

GUIDELINES FOR BUILDING CHURCH COMMUNITY AS A DISABLED INDIVIDUAL:

It can be nerve-wracking to enter a new social environment when your abilities/way of life has changed. I get it. I still dread being asked the question "What do you do?" because right now I don't have a traditional "job."

But the risk is worth it. Podcasts cannot pray for you, and no matter how fantastic the online sermon series was, it won't watch *Downton Abbey* with you when you are recovering from surgery. God has blessed me with some phenomenal friends during this season, and I met most of them through church. They are my extended family and the people I walk through life with.

Don't miss out on getting to know your fellow members of God's family! Once you decide to brave the butterflies, here are some guidelines that help me in new social settings:

1. Value Yourself:

Disability can make you feel very insecure—like you have nothing to contribute. But my mom always taught me that "there is nothing more attractive than confidence." It is true! People value those who value themselves. When you carry yourself with confidence, you send a message that there is something about you worth knowing.

Over the years, God has helped me fight many confidence battles to regain a sense of value. Together we have dealt with insecurities that made me overly sensitive to the slights/opinions of others. I have learned not to be embarrassed/ashamed of medical conditions and limitations that I didn't choose. I am more open about my challenges because God has shown me I have so much to offer in spite of, or in many cases, *because of* my experiences. Recovering my sense of worth began with valuing myself through

God's eyes. I made friends far more easily once I started loving/appreciating myself as a disabled person.

Additionally, church is a place where you belong. Christ has invited the poor, the crippled, the blind, and the lame to take part in his kingdom (Luke 14:15–23, Jas 2:1–5). The Bible proclaims that "those parts of the body that *seem to be weaker are indispensable* (1 Cor 12:22)." Not only has Jesus reserved you a seat, his word says that others will benefit from you being there!

When you feel like a burden, remember that Jesus calls you a blessing. Let his assessment of who you are boost your confidence as you go into social situations.

2. *Address the Elephant in the Room:*

My disabilities are mostly "invisible" to people who are around me for short periods of time. But I have a chronic cough due to reflux/esophageal dysmotility (trouble swallowing). I used to get embarrassed about explaining my cough and had my feelings hurt when people distanced themselves from me thinking I was sick.

Then COVID-19 happened. I had to be much more verbal about my cough if I did not want people to feel afraid. When I started coughing in church, I would simply tell my neighbors, "Don't worry, I am not going to get anyone sick. I have bad reflux." I could instantly see tension leave peoples' faces and their postures relax. Sharing became no big deal.

If you sense people are uncomfortable with your symptoms, set them at ease with a quick explanation and a smile.

3. *Allow Others to "See" You:*

Your medical condition is a challenge you are learning to live with—not who you are. When you are building community, let people "see" other sides to you. Tell people what you are passionate about, laugh over a funny memory or amusing YouTube video, or discuss your favorite book/sports team. Show others your thoughtful side by asking about their interests, take notes when you get in the car to drive home, and then follow-up with related questions the next time you see them. It always makes me want to pursue friendship with an acquaintance when they care enough to remember details about my life.

IDEAS FOR STAYING CONNECTED WHEN YOU ARE HOMEBOUND:

Sometimes disability or chronic illness requires us to be homebound for long periods of time. If you are in one of these seasons, it is wise to set up face-to-face interactions so you will have support and something to look forward to. Here are a few ideas:

- Many pastors will come (or send an elder/deacon) to give you communion when you are homebound. Contact your church about this possibility.

- If you have a close group of church friends, a small group, or are part of a Sunday school class, invite them to come watch the service with you. With a little creativity, there is a lot of flexibility for how this could work. If you are most comfortable with one or two people, your group may be willing to set up a rotation so you will see someone every week. Alternatively, perhaps the entire small group could come once a month. Give everyone a good experience by being respectful of your guests' comfort and time.

- When germ exposure is a concern, then absolutely embrace technology as a modern-day miracle. Make plans to discuss a sermon over the phone. Participate in an online Bible Study or virtual small group. This has never been more feasible than in a post-COVID world. Even my grandparents learned how to attend Sunday school via Zoom during the pandemic. I hope I am as tech savvy in my eighties!

- Send your pastor an *encouraging email* (no complaining) once a month. Thank them for a part of their sermon that spoke to you or lifted your spirits. Pastors have an extremely difficult job that puts them at high risk for emotional burnout. They need encouragement too! Staying in touch with the leadership of your church will help you feel more connected *and* help them think of you when you cannot attend in person.

Part 8

Transformed Through Trials

Now all of us, with our faces unveiled, reflect the glory of the Lord as if we are mirrors; and so we are being transformed, metamorphosed, into His same image from one radiance of glory to another, just as the Spirit of the Lord accomplishes it. —2 Cor 3:18 VOICE

NOTE TO READER:

As we begin the final leg of our journey together, let us remember that God does not cause our suffering (1 John 1:5). He never punishes his beloved children with sickness or uses it as some sort of psychotic teaching tool. Instead, suffering is a symptom of the brokenness of this world (1 John 5:19). Jesus warned in John 16:33 that "In this world you will have trouble."

Just don't stop there! For Jesus' very next words proclaim, "But take heart! I have overcome the world."

Jesus overcame our eternal suffering by taking the punishment for our sins upon himself (Isa 53:5). Furthermore, our loving Father has placed a time limit on sufferings' earthly reign (Rev 21:4). In the interim, we have a promise to hold on to. Jesus has already broken the power of suffering within a believer's life because he has turned the tables on our trials. Romans 8:28 says "that in all things God works for the good of those who love him, who have been called according to his purpose."

Jesus turns our troubles into opportunities to spiritually triumph. He redeems our pain and calls it purpose. Believing in Christ's love is our key to overcoming (1 John 5:5). Jesus is still the Resurrection King (Heb 13:8)!

Introduction:

Harness the Harvest

Dear brothers and sisters, when troubles of any kind come your way,
consider it an opportunity for great joy. For you know that when
your faith is tested, your endurance has a chance to grow. So let it
grow, for when your endurance is fully developed, you will be perfect
and complete, needing nothing. —Jas 1:2–4 NLT

HOW MANY CHURCH TESTIMONIES have you heard about mountaintop experiences? As Christians, we use this metaphor to revel in our pinnacle faith moments. These are the moments when God feels near enough to touch; as if you could stretch out your finger like Michelangelo's Adam and greet him E.T. style. Seasons so overflowing with God's goodness—you feel high on heaven's blessings.

Later alligator. I for one could float off on a cloud of euphoria just imagining mountaintop moments. But let's put a pin in that bliss and picture ourselves on the summit of a real mountain. Take a good look around. What do you actually see?

The jagged snow-covered peak around you is startlingly bleak. While the view is fantastic, the ground beneath your feet is barren. You spot the timberline thousands of feet below, but there is little life at your current elevation. Low temperatures, water locked inaccessibly in ice, and harsh winds stripping the boulders of soil deprive plants of the resources they need to grow. But from your bird's eye view, you can see that the valley glows green with life.

A green valley? That doesn't seem right because valleys symbolize our most difficult seasons. After all, it is descending the mountain that causes temperatures to rise and additional rain to fall on the land. Who wants to turn up the heat on their problems or weather more storms?

But as you head down the mountain trail, nature testifies that these are the right conditions for growth. Scrubby alpine plants and grasses give way to dense forests and wildflower meadows. The growing season lengthens, while the soil beneath your feet becomes rich and fertile. In direct contrast to the mountaintop, the lowlands teem with plant and animal life. Growth abounds in the valley.

ATTENTION VALLEY DWELLERS:

I have been a valley dweller for over a decade now. How about you? Living in a prolonged valley season is a challenging task. Did you ever envision yourself here? I certainly didn't sign up for chronic illness. To have a helpful conversation about how God can transform us through trials, we must acknowledge our honest human response to suffering. Frankly, growing is extremely painful. Valley growth coexists and evolves with complex emotions.

I've lived in the lowlands long enough to know that emotions have a valid role in the grieving process. It would be entirely inappropriate of me to belittle your pain by looking for the "bright" side of your circumstances when I have not lived through them. I have felt callously written-off, dehumanized, and even more alone when I was on the receiving end of such "help." I refuse to send you on your way by slapping a silver-linings Band-Aid on your suffering.

But I do hope it encourages you to hear how I have been transformed by disability. For many years I used God's promise from Romans 8:28 (*And we know that in all things God works for the good of those who love him, who have been called according to his purpose*) as a way to gloss over and run from my problems. I thought God would get rid of everything that wasn't good in my life. But there came a day when God broke through my grief enough to show me the heart of this promise. He is not guaranteeing an *escape from* our troubles, but a *way through* them.

God will not let the lives of his children be wasted, and I am staking my hope on his character. He loved me fiercely enough to give his one and only son for me. Therefore, I am convinced he would never allow me to suffer this much if he didn't have a plan to bring something far more precious *and* extraordinarily magnificent from it.

So I have made a decision: if I am going to be stuck in this valley, I want to harness the transformative power of my trials. I'm going to harvest them for everything they're worth. I am rolling up my sleeves and asking God tough questions:

What purpose is God working to achieve through my disabled life? What can I learn in the valley that I couldn't on the mountaintop? If I dig past my disappointed expectations, does chronic illness come with advantages? How has disability transformed me and influenced my understanding of God?

The final part of this book is a realization of how my chronic illnesses have spiritually shaped me. It is a genuine celebration of how my relationship with God has become exceedingly more vibrant in the valley. I feel like Jesus has steadily been opening a door to let light into a dark room. With increasing revelation, he is showing me how much I have changed and convincing me that my trials are opportunities. Each one can produce a harvest of joy.

However, no one could rush me to this point. Nor could I force my own grieving process to yield to the positive attitude I expected of myself as a person who takes faith seriously. My future prayer for you is that God opens your eyes in his perfect timing; That he dazzles you by completely redeeming your experience with disability or chronic illness.

Today, it is my prayer that the evidence of my own transformation ignites hope in your heart that it is possible for you too. May you begin to ask God your own tough questions.

In all this you greatly rejoice, though now for a little while you may have had to suffer grief in all kinds of trials. These have come so that the proven genuineness of your faith—of greater worth than gold, which perishes even though refined by fire—may result in praise, glory and honor when Jesus Christ is revealed. —1 Pet 1:6–7

Chapter 47

Difficulties Can Draw You
Closer to God

*The Lord is close to the brokenhearted and saves those who are
crushed in spirit. —Ps 34:18*

THE NEXT TIME YOU are gathered with a close group of family or friends ask,
"At what time in your life have you felt closest to God?"

Prepare to be surprised by what you hear. Until you have your own opportunity, my family invites you to time travel to Christmas Eve 2016. Join
us around my grandparents' fireplace for a little authorized eavesdropping.
As you pop marshmallows into your cocoa, my dad begins:

> When I needed open heart surgery at fifty-two, I could not stop
> thinking about how my father died at that same age. I was ter-
> rified I wouldn't get up from the operating table. The morning
> of the procedure, I woke to find an angel standing beside my
> hospital bed.
>
> I cannot even begin to describe the expression on the angel's
> face. It radiated God's love with a tangible intensity. The very air
> around me felt alive with warmth, and I knew everything was
> going to be ok. That one smile left a deep impression of God's
> care that carried me through six months of recovery.

My mom gestures to the quilt around her shoulders,

> When I had breast cancer, God's comforting embrace settled
> around me through the arms of his church. Friends drove me to
> doctors' appointments, mowed our lawn, and provided meals.
> I didn't even have to cook once during the year I had chemo
> treatments. It felt like being wrapped in a blanket of love.

Mema nods knowingly,

> God was my constant companion when I broke my femur and spent four months in a body cast. It was miserable to be helpless when I had a husband and three young children relying on me. Anxious to be back on my feet, I got up before my femur had fully healed. I broke it again. God was my only protection from complete despair. Day after day his spirit encouraged me that we could do this . . . together.

The fire crackles as my Grandaddy clears his throat,

> A few years ago, I was working beneath a friend's truck when the jack slipped. Four thousand pounds of steel crashed down on me. I could feel my skull starting to split as I cried out "Jesus!" At his name, the truck raised up just enough for me to scoot out from beneath it. My friend witnessed it and couldn't explain how I escaped being crushed to death. I am a dead man walking, by God's grace.

Joyful tears in our eyes, we shift our attention to Parker,

> God has faithfully comforted me each time Shannon and I have been lonely strangers in a new city. Developing quality friendships requires a time investment of shared experiences. That is challenging when your time is limited by chronic illness or caregiving. But God's taught me that he can provide for all of my needs, even while I am waiting on the blessings he has promised.

Take a minute to consider the similarities between my family members' stories. Do they reflect mountaintop moments? The thrill of spiritual highs, weddings, or births? No! Everyone in my family felt nearest to God in moments of pain, fear, and helplessness—moments when they needed a Savior.

Secondly, did you notice that four out of five of my relatives spoke about periods of prolonged struggle? They felt God's presence more tangibly during the most difficult months and years of their lives. There is something special about connecting with God in valley seasons.

THE MAGNETISM IN THE MESS:

How can our difficulties bring us closer to God? Is Jesus drawing nearer to us? Or are we reaching out for him?

Jesus promises to be with us always (Matt 28:20). He is especially concerned for the brokenhearted and for his children in trouble (Ps 34:18, Ps 9:9–10). He is accessible to everyone and knows each of us with startling intimacy (Luke 12:7). We can count on Christ's pursuit of us to be constant.

But my pursuit of God is far more changeable. It varies to accommodate my schedule, is bounded by my limitations, and fluctuates with my moods. Does this describe you? If Jesus' love for us never wavers, then perhaps it is our response that makes him feel closer or farther away.

Human beings often behave like magnets. Try this demonstration if you have two double-sided magnets on your fridge.

Let one magnet represent you and the other God. Every magnet has a positive and a negative side. Because God is always good, lay his magnet on the table positive side up.

What happens when you approach God with the positive side of your magnet? Feel the resistance? When your life is in a positive place, do you sometimes resist God's attempts to draw you closer because you are relying on your own resources?

For me this is not even a conscious choice . . . I still want to be growing in my relationship with God. But prior to disability, I had never faced a situation that could not be resolved by my own strength or with help from family/friends. As a result, I viewed God as a beloved resource instead of as an absolute necessity.

I was completely blindsided in my early twenties when I developed health problems that I was powerless against. I felt like Paul when he wrote to the Corinthians that:

> We were under great pressure, far beyond our ability to endure, so that we despaired of life itself. Indeed, we felt we had received the sentence of death. —2 Cor 1:8–9a

If verse 9 stopped with there, I would have been in a pitiable place indeed. But God's word continues . . .

> *But this happened that we might not rely on ourselves but on God,* who raises the dead. He has delivered us from such a deadly peril, and he will deliver us again. On him we have set our hope that he will continue to deliver us . . . —2 Cor 1:9b-10

Flip your magnet to the negative side and approach the positive God magnet. Do you feel the pull to come near?

Extended seasons of battle can position us to seek relief from God because there is magnetism in our messes—opposites often attract. In our weakness we depend on Jesus' strength. Facing life's uncertainties, we reach for his unfailing love. When others abandon us in the midst of trouble, we run to the one we know we can count on. Let go of your magnet and watch it cleave to the Father's side!

A SHIFT IN PERSPECTIVE:

My friend Amanda caught me off guard recently when she shared, "Shannon, I envy you."

Puzzled, I countered, "For what?"

Her response gave me pause:

> You know that I seriously injured my back a few years ago. Even though I was in pain and angry, I felt like God was so near to me during that season. Now that I'm better, I miss the closeness.

Reflecting on Amanda's words, I realized that disability has drawn me nearer to God than I ever thought possible. He used to be my life coach, but now he is my life's breath. I have always worshipped him for saving my soul, but now I sing his praises because he daily resurrects my life. Only Jesus could teach me to find joy in circumstances that should have crushed me.

I am in constant need of him and he is my "ever present help" moment by moment (Ps 46:1). Prayer connects us throughout the day as I ask him to help me get up, to have energy for work, to be able to swallow my food, to drive safely, etc. I have many days when I know that these simple tasks would be impossible without his strength. Every need he meets increases my awareness of how he is closer than I can imagine.

Amanda, thank you for reminding me that my intimacy with God is an advantage of the adversity I face. I was struck dumb by your challenge to think from the perspective of healing because it came with a shocking revelation. I realized that if God were to suddenly heal me, I would miss the closeness too.

Support systems falter. Loved ones don't always get your struggles. But Jesus always understands you *completely*. He is present in your pain every time. God's sympathetic ear is forever tuned to your cries and he refuses to let you fight alone. He will shoulder your grief when it is too intense, complex, and unpredictable for others. You cannot burn out his patience or his love for you. You will never tax his strength, there is no catch to his comfort, and there is no limit to his peace. It is Christ *alone* who perfectly understands your suffering. He is your most intimate friend.

Apply my husband's words from 2016 to your relationship with your Heavenly Father: "Developing a quality friendship requires a time investment of shared experiences." Dependence on God is not a disadvantage. It can be the catalyst that vibrantly enriches your bond.

In all their suffering he also suffered, and he personally rescued them.
In his love and mercy he redeemed them. He lifted them up and
carried them through all the years. —Isa 63:9 NLT

Chapter 48

Strengthened by Struggle

We can rejoice, too, when we run into problems and trials, for we know that they help us develop endurance. And endurance develops strength of character, and character strengthens our confident hope of salvation. —Rom 5:3–4 NLT

I HAD THE INCREDIBLE privilege of growing up on the Outer Banks of North Carolina. Born to a paradise of sea turtles, dolphins, and windswept beaches, I fell in love with God's beautiful world the moment my toes touched the sand. However, my very first memories are of the trees.

Live oak trees grow along the Southeastern Coast of the United States. Mature individuals have crowns spreading over one hundred feet and dominate their landscapes. Limbs as thick as trunks of lesser trees dip like wooden waves over the ground before gently sloping towards the sky.

My cousins and I preferred these majestic monsters to the playground equipment in our neighborhood park. We scampered among the branches pretending to be Pocahontas, pirates, or spies. Even as an adult, these giants overwhelm me with a desire to swing into their branches and let out a Tarzan yell.

The price of living in paradise is hurricanes—nature at her full fury. I have seen my dad (who is six feet of carpenter muscle) struggle to remain upright against winds of ninety miles per hour. At one hundred and forty mph, gusts can pick up limbs and drive them through pine trees like stakes. My teacher's house blew into the ocean during hurricane Isabel, and once water completely surrounded our sound-side home. I had to blink twice to make sure I wasn't dreaming when a neighbor paddled past our house in a kayak.

Surviving hurricanes is a particularly risky business for trees. Few species can withstand gale force winds, saltwater spray, and flooding. Just try drenching the next houseplant you want to murder with saltwater. It will shrivel up like a slug.

Yet special adaptations have allowed the Southern Live Oak to thrive in this harsh environment. Their leaves and roots have evolved to withstand salt. Low lying branches of dense foliage form protective windshields which route gusts over the trees. Deep roots anchor them to the earth and spread out into broad networks reaching even further than their branches. Impressive. But the most notable item on this formidable trees'resumé? Live oaks are famous for their strength.

Historically, live oak was the material of choice for wooden battleships. In 1794, it was used to build the USS Constitution. This ship has the honor of being the oldest commissioned naval vessel still afloat and you can tour her in the Boston Harbor. The USS Constitution is aptly nicknamed "Old Ironsides" because just one cubic foot of her dried live oak body weighs sixty-three pounds.[1] Live oak is clearly the unrivaled choice for hardest oak species when you consider that the runner up (Oregon White Oak) only weighs fifty-one pounds per dried cubic foot.[2] What is the secret to the live oak's strength?

HONED BY HURRICANES:

Live oaks are strong because they have spent their lives fighting hurricanes. They are nature's monuments proclaiming that God can use storms to make us stronger. Just like athletes must push their physical limits in order to increase their stamina, the oaks of the Outer Banks embody the "no pain, no gain" principle.

Your faith—or spiritual fitness—will also grow in response to stormy/ sweaty conditions. Pastor Steven Furtick puts it like this:

> Faith is like a muscle. To make a muscle strong, you work out. You push, you pull, you provide resistance with weights. Without resistance your muscles won't grow stronger, and neither will your faith.

1. Meier, "Live Oak," line 5.
2. Meier, "Oregon White Oak," line 5.

Trials offer the resistance you need for spiritual strength training. When your boundaries are tested, you have the chance to work out exactly who God is and what you can accomplish through his strength.

I just wish my faith could look like Thor's abs after one crisis crunch. But six pack abs don't show up overnight—that level of strength requires regular rigorous training. Likewise, live oaks must resist storms as saplings in order to develop the strength they need to withstand hurricanes as giants.

I feel a kinship with my favorite trees when I consider how life's storms have weathered me. Ten years ago, a single diagnosis of narcolepsy felt like a nightmare ripping my world apart. Fast forward through multiple disorders and only dealing with narcolepsy sounds like a dream. If all of my disorders had manifested simultaneously at the beginning of this unexpected journey, I honestly think I may have been put in a mental institution.

Instead, God used each fight to prepare me for the next battle. Like my oaks, Jesus has helped me adapt to make the most of this harsh way of life. He's taught me to lie low in prayer and in his protective presence when the winds blow their fiercest. To reach my roots down deep into his word and be anchored by his promises. To broaden the ways I experience him and increase the circle of family and friends I invite to pray for me.

Each hurricane I weather leaves behind new evidence of God's kindness towards me. And as this collection grows, it enables me to face the next storm with less fear. I find myself increasingly believing that,

> God is faithful; he will not let you be tempted beyond what you can bear. But when you are tempted, he will also provide a way out so that you can endure it. —1 Cor 10:13

THE FUTURE FORECAST:

That does not mean I am eager to spot more hurricanes on the horizon. This sapling would welcome some sunny days. It comforts me to know that Mother Teresa—one of the giants of our faith—shares this sentiment:

> I know God will not give me anything I can't handle. I just wish that he didn't trust me so much.

Respect for your transparency, Momma T. Your honest comment encourages me that you can both love God wholeheartedly *and* wrestle with gain that comes through pain.

However, to play devil's advocate against my saintly sister: I believe we often face challenges that are beyond our ability to cope with in our own strength. But when life gives us something we cannot handle, God gives us himself. He is the only one strong enough to bridge the gap of our inadequacies. First Corinthians 10:13 is clear that it is God's faithfulness and the power of his Holy Spirit within us that keeps us from being overcome. He is the one who opens doors for us when we are tempted to lose hope. He empowers us with peace. He is the source of our strength and the secret to every success.

God is our difference maker. He can bring triumph out of every tempest we encounter (Romans 8:28). It may take time to see beyond the storm clouds. But if we hold tightly onto our Father while we wait for the sun to rise, he will use what was meant to break us to make us more resilient. The hurricane will leave us standing stronger than if there had never been a storm at all.

Guess what the Bible says we will become? "Oaks of righteousness, a planting of the Lord for the display of his splendor (Isa 61:3b)." Ahhh-ahh-ahh-ahh (Tarzan yell), hallelujah!

You are their glorious strength. It pleases you to make us strong.
—Ps 89:17

Chapter 49
Crazy Gratitude

Every good and perfect gift is from above, coming down from the
Father of the heavenly lights, who does not change like shifting
shadows. —Jas 1:17

WHAT IS THE MOST hilarious "thank you" you have ever offered to God? During my severe digestive issues, I was writhing in bed with an abdomen painfully bloated with gas. I had only eaten a single cup of soup that evening, but hours later my stomach was still ballooned up. I looked like an expectant mother ready to give birth. Suddenly, I felt an overwhelming compassion for beached whales.

I cannot even describe how explosive the pressure felt. My muscles were too weak to expel the gas through my colon. Instead, I had been burping every thirty seconds for over three hours. I wished that I could become a cartoon, pop my stomach with a knitting needle, and fly around the room as I deflated. Through tears, moans, and gritted teeth, my husband and I prayed for relief.

Four answering trumpet blasts sounded like heavenly music to our ears. "Thank you, God," I exclaimed with the heartfelt gratitude of someone who has narrowly escaped imploding: "Thank you for those farts!" Parker and I looked at the sincerity on each other's faces, registered the absurdity of our praise, and burst into fits of laughter.

"Who thanks God for farts?" we choked through jovial tears. (Sorry Mom, but using the word poot, toot, passing gas, or making wind just doesn't pack the same punch.) It was the oddest "thank you" I have ever uttered, but at the same time I was profoundly grateful.

Gas is a gift. It is not until you cannot fart that you realize how crucial it is to the comfort of your body. I never imagined that I'd celebrate farts, or give my ancestors the vapors by writing about it. Life is so surprising. To this day, I am thankful for every toot. It is unexpected, crazy gratitude.

DELIVERANCE FROM ENTITLEMENT AND CONTROL:

At church we sing a hymn originally penned by James John Cummins in 1839. The chorus asks God, "By thy mercy, O deliver us, good Lord," from the hardships outlined in the verses. But the fourth verse asks for deliverance of another kind. It uniquely reads:

> When the world around is smiling,
> In the time of wealth and ease,
> Earthly joys our hearts beguiling,
> In the day of health and peace.[1]

Why would we need God's deliverance from times of ease? I struggled to understand this verse before I became disabled. But now I realize that when we do not need deliverance from our situation, we often need deliverance from our attitudes. When life is going well, it is easy to forget how quickly circumstances can fall apart. We treat blessing with entitlement.

As a healthy individual, I took wellness for granted as a normal part of the human experience. I seldom thought about or was thankful for the ways my body worked. It just wasn't on my radar.

Ironically, the disabilities that stripped me of many of my abilities also illuminated what I had left. Instead of giving God vague thanks for overall health, I now offer him praise for specific abilities: I can see, hear, and walk.

I appreciate that it takes thousands of complex biological processes working together for our bodies to function. Step outside of a small margin of error and—sayonara planet earth—hello pearly gates. The fact that the earth has nearly eight billion people indicates that God is an astonishingly proficient innovator, even within the limits of a decaying world. You and I, and 7,999,999,998 of our neighbors are alive in this moment because there is a lot more going right in our bodies than going wrong.

In addition to opening my eyes to the marvels of his craftsmanship, God has also been deepening my understanding of how involved he is in the outcome of my life. While I've never considered myself particularly prideful, I definitely had misplaced beliefs about the amount of control I had over my life before experiencing chronic illness.

1. Cummins, *Jesus, Lord of Life and Glory,* verse 4.

As a college freshman, I had zero doubt that I would be able to support myself as a teacher and be a positive contributor to my community. Reading this chapter's key verse (Jas 1:17), I would have been thankful for God's obvious blessings. But I also would have credited my own determination with earning the scholarships that allowed me to attend my expensive private university. After all, God helps those who help themselves, right?

Post chronic illnesses, I know that life can change in an instant. I did work hard to earn those scholarships, but God provided the context and circumstances I needed to succeed. He saw to it that I was born in the United States, blessed with twenty years of health, and placed in a family that valued education.

Would my hard work have gotten me far without his blessings? Not a chance. Now, I am pushing myself harder than I ever have but have little to show for it. I would struggle to financially support myself if it wasn't for God's gift of my kind, intelligent, and determined husband.

Desire and drive can do a lot, but they are not enough. Your blessings flow directly from God's hands. God is the one who gives you intellectual ability, talents, and favor. God orchestrates your circumstances, opportunities, and triumphs. And when storms stir up the complacent sands of our calm seasons, it is Jesus who ensures that our hurricanes are used to unearth hidden treasures. We owe everything to him. The words of Isaiah 26:12 are true, " . . . all that we have accomplished *you* have done for us."

Don't let this depress you. Let it liberate you. God is responsible for your well-being. Simply do your best, then hand over the reins of control. Allow disability to make you more aware of Christ's goodness and your hardships to remind you of the importance of living fully. Your every breath is a blessing from God's hand.

So what farts are you thankful for? Carpe Diem.

. . . give thanks in all circumstances; for this is God's will for you in
Christ Jesus. —1 Thess 5:18

Chapter 50

Contentedness

. . . whatever you do, do it all for the glory of God. —1 Cor 10:31

WHEN I WAS HEALTHY, I agonized over how to best spend my time. I always wanted to make the wisest choice in order to make the most of my life for God.

This idea sounds positive on paper, but it was very harmful in practice. I wasted a lot of time being indecisive because I was stressed about making a "wrong" decision. It was also hard to recharge. Anytime I chose to do an art project, pleasure read, or unwind with some tv, I couldn't enjoy it. I thought God only valued time I spent with him in prayer, worship, Bible study, or in service to others.

Keeping pace with my idea of a "Super Christian" was exhausting. I was paralyzed by feelings of selfishness when I dared to acknowledge my limits and plagued by burnout when I was getting it "right." (A great book on this topic is *Emotionally Healthy Spirituality* by Peter Scazzero.)[1]

This emotional baggage increased tenfold when I became disabled. How could I make the most of my time for Jesus now that I needed so much physical rest? Was it even fair to spend some of my limited energy on enjoyable activities when there were so many things I "should" be doing?

As I pondered these questions, a movement in the backyard caught my eye. A very determined squirrel was showing off his yoga moves in a valiant attempt to reach the seeds in my bird feeder. These furry jesters may be considered sneak thieves by most bird-lovers, but they are one of my favorite animals because they are hilarious to watch. The squirrel executed a perfect

1 See "Bibliography" for book details.

Half-Pigeon, Lord of the Dance, and Warrior III, before finally achieving snacking success in the One-Legged Downward Dog position. Chuckling at his antics, a half-formed query floated through my mind, "Why did God make squirrels?"

God surprised me with an immediate response, "To make you laugh! Isn't it fun to simply watch a squirrel being a squirrel?"

Smiling at this idea, I tried to return my attention to the original problem. Instead, thoughts of how joyful it is to watch squirrels kept scampering through my brain. They tumbled into reflections about why parents enjoy watching their child sleep. It should be an unremarkable pastime—the child is not actively trying to engage with her parents. But parents get tremendous pleasure out of viewing this ordinary act simply because they are watching the child they love.

That is when it hit home—just like the squirrels and the sleeping child— God enjoys watching me be the person he created me to be. Ps 104:31 NLT exclaims, "May the glory of the Lord continue forever! *The Lord takes pleasure in all he has made!*" God delights in his creations (you and me) so much he chose to emphasize this verse with an exclamation point.

It took disability slowing me down for me to finally realize that God loves me as a complete person. Yes, I am a spiritual being. But God also made me a physical, intellectual, emotional, and social being. He calls this good. He delights in the unique combination of personality traits, interests, and preferences that he wove together to make me (Ps 139:13–14).

I please God when I exercise the gifts he has given me and glorify him when I treasure the people he has placed in my life. He smiles when I take a walk with my husband, sing silly songs with my preschoolers, or exercise creativity through my artwork. I don't have to worry about taking time to rest or expending energy on activities that help me emotionally recharge. God delights in me whether I am studying about the land of Canaan or playing the Settlers of Catan board game with friends. My spirituality is not divorced from other aspects of who he created me to be.

This is the liberating power of the *"whatever you do"* mentioned in 1 Corinthians 10:31 (see this chapter's key verse). Every good and worthwhile pursuit can be done to the glory of God. Now everything in my life can be an act of worship because God designed me for balance. I proclaim the surpassing wisdom of my Creator when I gracefully accept this truth.

Since realizing that God loves all sides of me, I've spent a lot less time paralyzed by indecision and fear. Our relationship has grown deeper, more vibrant, and more personal. In this state of contentment, I am actually living
more fully for Jesus than when I was overly stressed about doing my best.

Saints, God loves your spiritual, sporty, silly, scholarly, and yes, even
your squirrely sides! Take time to ponder this truth. Ask him to give you the
freedom of knowing how much he delights in the details of who he made
you to be. God does not require you to be a superhuman. He simply wants
you to be a human who loves him through *whatever* it is you do.

*Moreover, when God gives someone wealth and possessions, and
the ability to enjoy them, to accept their lot and be happy in their
toil—this is a gift of God. They seldom reflect on the days of their life,
because God keeps them occupied with gladness of heart.*
—Eccl 5:19–20

Chapter 51

The Gift of Priorities

Martha, Martha," the Lord answered, "you are worried and upset about many things, but few things are needed—or indeed only one. Mary has chosen what is better, and it will not be taken away from her." —Luke 10:41–42

ARE YOU RESIDING IN a prison of people-pleasing? No judgment here, you are talking to an original inmate. Until my late college years, the word "no" did not exist in my vocabulary. I helped start and lead a contemporary worship service at my church. I was a tutor, Sunday school teacher, and small group leader. I competed in math competitions, volunteered at an animal therapy farm, and studied abroad—all while taking an aggressive load of honors courses.

I had the energy to keep up with a demanding schedule at the time. But I didn't have the maturity to realize that the people I chose to please were not always the people who mattered most.

Case in point: the night of my younger sister's chorus concert. I'd been working on my math homework for over two hours and was stuck on the last problem. I couldn't stomach disappointing my teacher by turning in an incomplete assignment. So while my sister sang, I continued to grapple with the monster math problem outside in our minivan.

Sheryl is a tough cookie. She rarely crumbles. But I could see the hurt plainly etched on her face when she slid open the car door and murmured, "You weren't there."

I would like to tell you that in that moment I realized I'd made the wrong choice. Instead, I fiercely defended my decision, rubbing more salt in my sister's wound. Karma was coming.

The following day at school, my math teacher said he did not mean to assign the last problem. A misprint made it unsolvable. I was the only one of my classmates who had even attempted it. I brought three pages of painstaking work up to my teacher, sure that he would praise me for going above and beyond. Do you know what that frustrating man said? "I'm sorry you chose to spend your time that way."

Now that I have more life experience, I am frustrated that misplaced priorities caused me to spend my time that way too. I was trying not to disappoint a teacher who didn't really care about my efforts. In the process, I let down my sister whom I care for deeply.

Disability slammed the brakes on my fast-paced life. Used to fourteen productive hours a day, I was reduced to three constructive hours *on my good days*. I felt like I was front row center in a priorities crash course being taught by X-men's Wolverine: low energy, required rest, and muscle weakness slashed my schedule to ribbons. No longer able to do it all, I was forced to prioritize what was most important.

By limiting my abilities as a young adult, God quickly taught me that time is a precious commodity not to be squandered. Regardless of our productivity, prestige, or salary, we can never earn more hours on this earth. Prioritizing time wisely is paramount to a life well lived.

How can we be like Mary and choose what is most important amidst the distractions of a busy life? How do we pick between good opportunities while balancing our needs? Trial and error taught me what Lysa Terkhust teaches in her book, *The Best Yes*.[1] When you say "yes" to an activity or person, you inevitably say "no" to something or someone else.

In the context of disability, this truth is even more magnified. If I do not carefully consider my "best yes," I quickly jeopardize my most important relationships and purposes. Saying "yes" to mopping my floors may result in saying "no" to the company I was trying to impress in the first place. Agreeing to sing in the church choir may prevent me from developing deeper relationships by joining a small group. Parker and I wish that every weekend we could say "yes" to church, a date, errands, and seeing friends. But it is only realistic for us to pick two of these activities at most. There is so much we want to do and so little time.

---

1 See "Bibliography" for book details.

To make the most of my time when my energy is good, I have three top priorities. Anything else is nonessential.

1. *My Relationship with God.*

2. *People:* My spouse tops everyone else. Parker daily takes care of me with such selflessness and grace, it is important that I look out for him.

3. *My God Given Work:* For seven years, this was teaching preschool. Now it is finishing this book, spending time with my godchildren, and keeping the house in a habitable state.

Even juggling these three priorities requires compromise. Sometimes Parker and I skip church to save energy for a date because we know that God wants us to invest in our marriage. During Parker's busy season, prioritizing him can mean disappointing other people I love. It is not easy to cancel plans with friends so that I can do the grocery shopping he normally helps me with; or to say no to family visits to protect him from the additional work having company creates. However, I know that when Parker's work slows down, he will shoulder some of my housework to give me more time to spend writing or with other people. Navigating all this give and take is tough for a rehabilitating people pleaser.

I don't always get this constant balancing act right. But learning to prioritize well has been worth the challenge. Jesus says that we are the light of the world (Matt 5:14). Think of yourself as a lightbulb. A single lightbulb within a large warehouse barely illuminates anything because its light is spread too thin. But if that light is given boundaries and concentrated, it becomes a focused laser beam. A laser beam can cut through steel, shape diamonds, cauterize wounds, and restore eyesight. It is capable of permanently marking everything it touches with the intensity of its light.

This is the gift and power of prioritizing well: a life that is effective *because it is focused*. Without the distractions of an overfilled schedule, eternal investments now claim my attention. I am teaching my students that they are precious to Jesus. I'm nurturing my marriage. I have deeper friendships. I am praying more, learning to appreciate gradual transformation, and increasingly tuned into God's purposes for me. I'm more aware of the people around me; recognizing situations when I need to stop what I am doing to meet the needs of a neighbor or stranger.

Prioritizing well glorifies God, but it is also for my gain. Without disability, I would have been the person who kept saying "yes" to every opportunity that came my way. I could have spent my time on earth trading what is most important for the busyness of everyday life.

Thank you, Jesus, for saving me from this fate when my adult life was just beginning. Because now I have a different story. You captured my attention and in doing so redeemed decades of my life. Thank you for teaching me to bank heavenly treasure by valuing people. I owe countless cherished memories to this lesson.

My friend, I know it is frustrating to be limited. But only God is limitless and capable of doing all things well. If we place our limits in his hands, he will turn them to our advantage. He will, "Teach us to number our days, that we may gain a heart of wisdom (Ps 90:12)."

Allow him to bless you by turning your attention towards what is most important. Take time today to examine your priorities. Identify your top three. Where you choose to focus your time and energy is where you will leave your mark. Shine bright.

Let your light shine before others, that they may see your good deeds and glorify your Father in heaven. —Matt 5:16

Chapter 52

You Are Uniquely Equipped
to Comfort Others

*Praise be to the God and Father of our Lord Jesus Christ, the Father
of compassion and the God of all comfort, who comforts us in all
our troubles, so that we can comfort those in any trouble with the
comfort we ourselves receive from God. —2 Cor 1:3–4*

*When you are in the dark, listen and God will give you a very pre-
cious message for someone else when you are in the light.
—Oswald Chambers, My Utmost for His Highest*

"An unrecognized advantage is an unrecognized reward."[1] What advantage do you and I, as disabled/chronically ill persons, have to share with
others? Our undeniably unique stories. Your life experience gives you a dis-
tinctive voice and point of view. You can connect with people facing medical
challenges on a level that is impossible for those who have not been in your
shoes.

Consider Alcoholics Anonymous. Would it make sense for a recovering alcoholic to have a mentor who has never had an addiction? No way.
The program's success comes from coupling a struggling alcoholic with a
sponsor who has made tough choices to stay sober. As a seasoned warrior in
the fight against addiction, the mentor can share battle strategies, help guard
against pitfalls, and support his mentee during weak moments. The mentee
sees his/her sponsor as living proof that sobriety is possible. Relatability is
the cornerstone of their partnership.

---

1. Pastor Steven Furtick

Similar experiences build bridges. Somewhere, there is a person struggling who your voice will reach when all other voices fail. Your message of hope will be the one to break through because you can meaningfully relate to their suffering.

My friend, Marie, recently shared how her father has been losing motor control due to Parkinson's disease. She was frustrated with how her mom, Debra, was handling the situation:

> I know my mom loves my dad, but she is refusing to make changes to accommodate his condition. He can't get around the house safely anymore. He keeps falling and hurting himself when she is at work.
>
> My brother and I think it is time for them to move to an assisted living facility. He needs someone to check on him when she's not home. But she keeps insisting that they are fine and that she does not want to leave our childhood home. Why can't she acknowledge that he needs help? I just don't get it.

I began to have a sneaking suspicion that Debra was experiencing more than outright denial or excessive nostalgia. She was covering up fear. Her refusal to make appropriate accommodations reminded me of a time when I delayed my treatment needs because I was afraid. I didn't want to accept my new circumstances. For as long as possible, I avoided making lifestyle changes that would also make my disabilities terrifyingly real.

As a Christian, I was grappling with an additional fear. I had faith that God could heal me and believed he wanted me to be well. Would I be giving up on God if I started making accommodations for my disorders? Would that be letting sickness win?

God exposed this as a lie when he taught me to have a more balanced view of healing.[2] Believing in God's ability to redeem our pain can require more faith than believing in his power to heal. It takes tremendous trust to allow Jesus to show you how to live well when life hits you with an unexpected challenge.

Eventually, I realized that refusing treatment was slowing my sanctification process. I was burning myself out fighting a losing battle. I would never learn to live well with chronic illness if I kept pretending that I wasn't sick. Nor would I discover the purposes God wanted to bring out of my suffering.

---

2. See Chapter 19, "Cultivate a Balanced View of Healing."

Reminded of how tenderly God helped me face my own fears, I texted Marie these words to share with her mom:

> *Accepting your limitations does not mean you're giving up on God or being defeated by disability. Instead, acceptance allows you to make the most of your situation. By recognizing your limitations in this season, God can help you and your husband move towards your best life together.*

I encouraged Marie to help Debra focus on what she would gain. While it would be sad to leave the home where her children grew up, her memories would come with her. Moving would be a lot of work, but in return she'd get much needed help. An assisted living facility would give Debra freedom to leave the house without worrying about her husband. She'd have more time to pursue her own interests. Her marriage would benefit as her husband felt cared for and secure in their new home. Moving would be a win for both of them.

Debra said these were exactly the words she needed to hear. But I only knew to speak them because I could relate to her situation. My own experiences as a chronically ill Christian prepared me to pick up on her unspoken fears.

Three months later, it is my great joy to announce that Marie's parents have finalized plans to move in the new year. Seeing God use the comfort he gave me to make life easier for someone else is the best Christmas present I could ask for. Because, like the birth of Jesus, it is the gift of redemption.

Luke 19:10 says that Jesus came to "seek and to save the lost." All Christians are called to join Christ in this work. Through your unique experience, God has equipped you to reach a special niche. You speak the language of chronic illness or disability.

Each of you must bring a gift in proportion to the way the Lord your God has blessed you. —Deut 16:17

THE SOURCE OF OUR COMFORT:

If you find the idea that God can use your heartaches to reach others insensitive, I understand. I have moments when the heaviness of my struggle seems to outweigh any good God has brought from it. Please know I am not attempting to gloss over the brutalities of a disabled life.

But I would like to encourage you that—as time has passed—God has been working in my heart to make me more consistently excited about the beauty he is birthing from my brokenness. This has been a gradual and imperfect process. These paragraphs from *Hope for the Caregiver* by Peter Rosenberger, accurately portray how I wrestle with this idea:

> Over the years, others have tried to offer consolation to Gracie and me when they see the challenges we live with.
>
> "I hate what you have to go through, but look at the testimony . . . "
>
> "Your burdens are great, but look what God has done through you all . . . "
>
> "God clearly has a plan and purpose for all this, or you wouldn't be here . . . "
>
> I appreciate the sentiment behind those statements, but they are just that: sentiment, and sentiment is not hope. A great testimony and even a powerful ministry to Gracie's fellow amputees is not a consolation prize for the harshness of our lives. As wonderful as our work is, that is not what strengthens our hearts during brutal times. Our consolation has to be greater than simply doing good works and even having a great message . . .
>
> When your wife is seizing, going into respiratory arrest, screaming in agony, or listlessly looking off and living in a place where she can't be reached, no ministry or testimony provides consolation in those moments. What I hang my hat on is far greater than those things- and that's what helps me push back against the hopelessness.
>
> I depend upon a greater source of hope and consolation than what my mind, and the minds of others, can fully comprehend . . . [3]

What is this source of hope? Because I agree with Peter: knowing that someone else has been helped by my suffering is not enough compensation on its own. However, it is evidence. When I see God redeem my problems for his purposes, it births hope in my heart. A hope founded—not in the possibilities of what God is doing through me—but in God himself.

We worship a God for whom nothing is impossible. No situation is beyond the reach of his resurrection power. He loves his children with an

---

3. Rosenberger, *Hope for the Caregiver*, excerpts from pages 44–45.

unfailing love and continually works on our behalf. Every bit of evidence of his redemptive power at work in my life fuels my faith in his infinite greatness and unerring goodness. Such kindness is a foretaste of his promise that all suffering will end and that heavenly rewards will truly outweigh our earthly sorrows. We do not fully comprehend his promises. But every blessing the Lord reclaims from brokenness builds our trust in the promise maker: *Jesus—the only sure foundation for our hope.*

I pray that God, the source of hope, will fill you completely with joy and peace because you trust in him. Then you will overflow with confident hope through the power of the Holy Spirit.
—Rom 15:13 NLT

Chapter 53
More Blessings Available to You Now

On your feet wear the Good News of peace to help you stand strong.
—Eph 6:15

EMBARRASSING CONFESSION: I WAS a sophomore in high school before I realized that the Super Bowl was a football game. Monks know more about marriage than I do about sports. But an athletic fact I am absolutely certain about is that I have never seen an Olympic runner race in flip flops.

We need the best shoes when we are facing fierce competition. Shoes that can take the strain. As I look ahead at my Christian race, I realize I may have fifty to sixty years of running with chronic illness left. *Dang.* That is a long trot to the finish line. I'm gonna need more than Nikes to just do this.

Sure, heavenly rewards are a powerful incentive. But can rewards half a century away carry us through daily suffering? Especially when weariness tempts us to give up or coast through life while we wait for something better? Is revelation of how God's transformed our past trials enough to persevere if there is no fresh fuel between now and the finish line?

Frankly, I need more for this strenuous race—because *how* I run counts. To run well, I need God's mercy watching over my every step. I need to know his blessings are available to me today. I need his assurance that somehow "I will see the goodness of the Lord in the land of the living (Ps 27:13)." How about you?

Good news . . . Jesus has kicks for that. His favor isn't just in your future. He has good things waiting for you this day. So sink your toes into how your Savior is blessing you now. May these promises from your "ever present help (Ps 46:1)" revive your spirit and refresh your strength.

I tell you, now is the time of God's favor, now is the day of salvation.
—2 Cor 6:2b

BLESSINGS GOD HAS FOR YOU TODAY:

God blesses you for waiting:

Yet the Lord longs to be gracious to you; therefore he will rise up to show you compassion. For the Lord is a God of justice. Blessed are all who wait for him! —Isa 30:18

You are blessed with God's presence:

A Message from the high and towering God, who lives in Eternity, whose name is Holy: "I live in the high and holy places, but also with the low-spirited, the spirit-crushed, And what I do is put new spirit in them, get them up and on their feet again." —Isa 57:15 MSG

For the Lord your God is the one who goes with you to fight for you against your enemies to give you victory. —Deut 20:4

God is our refuge and strength, an ever-present help in trouble. —Ps 46:1

You are blessed by God's Spirit—who resides within you:

And I will ask the Father, and he will give you another Helper, to be with you forever, even the Spirit of truth, whom the world cannot receive, be-cause it neither sees him nor knows him. You know him, for he dwells with you and will be in you. I will not leave you as orphans; I will come to you. —John 14:16–18 ESV

And hope does not put us to shame, because God's love has been poured out into our hearts through the Holy Spirit, who has been given to us. —Rom 5:5

In the same way, the Spirit helps us in our weakness. We do not know what we ought to pray for, but the Spirit himself intercedes for us through word-less groans. And he who searches our hearts knows the mind of the Spirit, because the Spirit intercedes for God's people in accordance with the will of God. —Rom 8:26–27

But when he, the Spirit of truth, comes, he will guide you into all the truth. —John 16:13a

But the Counselor, the Holy Spirit—the Father will send Him in My name— will teach you all things and remind you of everything I have told you. —John 14:26

But if Christ is in you, then even though your body is subject to death be- cause of sin, the Spirit gives life because of righteousness. And if the Spirit of him who raised Jesus from the dead is living in you, he who raised Christ from the dead will also give life to your mortal bodies because of his Spirit who lives in you. —Rom 8:10–11

In him you also, when you heard the word of truth, the gospel of your salva- tion, and believed in him, were sealed with the promised Holy Spirit, who is the guarantee of our inheritance until we acquire possession of it, to the praise of his glory. —Eph 1:13–14 ESV

God offers you his rest:

Come to me, all you who are weary and burdened, and I will give you rest. —Matt 11:28

I will refresh the weary and satisfy the faint. —Jer 31:25

God promises his comfort:

God blesses those who mourn, for they will be comforted. —Matt 5:4 NLT

He heals the brokenhearted and binds up their wounds [healing their pain and comforting their sorrow]. —Ps 147:3 AMP

When doubts filled my mind, your comfort gave me renewed hope and cheer. —Ps 94:19

Lord, you know the hopes of the helpless. Surely you will hear their cries and comfort them. —Ps 10:17 NLT

For the more we suffer for Christ, the more God will shower us with his comfort through Christ. —2 Cor 1:5 NLT

You are blessed as God strengthens you:

He gives strength to the weary and increases the power of the weak. —Isa 40:29

My health may fail, and my spirit may grow weak, but God remains the strength of my heart; he is mine forever. —Ps 73:26 NLT

We can rejoice, too, when we run into problems and trials, for we know that they help us develop endurance. And endurance develops strength of character, and character strengthens our confident hope of salvation. —Rom 5:3–4 NLT

Every test that you have experienced is the kind that normally comes to people. But God keeps his promise, and he will not allow you to be tested beyond your power to remain firm; at the time you are put to the test, he will give you the strength to endure it, and so provide you with a way out. —1 Cor 10:13 GNT

Chapter 54

What Joy Awaits

Let us run with endurance the race God has set before us. We do this by keeping our eyes on Jesus, the champion who initiates and perfects our faith. Because of the joy awaiting him, he endured the cross, disregarding its shame. Now he is seated in the place of honor beside God's throne. —Heb 12:1–2

THE MERCIES GOD MAKES available to us now empower us to follow the example of Jesus. Our team captain runs this race beside us as an experienced athlete. He picks us up when we stumble and continually encourages us through the long, hot miles. Finally, Jesus has one final tip to keep us moving forward when the troubles of this life become too much. Christ calls us to lift our eyes to the finish line and remember what we are fighting for.

Hebrews 12:1–2 says that Jesus was able to endure the cross because he could see beyond it. He trusted his Father to raise him in victory over death. But the road to triumph was not easy. Jesus had to willingly endure torture, being forsaken by the Father, and descending into hell. How did he find the strength to go through with such a sacrifice?

Jesus' strength came from remembering the reward he was fighting for: *you*. The Passion Translation puts it most beautifully,

> His example is this: Because his heart was focused on the joy of knowing that you would be his, he endured the agony of the cross and conquered its humiliation, and now sits exalted at the right hand of the throne of God! —Heb 12:2b TPT

Jesus braved unprecedented suffering for the "joy of knowing that you would be his." Fixing his thoughts on you enabled him to push past the physical and emotional pain of the cross. Likewise, God restrained himself while his beloved son was murdered by "wicked men" so that many sons and daughters could come home to heaven (Acts 2:23–24, Heb 2:9–10). We are the priceless treasures that motivated both God the Father and Christ the Son.

This is the strength of the love that fights for us. This is the character of God.

How thankful I am for his undeserved mercy. Because on bad days, when I've lost my voice from coughing or when I am hungry but can't eat, I question whether or not Christ had an edge to coping. I mean Jesus had God on speed dial. He preapproved the resurrection plan and knew exactly what was awaiting him in paradise. That kind of insider knowledge is gold when you are suffering.

So if I have to fight hard, I want to know exactly what I am fighting for. Who's with me? After all, every Christian has been given right standing with God, a home in heaven, and has become heir to the promises of Christ. But what rewards are specifically waiting for those who suffer?

In the process of answering this question, I have learned something about God: he is a remarkably bad secret keeper. He loves us too much to keep us completely in the dark and cannot resist dropping hints to point us in the right direction. His word is full of spoilers about our glorious future. Like Christ, we know exactly how our story ends/begins.

May these verses inspire you to follow the example of your champion, Jesus, as you anticipate the rewards God has promised to you. May the brightness of your future propel you towards hope even amidst earthly suffering. At times when you want more details, remind yourself that the outcome of your life is in the hands of a God who gave his very life for you. You are his most precious love. Surely, he has reserved the very best for his treasure.

BLESSINGS TO COME: *ITALICS HIGHLIGHT THE JOYS THAT AWAIT YOU.*

For our light and momentary troubles are achieving for us an *eternal glory that far outweighs them all.* —2 Cor 4:17

I consider that our present sufferings are *not worth comparing with the glory that will be revealed in us.* —Rom 8:18

Now we live with great expectation, and *we have a priceless inheritance—an inheritance that is kept in heaven for you, pure and undefiled, beyond the reach of change and decay.* And through your faith, God is protecting you by his power until you receive this salvation, which is ready to be revealed on the last day for all to see. So be truly glad. There is *wonderful joy ahead,* even though you must endure many trials for a little while. These trials will show that your faith is genuine. It is being tested as fire tests and purifies gold—though your faith is far more precious than mere gold. *So when your faith remains strong through many trials, it will bring you much praise and glory and honor on the day when Jesus Christ is revealed to the whole world.* —1 Pet 1:3–7 NLT

God blesses those who patiently endure testing and temptation. Afterward they will *receive the crown of life* that God has promised to those who love him. —Jas 1:12 NLT

We give *great honor* to those who endure under suffering. For instance, you know about Job, a man of great endurance. You can see how the Lord was kind to him at the end, for the Lord is full of tenderness and mercy. —Jas 5:11 NLT

Instead of your shame you will receive a double portion, and instead of disgrace you will rejoice in your inheritance. And so you will *inherit a double portion in your land, and everlasting joy will be yours.* —Isa 61:7

If we endure hardship, *we will reign with him.* —2 Tim 2:12 NLT

The Spirit of the Sovereign Lord is on me, because the Lord has anointed me to proclaim good news to the poor. He has sent me to bind up the brokenhearted, to proclaim freedom for the captives and release from darkness for the prisoners, to proclaim the year of the Lord's favor and the day of vengeance of our God, *to comfort all who mourn, and provide for those who grieve in Zion— to bestow on them a crown of beauty instead of ashes, the oil of joy instead of mourning, and a garment of praise instead of a spirit of despair. They will be called oaks of righteousness, a planting of the Lord for the display of his splendor.* —Isa 61:1–3

I heard a loud shout from the throne, saying, "Look, God's home is now among his people! He will live with them, and they will be his people. *God himself will be with them. He will wipe every tear from their eyes, and there will be no more death or sorrow or crying or pain.* All these things are gone forever." And the one sitting on the throne said, "*Look, I am making every-thing new!*" —Rev 21:3–7 NLT

Confessions from the Valley

WHEN I WEIGH THE evidence of my transformation against my trials, was it worth it? Am I genuinely willing to be shaped by suffering to secure heavenly rewards I don't fully understand? Honestly . . . it is a close call.

I've had over a decade to adjust to living with chronic illness. It took time for my intense grief to heal enough for me to begin perceiving God's goodness. But now I can clearly see that I would not be the same person if I had stayed on the mountaintop. No number of sermons, Bible studies, mission trips, or prayers would have produced the same harvest in my spirit.

God's most shocking surprise? I like who I am on the inside now *better*. So much better, that I'm beginning to accept the suffering it took to get me here.

It blows my mind to live such a spiritually complex reality. I long to be back on the mountain. I absolutely carry the hope of healing in my heart. I still get frustrated by my limitations. But most of all, I am utterly dumbfounded to find myself at a crossroads I never thought I would reach. I can look you in the eye and truthfully answer, "Yes, my life has been richer because of disability." I am thankful for how narcolepsy, POTS, and gastroparesis have helped me truly discover Jesus.

God's unending mercy allows me to simultaneously desire healing and accept a future that I once thought was unimaginable. The goodness I've seen come from the last ten years fuels my faith that Jesus will continue to redeem any suffering he allows into my life. And while I'm nervous about how that may stretch me, I am just a little more excited about his rewards. Christ keeps changing me in ways I never thought were possible. How has he enabled all of these truths and emotions to coexist in my heart?

LIKE OUR FATHER:

Does this describe you? Perhaps your ability to both mourn what you have lost and hope in what you've gained is just one more sign that you are made in God's image. In fact, your very complex emotions about disability reflect the Lord's heart towards your experiences.

God hates your suffering too. He mourns your sorrows and has compassion on how confusing it is to be human. Remember that he stayed his hand while Jesus' body was wounded in order to open the way for your body to be healed and made whole (Isa 53:4–5 AMPC). God obviously wants you to be healthy.

However, Christ's blood was also shed for your soul. As the part of you destined to live with him forever, your spirit is God's highest priority. You were chosen to be conformed into the image of Christ with ever increasing holiness as you transform from "one radiance of glory to another (2 Cor 3:18 VOICE)."

Sometimes suffering enters this process. God does not initiate it; it is just part of our broken world. But as a believer, you have God's assurance that when suffering comes into your life, it can only operate within the protective parameters of his love. Every trial is under the umbrella of "all things" God is working together for your spiritual good (Rom 8:28). Any curse that has the audacity to trouble his beloved child will pay dearly—it is destined to be a blessing by the time your magnificent Father is finished.

Be encouraged that God understands how painful transformation can be. He has compassion for your complex emotions towards suffering because he is juggling them too. He balances entering into your immediate hurts while watching over your eternal welfare. He cares for you deeply, yet encourages you to press through your trials knowing that they will make you perfect and complete. He is calling you heavenward into Christ's glory, but promises to be with you until you cross the finish line. His precious promises await those who persevere. Your valley of suffering will become a place of victory.

Lord Jesus,
Give us gladness in proportion to our former misery!
Replace the evil years with good (Ps 90:15 NLT).
Amen.

Conclusion
Comfort for the Road

FELLOW WARRIOR, THANK YOU for including me in your faith journey. Your endeavor to keep believing in the midst of suffering is precious to God. How beautiful and brave you are! I pray that God's love has comforted you within these pages and that you have found strength to keep seeking his face.

And dear friend, on days when you wonder how you will keep going, remember my mom's encouraging words towards a stranger,

> *I know today is really tough, but you're not alone. Just keep taking it one day at a time, and you will make it through this. I promise things are going to get better.*

Take her words to heart, for they echo God's heart towards you . . .

HOLD FAST TO THESE TRUTHS:

- *"I know today is really tough, but you're not alone."*

    The Lord is close to the brokenhearted and saves those who are crushed in spirit. —Ps 34:18

- *"Just keep taking it one day at a time, and you will make it through this."*

    I can do everything through Christ, who gives me strength. —Phil 4:13 NLT

- *"I promise things are going to get better."*

"For I know the plans I have for you," declares the Lord, "plans
to prosper you and not to harm you, plans to give you hope and a
future." —Jer 29:11

God has spoken. These are your promises. He holds your past disappointments, your present troubles, and your future dreams within the care
of his unfailing love. He enfolds you in the protection of his never-ending
embrace. Trust yourself to the arms of Jesus and he will carry you to brighter
days.

THE MIRACLE I SEE NOW:

Have circumstances gotten better for me? Be encouraged by what I see now
when I look back at my twelve years with disability:

Today, I see what God *has done* for me instead of what he *has not*. I
see Jesus fighting my enemies when they were too strong for me. Beckoning
me beyond the fear, disappointment, anxiety, and anger of those first most
difficult years.

I see Christ's love daily radiating to me through Parker's eyes: God's
profound mercy in the gift of such a caring and steadfast husband for this
journey. I am equally thankful for his provision of supportive parents, family, and friends. They form my circle of joy and keep me surrounded by
prayer.

I see God's hands working wonders on my behalf as time after time
outrageous "coincidences" connected me to doctors, medical therapies, and
surgeries that helped me gain quality of life. My days have been easier in
recent years as my energy, hydration, and ability to eat have improved.

I see evidence of God's faithfulness when I look out at my beautiful
flower garden or stroke Vinny's (the cat who "adopted" us) velvety fur. I
celebrate how he has given me back pieces of my life which I feared were lost
forever. Every restored desire is a victory.

I see answered prayers as Jesus fills my days with purpose and gives me
new dreams. It amazes me that—not only am I still standing—but standing
taller because of his strength. God has used my wounds to shape me into a
warrior.

Finally, I marvel at the exquisite kindness of my Redeemer. He took
me—when I thought my life was over—and taught me to love it again. It
would have been so easy for me to be joyful if the Lord had healed me with

a snap of his fingers. But finding myself genuinely fulfilled in the midst of suffering is a gift of God's most extraordinary grace.

For all these blessings, I sing Christ's praise! Hosanna to him in the highest! Do you realize what it is that I see when I add the evidence of the past twelve years together? I see his resurrection power at work in me. And that, my friend, is the greatest miracle.

I believe God is just beginning; that he is working resurrection for you too. I sincerely hope that includes healing. But, one way or the other, things are going to get better. His plans for you are immeasurably good. May God bless you and keep you until you clearly see evidence of his resurrection in your life. I cannot wait to hear your story.

> *I pray that from his glorious, unlimited resources he will empower you with inner strength through his Spirit. Then Christ will make his home in your heart as you trust in him. Your roots will grow down into God's love and keep you strong. And may you have the power to understand, as all God's people should, how wide, how long, how high, and how deep his love is. May you experience the love of Christ, though it is too great to understand fully. Then you will be made complete with all the fullness of life and power that comes from God.*
>
> *Now all glory to God, who is able, through his mighty power at work within us, to accomplish infinitely more than we might ask or think. Glory to him in the church and in Christ Jesus through all generations forever and ever! Amen.* —Eph 3:16–21 NLT

With Blessings of Christ's Love,

Shannon Cramer

Appendix 1

Overcome Lies with God's Truth

LIE—*GOD DOESN'T LOVE ME.*

The Scriptures say: (Emphasis added.)

For God so loved the world that he gave his one and only Son, that whoever believes in him shall not perish but have eternal life. For God did not send his son into the world to condemn the world, but to save the world through him. —John 3:16–17

"I am in them and you are in me. May they experience such perfect unity that the world will know that you sent me and that you love them as much as you love me." —John 17:23 NLT *(While praying for believers, Jesus acknowledges that God's love for you is equal to the love God has for Jesus. Incredible!)*

Greater love has no one than this, that he lay down his life for his friends. —John 15:13

Whoever does not love does not know God, because God is love. This is how God showed his love among us: He sent his one and only Son into the world that we might live through him. This is love: not that we loved God, but that he loved us and sent his Son as an atoning sacrifice for our sins. —1 John 4:8–10

How great is the love the Father has lavished on us that we should be called children of God! And that is what we are! —1 John 3:1

I have loved you with an everlasting love; I have drawn you with unfailing kindness. —Jer 31:3

For great is your love, reaching to the heavens: your faithfulness reaches to the skies. —Ps 57:10

Praise be to God, who has not rejected my prayer or withheld his love from me! —Ps 66:20

For the Lord is good and his love endures forever; his faithfulness continues through all generations. —Ps 100:5

But from everlasting to everlasting the Lord's love is with those who fear him . . . —Ps 103:17a

LIE—*WHEN BAD THINGS HAPPEN, IT MEANS GOD DOESN'T LOVE ME.*

The Scriptures say:

For he [God] does not willingly bring affliction or grief to the children of men. —Lam 3:33

And we know that in all things God works for the good of those who love him, who have been called according to his purpose. —Rom 8:28

Fear not, for I have redeemed you; I have summoned you by name; you are mine. When you pass through the waters, I will be with you; and when you pass through the rivers, they will not sweep over you. When you walk through the fire, you will not be burned, the flames will not set you ablaze. For I am the Lord, your God, the Holy One of Israel, your Savior. —Isa 43:1–3

Blessed is the man who perseveres under trial, because when he has stood the test, he will receive the crown of life that God has promised to those who love him. —Jas 1:12

Who shall separate us from the love of Christ? Shall trouble or hardship or persecution or famine or nakedness or danger or sword? . . . No, in all these things we are more than conquerors through him who loved us. For I am convinced that neither death nor life, neither angels nor demons, neither the present nor the future, nor any powers, neither height nor depth, nor anything else in all creation, will be able to separate us from the love of God that is in Christ Jesus our Lord. —Rom 8:35, 37–39

LIE—*WHEN BAD THINGS HAPPEN, IT MEANS GOD IS PUNISHING ME.*

The Scriptures say:

A righteous man may have many troubles but the Lord delivers him from them all. —Ps 34:19

I have told you these things, so that in me you may have peace. In this world you will have trouble. But take heart! I have overcome the world. —John 16:33

As he went along, he saw a man blind from birth. His disciples asked him, "Rabbi, who sinned, this man or his parents, that he was born blind?" "Neither this man nor his parents sinned," said Jesus, "but this happened so that the work of God might be displayed in his life." —John 9:1–3

For God chose to save us through our Lord Jesus Christ, not to pour out his anger on us. —1 Thess 5:9 NLT

LIE—*GOD HAS FORGOTTEN ME.*

The Scriptures say:

. . . He [God] does not forget the cry of the afflicted. —Ps 9:12 HCSB

But God will never forget the needy; the hope of the afflicted will never perish. —Ps 9:18

But Zion said, "The Lord has forsaken me, the Lord has forgotten me." "Can a mother forget the baby at her breast and have no compassion on the child she has borne? Though she may forget, I will not forget you! See, I have engraved you on the palms of my hands; your walls are ever before me. —Isa 49:14–16

Are not five sparrows sold for two pennies? Yet not one of them is forgotten by God. Indeed, the very hairs of your head are all numbered. Don't be afraid; you are worth more than many sparrows. —Luke 12:6–7

LIE—*GOD DOESN'T HEAR MY PRAYERS.*

The Scriptures say:

You heard my plea: "Do not close your ears to my cry for relief." You came near when I called you, and you said, "Do not fear." —Lam 3:56–57

For he has not despised or scorned the suffering of the afflicted one; he has not hidden his face from him but has listened to his cry for help. —Ps 22:24

You, Lord, hear the desire of the afflicted; you encourage them, and you listen to their cry . . . —Ps 10:17

The Lord hears his people when they call to him for help. He rescues them from all their troubles. —Ps 34:17 NLT

People of Zion, who live in Jerusalem, you will weep no more. How gracious he will be when you cry for help! As soon as he hears, he will answer you. —Isa 30:19

This is the confidence we have in approaching God: that if we ask anything according to his will, he hears us. And if we know that he hears us—whatever we ask—we know that we have what we asked of him. —1 John 5:14–15

LIE—*GOD IS FAR AWAY AND DOESN'T CARE ABOUT MY PAIN.*

The Scriptures say: (Context added.)

I will be glad and rejoice in your unfailing love, for you have seen my troubles, and you care about the anguish of my soul. —Ps 31:7

The righteous cry out, and the Lord hears them; he delivers them from all their troubles. The Lord is close to the brokenhearted and saves those who are crushed in spirit. —Ps 34:17–18

He [*God or Jesus*] tends his flock like a shepherd: He gathers the lambs in his arms and carries them close to his heart. —Isa 40:11

You've kept track of my every toss and turn through the sleepless nights, Each tear entered in your ledger, each ache written in your book. —Ps 56:8 MSG

In all their suffering he also suffered, and he personally rescued them. In his love and mercy he redeemed them. He lifted them up and carried them through all the years. —Isa 63:9 NLT

As a father has compassion on his children, so the Lord has compassion on those who fear him. —Ps 103:13

The Lord is near to all who call on him, to all who call on him in truth. —Ps 145:18

But now in Christ Jesus you who once were far away have been brought near by the blood of Christ. —Eph 2:13

LIE—*GOD IS NEVER GOING TO RESCUE ME.*

The Scriptures say:

. . . say to those with fearful hearts, "Be strong, do not fear; your God will come, he will come with vengeance; with divine retribution he will come to save you." —Isa 35:4

Though you have made me see troubles, many and bitter, you will restore my life again; from the depths of the earth you will again bring me up. —Ps 71:20

But you, God, see the trouble of the afflicted; you consider their grief and take it in hand. —Ps 10:14

The Lord is a refuge for the oppressed, a stronghold in times of trouble. Those who know your name trust in you, for you, Lord, have never forsaken those who seek you. —Ps 9:9–10

LIE—*BECAUSE I AM WEAK, I AM WORTHLESS.*

The Scriptures say: (Context added.)

But God chose the foolish things of the world to shame the wise; God chose the weak things of the world to shame the strong. He chose the lowly things of this world and the despised things—and the things that are not—to nullify the things that are, so that no one may boast before him. —1 Cor 1:27–29

(God's response when Paul asks him to remove the "thorn in his flesh"—Paul's physical illness.) But he said to me, "My grace is sufficient for you, for my power is made perfect in weakness." Therefore I will boast all the more gladly about my weaknesses, so that Christ's power may rest on me. That is why, for Christ's sake, I delight in weaknesses, in insults, in hardships, in persecutions, in difficulties. For when I am weak, then I am strong. —2 Cor 12:9–10

On the contrary, those parts of the body that seem weaker are indispensable. —1 Cor 12:22

But many who are first will be last, and many who are last will be first. —Matt 19:30

LIE—*I AM A FAILURE.*

Note to Reader:
I often heard this lie in response to the inadequacy I felt on becoming disabled.
I am referring to failure in terms of a general sense of identity that labeled my
whole life. Grieving the vision I had for the way my life was "supposed" to be,
made me feel like I was coming up short as a wife, daughter, professional, and
friend. The verses below reassured me of my value to God and helped me love
myself again. May they help you see yourself through God's eyes.

The Scriptures say: (Context added.)

For we are God's masterpiece. He has created us anew in Christ Jesus, so we
can do the good things he planned for us long ago. —Eph 2:10 NLT

But now, this is what the Lord says— he who created you, Jacob, he who
formed you, Israel: "Do not fear, for I have redeemed you; I have summoned
you by name; you are mine. —Isa 43:1

See, I have engraved you on the palms of my hands; your walls are ever
before me. —Isa 49:16

. . . He [*God*] who began a good work in you will carry it on to completion
until the day of Christ Jesus. —Phil 1:6

My flesh and my heart may fail, but God is the strength of my heart and my
portion forever. —Ps 73:26

But you are a chosen people, a royal priesthood, a holy nation, God's special
possession, that you may declare the praises of him who called you out of
darkness into his wonderful light. —1 Pet 2:9

Who will bring any charge against those whom God has chosen? It is God
who justifies. —Rom 8:33

Listen, my dear brothers and sisters: Has not God chosen those who are
poor in the eyes of the world to be rich in faith and to inherit the kingdom
he promised those who love him? —Jas 2:5

He will take pity on the weak and the needy and save the needy from death. He will rescue them from oppression and violence, for precious is their blood in his sight. —Ps 72:13–14

LIE—*MY CONDITION MAKES ME A BURDEN TO MY SPOUSE. I'M NOT A BLESSING.*

The Scriptures say: (Context added.)

He who finds a wife finds what is good and receives favor from the Lord. —Prov 18:22

The Lord God said, "It is not good for the man to be alone. I will make a helper suitable for him." —Gen 2:18 (*God said this before making Eve.*)

"But at the beginning of creation God made them male and female. For this reason a man will leave his father and mother and be united to his wife, and the two will become one flesh. So they are no longer two, but one flesh. Therefore what God has joined together, let no one separate." —Mark 10:6–9 (*Jesus' words.*)

Two are better than one, because they have a good return for their labor: If either of them falls down, one can help the other up. But pity anyone who falls and has no one to help them up. Also, if two lie down together, they will keep warm. But how can one keep warm alone? Though one may be overpowered, two can defend themselves. A cord of three strands is not quickly broken. —Eccl 4:9–12

Live happily with the woman you love through all the meaningless days of life that God has given you under the sun. The wife God gives you is your reward for all your earthly toil. —Eccl 9:9 NLT

LIE—*I AM HOPING IN THE LORD IN VAIN.*

The Scriptures say: (Emphasis added.)

The Lord is good to those whose hope is in him, to the one who seeks him. —Lam 3:25

Therefore, my dear brothers and sisters, stand firm. Let nothing move you. Always give yourselves fully to the work of the Lord, because you know that your labor in the Lord is not in vain. —1 Cor 15:58

" . . . Then you will know that I am the Lord; those who hope in me will not be disappointed." —Isa 49:23

The Lord will surely comfort Zion and will look with compassion on all her ruins; he will make her deserts like Eden, her wastelands like the garden of the Lord. Joy and gladness will be found in her, thanksgiving and the sound of singing. —Isa 51:3

The cowering prisoners will *soon* be set free; they will not die in their dungeon, nor will they lack bread. —Isa 51:14

A horse is a vain hope for deliverance; despite all its great strength it cannot save. But the eyes of the Lord are on those who fear him, on those whose hope is in his unfailing love, to deliver them from death and keep them alive in famine. —Ps 33:17–19

I sought the Lord, and he answered me; he delivered me from all my fears. —Ps 34:4

LIE—*CIRCUMSTANCES WILL NEVER CHANGE OR GET BETTER. THEY WILL ALWAYS BE THE SAME.*

The Scriptures say:

For no one is cast off by the Lord forever. Though he brings grief, he will show compassion, so great is his unfailing love. —Lam 3:31–32

As God's co-workers we urge you not to receive God's grace in vain. For he says, "In the time of my favor I heard you, and in the day of salvation I helped you." I tell you, now is the time of God's favor, now is the day of salvation. —2 Cor 6:1–2

Forget the former things; do not dwell on the past. See, I am doing a new thing! Now it springs up; do you not perceive it? I am making a way in the desert and streams in the wasteland. —Isa 43:18–19

. . . weeping may stay for the night, but rejoicing comes in the morning. —Ps 30:5

Those who sow in tears will reap with songs of joy. —Ps 126:5

I waited patiently for the Lord; he turned to me and heard my cry. He lifted me out of the slimy pit, out of the mud and mire; he set my feet on a rock and gave me a firm place to stand. He put a new song in my mouth, a hymn of praise to our God. Many will see and fear and put their trust in the Lord. —Ps 40:1–3

And the God of all grace, who called you to his eternal glory in Christ, after you have suffered a little while, will himself restore you and make you strong, firm and steadfast. —1 Pet 5:10

Appendix 2

Principles of Positive Prayer

POSITIVE PRAYER PRINCIPLE #1 — GOD'S WORD IS POWERFUL BECAUSE . . .

God's words/promises are true:

God's way is perfect. All the Lord's promises prove true. —Ps 18:30 NLT

For the word of the Lord holds true, and we can trust everything he does. —Ps 33:4 NLT

God's word has authority:

The LORD merely spoke, and the heavens were created. He breathed the word, and all the stars were born. —Ps 33:6 NLT

Let the whole world fear the LORD, and let everyone stand in awe of him. For when he spoke, the world began! It appeared at his command. —Ps 33:8–9

God's word is alive and accomplishes his will:

For the word of God is alive and active. Sharper than any double-edged sword, it penetrates even to dividing soul and spirit, joints and marrow; it judges the thoughts and attitudes of the heart. —Heb 4:12

As the rain and the snow come down from heaven, and do not return to it without watering the earth and making it bud and flourish, so that it yields seed for the sower and bread for the eater, so is my word that goes out from my mouth: It will not return to me empty, but will accomplish what I desire and achieve the purpose for which I sent it. —Isa 55:10–11

God's word is flawless, permanent, and invincible:

Every word of God is flawless; he is a shield to those who take refuge in him. —Prov 30:5

The grass withers and the flowers fall, but the word of our God endures forever. —Isa 40:8

For the word of God will never fail. —Luke 1:37

God's word is life-giving. It sustains, heals, and fuels us:

Jesus answered, "It is written: 'Man shall not live on bread alone, but on every word that comes from the mouth of God.'" —Matt 4:4

The Son is the radiance of God's glory and the exact representation of his being, sustaining all things by his powerful word. —Heb 1:3

Your new life will last forever because it comes from the eternal, living word of God. —1 Pet 1:23 NLT

The Sovereign Lord has given me a well-instructed tongue, to know the word that sustains the weary. He wakens me morning by morning, wakens my ear to listen like one being instructed. —Isa 50:4

He sent forth his word and healed them; he rescued them from the grave. —Ps 107:20

Your promise revives me; it comforts me in all my troubles. —Ps 119:50

His word protects us and is a victorious weapon against evil: (Commentary added.)

His faithful promises are your armor and protection. —Ps 91:4 NLT

Take the helmet of salvation and the sword of the Spirit, which is the word of God. —Eph 6:17 *(Ephesians 6 exhorts believers to put on the armor of God to protect themselves from evil. Paul says God's word is the sword of the Spirit—which is noteworthy because it is the only offensive weapon listed.)*

I have written to you who are young in the faith because you are strong. God's word lives in your hearts, and you have won your battle with the evil one. —1 John 2:14 NLT

God's word prepares us to do his work:

All Scripture is God-breathed and is useful for teaching, rebuking, correcting and training in righteousness, so that the servant of God may be thoroughly equipped for every good work. —2 Tim 3:16–17

POSITIVE PRAYER PRINCIPLE #2—PRAYER IS POWERFUL BECAUSE . . .

Prayer pleases God: (Commentary added.)

The Lord detests the sacrifice of the wicked, but the prayer of the upright pleases him. —Prov 15:8

Cornelius stared at him in fear. "What is it, Lord?" he asked. The angel answered, "Your prayers and gifts to the poor have come up as a memorial offering before God." —Acts 10:4

I urge, then, first of all, that petitions, prayers, intercession and thanksgiving be made for all people— for kings and all those in authority, that we may live peaceful and quiet lives in all godliness and holiness. This is good, and pleases God our Savior . . . —1 Tim 2:1–3 *(Intercessory prayer is praying for others.)*

Jesus valued prayer:

During the days of Jesus' life on earth, he offered up prayers and petitions with fervent cries and tears to the one who could save him from death, and he was heard because of his reverent submission. —Heb 5:7

But Jesus often withdrew to lonely places and prayed. —Luke 5:16

Prayer helps us communicate and connect with God: (Commentary added.)

Do not be anxious about anything, but in every situation, by prayer and petition, with thanksgiving, present your requests to God. —Phil 4:6

Then you will call on me and come and pray to me, and I will listen to you. —Jer 29:12

Again, I tell you that if two of you on earth agree about anything you ask for, it will be done for you by my Father in heaven. For where two or three come together in my name, there am I with them. —Matt 18:19–20 *(Prayer helps us connect with God and strengthens bonds between believers.)*

Prayer gives us strength to fight temptation: (Context added.)

Keep watch and pray, so that you will not give in to temptation. For the spirit is willing but the body is weak! —Matt 26:41 NLT *(Jesus' instruction to Peter in the garden of Gethsemane.)*

Prayer invites God's favor:

But when you pray, go into your room, close the door and pray to your Father, who is unseen. Then your Father, who sees what is done in secret, will reward you. —Matt 6:6

Then many will give thanks on our behalf for the gracious favor granted us in answer to the prayers of many. —2 Cor 1:11

Our prayers can work together with God's will to affect change:

On him we have set our hope that he will continue to deliver us, as you help us by your prayers. —2 Cor 1:10

For I know that through your prayers and God's provision of the Spirit of Jesus Christ what has happened to me will turn out for my deliverance. —Phil 1:19

And the prayer offered in faith will make the sick person well; the Lord will raise them up. If they have sinned, they will be forgiven. Therefore confess your sins to each other and pray for each other so that you may be healed. The prayer of a righteous person is powerful and effective. —Jas 5:15–16[1]

1. A Word of Caution:

I debated whether I should include James 5:15–16. Taken in the wrong context, these verses can be very damaging. Many faithful people who belong to Jesus still have unanswered prayers. (If you need a refresher, revisit Chapter 9 "Responding to Accusations of 'Not Enough Faith.'")

As the next verse from 1 John reminds us, it is not just our prayers that matter, but God's will. God cares about your body, but his first priority is always to transform your heart and soul into who he created you to be. Your earthly body will wear out, but your soul will live eternally in the new heavenly body he has prepared for you (1 Cor 14:42–44).

This is the confidence we have in approaching God: that if we ask anything according to his will, he hears us. And if we know that he hears us—whatever we ask—we know that we have what we asked of him. —1 John 5:14–15

God sees shaping your forever soul as a very worthwhile investment, but he never intended for you to suffer. One way he redeems suffering is by using it to bring out the strength of your spirit (Rom 8:28). He turns the tables on your temporary trials by producing eternal treasures within you. Good fathers don't let anyone mess with their kids and get away with it.

POSITIVE PRAYER PRINCIPLE #3—YOU HAVE GOD'S ATTENTION.

God's promises are for you. You are his child and an heir through Christ:

This mystery is that through the gospel the Gentiles are heirs together with Israel, members together of one body, and sharers together in the promise in Christ Jesus. —Eph 3:6

So you are no longer a slave, but God's child; and since you are his child, God has made you also an heir. —Gal 4:7

Now if we are children, then we are heirs—heirs of God and co-heirs with Christ, if indeed we share in his sufferings in order that we may also share in his glory. —Rom 8:17

 . . . having been justified by his [*Christ's*] grace, we might become heirs having the hope of eternal life. —Titus 3:7

I pray that the eyes of your heart may be enlightened in order that you may know the hope to which he has called you, the riches of his glorious inheritance in his holy people, and his incomparably great power for us who believe. —Eph 1:18–19

His divine power has given us everything we need for a godly life through our knowledge of him who called us by his own glory and goodness. Through these he has given us his very great and precious promises, so that through them you may participate in the divine nature, having escaped the corruption in the world caused by evil desires. —2 Pet 1:3–4

Because Christ is your righteousness, you can confidently ask for help:

For we do not have a high priest who is unable to empathize with our weaknesses, but we have one who has been tempted in every way, just as we are—yet he did not sin. Let us then approach God's throne of grace with confidence, so that we may receive mercy and find grace to help us in our time of need. —Heb 4:15–16

It is because of him [*God*] that you are in Christ Jesus, who has become for us wisdom from God—that is, our righteousness, holiness and redemption. —1 Cor 1:30

God is watching over you 24/7:

"For the eyes of the Lord are on the righteous and his ears are attentive to their prayer, but the face of the Lord is against those who do evil." —1 Pet 3:12

He will not let you stumble; the one who watches over you will not slumber. Indeed, he who watches over Israel never slumbers or sleeps. —Ps 121:3–4

No detail of your life is beneath God's notice:

The LORD directs the steps of the godly. He delights in every detail of their lives. —Ps 37:23 NLT

Are not five sparrows sold for two pennies? Yet not one of them is forgotten by God. Indeed, the very hairs of your head are all numbered. Don't be afraid; you are worth more than many sparrows. —Luke 12:6–7

Appendix 3

Prayers for the Dark Night of the Soul

ADDITIONAL "HAIL MARY" VERSES:

May God himself, the God of peace, sanctify you through and through. May your whole spirit, soul and body be kept blameless at the coming of our Lord Jesus Christ. The one who calls you is faithful, and he will do it. —1 Thess 5:23–24

Because of the Lord's great love we are not consumed, for his compassions never fail. —Lam 3:22

Now it is God who makes both us and you stand firm in Christ. He anointed us, set his seal of ownership on us, and put his Spirit in our hearts as a deposit, guaranteeing what is to come. —2 Cor 1:21–22

He will not let your foot slip— he who watches over you will not slumber. —Ps 121:3

To him who is able to keep you from stumbling and to present you before his glorious presence without fault and with great joy— to the only God our Savior be glory, majesty, power and authority, through Jesus Christ our Lord, before all ages, now and forevermore! Amen. —Jude 1:24–25

Cast your cares on the Lord and he will sustain you; he will never let the righteous be shaken. —Ps 55:22 *(Remember, your righteousness doesn't depend on your efforts or feelings. Romans 3:22-24 says you are made righteous through faith in Jesus' sacrifice for you.)*

He rescued me from my powerful enemy, from my foes, who were too strong for me. —Ps 18:17

Our lives are in his hands, and he keeps our feet from stumbling. —Ps 66:9

When my spirit grows faint within me, it is you who watch over my way. —Ps 142:3

Where can I go from your Spirit? Where can I flee from your presence? If I go up to the heavens, you are there; if I make my bed in the depths, you are there. If I rise on the wings of the dawn, if I settle on the far side of the sea, even there your hand will guide me, your right hand will hold me fast. —Ps 139:7–10 *(Wherever you are in life, God holds you fast.)*

We were under great pressure, far beyond our ability to endure, so that we despaired of life itself. Indeed, we felt we had received the sentence of death. But this happened that we might not rely on ourselves but on God, who raises the dead. —2 Cor 1:8–9

Appendix 4

My Favorite . . .

MY FAVORITE . . .

Online Pastors:

Whether you are craving a deeper understanding of God or some extra encouragement, these pastors always breathe fresh life into my spirit:

- Pastor Steven Furtick of *Elevation Church* in Charlotte, North Carolina:
  My MVP pick (Most Valuable Pastor). God fearlessly speaks through Pastor Steven to the most hidden places of your heart. I appreciate that his powerful preaching tackles nuances and the complexities of being human. His sermon, "What Do We Do When God Lets Us Down?" changed my life and allowed me to move forward at a time when I felt incredibly disappointed in God. Every time I hear him speak; God inspires me. That's an impressive track record when I've been listening for more than a decade! Find sermons at *elevation-church.org* or *stevenfurtick.com.*

- Pastor Joseph Prince of *New Creation Church* in Singapore:
  A gifted speaker and talented teacher who has a clear heart for God's Word. He uses his understanding of biblical languages to bring verses to life by illuminating how richly they convey God's love. Whenever I listen to Pastor Prince, I know I will come to a deeper understanding of how Jesus is everything. Learn more at *josephprince. org.*

- Christine Caine: activist, evangelist, and contributor to *Hillsong Church*:
  A powerful voice for heaven from down under (she's Australian). If God ever gives me the chance to speak, it is my prayer to preach with the strength, piercing truth, boldness, and wisdom of this woman. Not only is she the most remarkable woman I've ever heard preach, Christine is one of the most spirit-filled speakers of today, *period.* Visit *christinecaine.com.*

Worship Bands:

YouTube is my favorite streaming platform for a more church-like experience. You can find a version of most songs which includes lyrics so that you can stream from your TV and sing along.

- Music Meets Heaven " . . . apart from You I have no good thing!":
  A YouTube channel dedicated to promoting Christian music from many artists. All of the videos include lyrics and a soothing natural background to create a worshipful experience.

- Elevation Worship: Church based in Charlotte, North Carolina.
- Bethel Worship or Bethel Music: Church based in Redding, California.
- CityAlight: Music ministry based out of St. Paul's Castle Hill Church in Australia.
  All of their songs are biblically rooted and easy to sing along with.

Bibles/Study Tools:

- *The Beyond Suffering Bible* New Living Translation:
  A Bible with commentary for readers with disabilities and chronic illnesses. This project was spearheaded by Joni Eareckson Tada who is a beacon of faith to the disabled community. She became a quadriplegic at seventeen, endures bouts of chronic pain, and has survived breast cancer. Despite all her challenges, she burns ever brighter for Jesus.

- *Praying God's Word* by Beth Moore:
  Learn the powerful practice of adapting Bible verses into personal prayers.

- *The Bible Promise Book: One Thousand Promises from God's Word* New Life Version:
  Quick reference guide with biblical promises grouped by topic.

- *Words of Wisdom: From Living Psalms and Proverbs* Paraphrased by Kenneth N. Taylor:
  Read through the Psalms and Proverbs in a month in this absolutely beautiful translation. I picked up *Words of Wisdom* when I was first diagnosed and deeply depressed. With God's word split conveniently into days, it was easy to read at a time I felt numb. I absolutely immersed myself in this book until God's promises began to reignite my spirit. It also includes a small topical index to help you find Psalms/Proverbs for specific needs.

Devotionals:

- *Jesus Calling Series* by Sarah Young:

    Written as if Jesus is speaking directly to you, this is my absolute favorite series. The devotions read like love letters, masterfully capturing God's truth and heart towards you. Sarah Young coped with declining health as she was writing the series and was finally diagnosed with Lyme Disease. She is also a trained counselor. The devotions are quick enough for your most tired days, especially if you opt for the editions that print out the entire Bible verse. The series includes:

    Jesus Calling: Enjoying Peace in His Presence

    Dear Jesus: Seeking His Light in Your Life

    Jesus Lives: Seeing His Love in Your Life

    Jesus Today: Experience Hope through His Presence

    Jesus Always: Embracing Joy in His Presence

- *Beside Bethesda: 31 Days Toward Deeper Healing* by Joni Eareckson Tada
- *The Healing Power of the Holy Communion—A 90-Day Devotional* by Joseph Prince:

    Jesus instructed his disciples to remember his sacrifice on the cross by taking communion. We associate this act of Holy celebration with forgiveness of sins, but did you know Jesus also died for your diseases? Isaiah 53:5 says that, "by his *[Jesus']* wounds we are healed." Learn how communion is a God-given gift for claiming Christ's promises.

On Suffering and Healing:

- *A Place of Healing: Wrestling with the Mysteries of Suffering, Pain, and God's Sovereignty* by Joni Eareckson Tada:

    This book offers a thoughtful examination on why God allows suffering from an author who has triumphantly faced more adversity than I can comprehend.

On Positive Thinking and Mental Health:

- *Battlefield of the Mind: Winning the Battle in Your Mind* by Joyce Meyer
- *Crash the Chatterbox* by Steven Furtick

Inspirational Reads:

- *Fear Not Promise Book: For I Am with You Always* by Max Lucado:
  Collection of Bible verses and quotes to help you find peace in God's promises.

- *He Still Moves Stones* by Max Lucado:
  Biblical portraits of how God does the impossible for his beloved children.

Bibliography

Associated Press. "Mother Teresa Gets Pacemaker, Is 'Fine.'" *Los Angeles Times,* December 2, 1989. https://www.latimes.com/archives/la-xpm-1989-12-02-mn-312-story.html

Attenborough, David, narrator. *Africa.* Season 1, episode 1, "Kalahari." Aired January 2, 2013, on BBC.

Attenborough, Richard, dir. *Shadowlands.* Price Entertainment, 1993. Distributed by Warner Bros., 1993.

Benson, Kyle. "The Magic Relationship Ratio, According to Science." The Gottman Institute. October 4, 2017. https://www.gottman.com/blog/the-magic-relationship-ratio-according-science/.

Bloom, John. "Jesus Understands Loneliness." *desiringGod.org.* October 12, 2012. https://www.desiringgod.org/articles/jesus-understands-loneliness.

Bondy, Filip. "Kerry Strug Stands Tall on Injured Ankle, Leads U.S. Gymnastics to Team Gold at 1996 Olympics." *New York Daily News,* July 24, 1996. https://www.nydailynews.com/sports/more-sports/kerri-stands-tall-sprained-ankle-article-1.2015138.

Cummins, James John. *Jesus, Lord of Life and Glory.* First published 1839. Reprinted in *Trinity Hymnal (Rev. ed.)* #569. Suwanee, GA: Great Commission, 1990.

Dysautonomia International. "Postural Orthostatic Tachycardia Syndrome." Accessed July 13, 2021. http://www.dysautonomiainternational.org/page.php?ID=30.

Fincher, David, dir. *The Curious Case of Benjamin Button.* Hollywood, CA: Paramount, 2008.

Frantz, Laura. *Love's Fortune.* Grand Rapids, MI: Revell, 2014.

Jabr, Ferris. "How Does a Caterpillar Turn into a Butterfly." *Scientific American.* August 10, 2012. https://www.scientificamerican.com/article/caterpillar-butterfly-metamorphosis-explainer/.

Jerajani, H. R., et al. "Hematohidrosis: A Rare Clinical Phenomenon." *Indian Journal of Dermatology* 54, no. 3 (July–September 2009) 290–92. https://www.ncbi.nlm.nih.gov/pmc/articles/PMC2810702/#CIT6.

Joni and Friends. (n.d.) "Our History." Accessed July 14, 2021. https://www.joniandfriends.org/about/our-history/.

Kaneda, Toshiko, and Carl Haub. "How Many People Have Ever Lived on Earth?" Population Reference Bureau. Updated May 18, 2021. https://www.prb.org/articles/how-many-people-have-ever-lived-on-earth/.

Lewis, C. S. *The Lion, the Witch, and the Wardrobe.* First published 1950. Reprinted New York, NY: HarperCollins, 1994.

Madden, John, dir. *The Best Exotic Marigold Hotel*. London: Blueprint, 2011. Distributed by Fox Searchlight, 2012.

McGrath, Alister. *C. S. Lewis – A Life: Eccentric Genius, Reluctant Prophet*. Carol Stream, IL: Tyndale, 2013.

Meier, Eric. "Live Oak." The Wood Database. Accessed July 29, 2021. https://www.wood-database.com/live-oak/.

———. "Oregon White Oak." The Wood Database. Accessed July 29, 2021. https://www.wood-database.com/oregon-white-oak/.

Miller, Michael Craig. "In Praise of Gratitude." *Harvard Health* (blog). *Harvard Health Publishing*, November 21, 2012. https://www.health.harvard.edu/blog/in-praise-of-gratitude-201211215561.

Moore, Beth. *Praying God's Word: Breaking Free from Spiritual Strongholds*. Nashville, TN: B&H (2000) 2009. Citations refer to the 2009 edition.

Murray, Andrew. *Abide in Christ*. New Kensington, PA: Whitaker, 1979.

Nouwen, Henri. *Lifesigns: Intimacy, Fecundity, and Ecstasy in Christian Perspective*. New York City, NY: Doubleday, 1986.

Renn, Stephen D., ed. *Expository Dictionary of Bible Words*. Peabody, MA: Hendrickson, 2005.

Ribeiro, Marta. "6 Celebrities Who Lived with Parkinson's Disease." *Parkinson's News Today*, July 25, 2017. https://parkinsonsnewstoday.com/social-clips/six-celebrities-parkinsons-disease/

Rosenberger, Peter. *Hope for the Caregiver: Encouraging Words to Strengthen Your Spirit*. Brentwood, TN: Worthy Inspired, 2014.

Patterson, Jim. "Worship Is Good for Your Health: Vanderbilt Study." *Vanderbilt University Research News*, May 31, 2017. https://news.vanderbilt.edu/2017/05/31/worship-is-good-for-your-health-vanderbilt-study/.

Scazzero, Peter. *Emotionally Healthy Spirituality: It's Impossible to be Spiritually Mature While Remaining Emotionally Immature*. Grand Rapids, MI: Zondervan, 2006.

Sun, Eryn. "Joni Eareckson Tada on Wilberforce Award, 'Better Off Dead Than Disabled' Mentality." *The Christian Post*, March 16, 2012. https://www.christianpost.com/news/joni-eareckson-tada-on-wilberforce-award-better-off-dead-than-disabled-mentality-71536/.

Ten Boom, Corrie. *Amazing Love*. First published 1953. Reprinted Fort Washington, PA: CLC, 2010.

TerKeurst, Lysa. *The Best Yes: Making Wise Decisions in the Midst of Endless Demands*. Nashville, TN: Nelson, 2014.

Printed in the USA
CPSIA information can be obtained
at www.ICGtesting.com
LVHW010450020224
770553LV00003B/3